THE DEFENSE LAWYER

For a complete list of books by James Patterson, as well as previews of upcoming books and more information about the author, visit JamesPatterson.com or find him on Facebook.

THE DEFENSE LAWYER

THE BARRY SLOTNICK STORY

JAMES PATTERSON
AND BENJAMIN WALLACE

Little, Brown and Company

New York Boston London

Little, Brown and Company
Hachette Book Group
1290 Avenue of the Americas, New York, NY 10104
littlebrown.com

First edition: December 2021

Little, Brown and Company is a division of Hachette Book Group, Inc. The Little, Brown name and logo are trademarks of Hachette Book Group, Inc.

The publisher is not responsible for websites (or their content) that are not owned by the publisher.

The Hachette Speakers Bureau provides a wide range of authors for speaking events. To find out more, go to hachettespeakersbureau.com or call (866) 376-6591.

ISBN 978-0-316-49437-3 (hc) / 978-0-759-55515-0 (large print)
LCCN 2020949148

10 9 8 7 6 5 4 3 2 1

FRI

Printed in Canada

THE DEFENSE LAWYER

PROLOGUE

CHAPTER 1

It was only around 4:30 p.m. on a Thursday, but Barry Slotnick had an early dinner to get to in the city before going home to Scarsdale, the affluent New York suburb where he lived with his family: his wife of nineteen years, Donna, and their four children. As Slotnick gathered his belongings, his eyes flitted over the framed illustrations on his walls, courtroom artists' renderings of Slotnick arguing cases on behalf of a gallery of rogues.

His gaze kept returning to the windows. One of the reasons he'd moved here to the Transportation Building was for the views. From his corner office on the twenty-first floor, Slotnick could take in a sweeping panorama that encompassed downtown Manhattan, the East River, and the Brooklyn Bridge. It never got old.

He said goodbye to his assistant, Pam, and stepped into the elevator. Moments later, he exited the building. Slotnick cut an impressive figure. He was six feet one and meticulously groomed, with a distinguished smattering of salt creeping into his neatly clipped beard. Despite the steamy July weather, he wore a tailored three-piece wool suit, a crisp white shirt, and a red power tie. The shirt cuffs, peeking out from the sleeves of his suit jacket, revealed a tastefully stitched monogram: BIS. It was a look befitting a man who was at that moment the most famous criminal-defense lawyer in America.

Slotnick stepped out on lower Broadway. He started to turn right, then glanced at his wedding ring, a trick he had come to rely on. Since childhood, he'd had a form of dyslexia that made him hopeless at distinguishing left from right. By remembering that his wedding ring was on his left hand, he was able to navigate well enough. He turned in the opposite direction and began making his way across the street toward City Hall Park, a shaded plaza where his driver, Roberto, sat waiting to ferry his boss to his next appointment.

Slotnick's life was often stressful, but if there was ever a time when the forty-eight-year-old attorney might feel entitled to a rest, it was now, in the summer of 1987. Over the previous nine months, Slotnick had quarterbacked the successful defense in two of the most daunting and controversial trials in memory. First had come the prosecution of John Gotti, the dapper boss of the Gambino crime family, as part of an almost unprecedented legal onslaught against the Mafia by the federal government. Just a few weeks earlier, Slotnick had represented Bernhard Goetz, a white electronics engineer who had shot four Black kids he believed were about to mug him in a New York City subway car, in what was called the Trial of the Century (O. J. Simpson was still just a football star turned rental-car spokesman). But instead of resting after those two high-profile cases, Slotnick was busier than ever, carrying an alligator-skin briefcase in each hand. As he reached the car, a black Cadillac Fleetwood, Roberto popped the trunk from his seat behind the wheel, and Slotnick began putting the briefcases into it.

Just then, he felt a jolt, a searing sting in his back.

CHAPTER 2

The pain was sharp and sudden and had force behind it, like a knife thrust. Turning, Slotnick saw a man in a motorcycle helmet, its dark faceplate pulled down, swinging a blunt wooden object wrapped in newspapers toward his head.

Instinctively, he raised his left arm to deflect the blow. The weapon connected with his wrist, sending a shock of pain up his arm and a stab of fear through his whole body.

Although Slotnick was an urbane lawyer known for his twenty-five-hundred-dollar Fioravanti suits, he was not unacquainted with violence. He'd had a couple of close brushes with death many years earlier—first when a bomb exploded at his office, and then when a client was gunned down while standing right next to him. But Slotnick had never been personally assaulted—until right now.

He ran into the park to escape but had traveled only a few yards when the assailant caught up with him, raining blows on his back and arms with the weapon, which Slotnick thought might be a baseball bat with a nail sticking out of it. As bystanders approached, the assailant fled—jumping on a waiting motorcycle piloted by a helmeted accomplice—and sped away.

Slotnick stumbled back to the safety of his car, where Roberto apologized for not having been able to help. It had all happened so fast. Roberto had frozen and had only just managed to unfasten his seat belt.

"I think my arm is broken," Slotnick said. "Take me to the hospital."

As Roberto drove, Slotnick inventoried the damage. His left hand throbbed. There were puncture wounds to his right arm. His back and arms felt covered with cuts and bruises.

And he now noticed that his fifteen-thousand-dollar gold Piaget Polo watch had been lost in the scuffle.

At New York Infirmary–Beekman Downtown Hospital, an orthopedic surgeon X-rayed Slotnick's arm and found the fracture. Then Slotnick's nephew Rich, a Wall Street trader and martial arts black belt, arrived at the hospital, having heard about the attack on a newswire. "Oh," Slotnick said. "Karate boy shows up *now*."

Stuart Slotnick, a rising senior at Scarsdale High, was working the register at Sam Goody in the Galleria in White Plains when his friend Eddie called.

Eddie was so distraught he could barely speak. "Your dad was attacked," he finally managed. "I saw it on the news."

Stuart immediately called his mother. "Everything's okay," Donna assured him. "His wrist is broken, but he's okay."

At the record store, Stuart's manager came up to him and said, "You should call home."

"I know already," Stuart said.

Everyone at the job knew who Stuart's dad was.

CHAPTER 3

More than a dozen newspapers from around the country were fanned out in front of Slotnick on his glass-topped desk the next morning. He was back in the office, and his assistant, Pam, had gotten them from a nearby newsstand that carried papers from around the country. Once she plunked them down in front of her boss, Slotnick awkwardly began flipping through the papers with his right hand. His left arm was immobilized in a sling.

Friday wasn't the worst day to be in the news. That was Saturday, where news went to die. But Slotnick's preferred day was Tuesday. The Monday dam burst of pent-up weekend news was over, clearing the way for more column inches and better play, and it was still early enough in the week for slowpoke journalists to do follow-up coverage.

The *New York Times* had the story on the first page of the Metropolitan News section: SLOTNICK HURT IN ATTACK LEAVING HIS OFFICE.

Slotnick nodded approvingly.

The New York *Daily News* had it on page 2: SLOTNICK BEATEN: THUG ATTACKS GOETZ' LAWYER.

Not bad, either.

There was nothing by Breslin, but that was probably a good thing. Jimmy Breslin, the famous newspaper columnist, tended to be snide whenever he mentioned Slotnick. Besides, Breslin was moving from the *Daily News* to *Newsday,* so Slotnick guessed himself to be a beneficiary of Breslin's hiatus.

Both wire services, AP and UPI, had run stories, which meant that the news of Slotnick's attack had been picked up by papers all over North America, from Mississippi to Nebraska to Quebec.

The *Philadelphia Daily News:* GOETZ LAWYER BATTERED: POLICE AT A LOSS FOR MOTIVE IN ATTACK.

The *Palm Beach Post:* BIKER WITH BASEBALL BAT CLUBS GOETZ'S LAWYER ON NYC STREET.

Slotnick paused to study a large photo accompanying one of the articles. Other than the sling, he looked perfectly put together, his tie elegantly knotted, not a hair out of place. He appreciated that every headline referred to him as "Goetz's lawyer" or the "subway gunman's lawyer." It showed he'd moved beyond the headlines that referred to him as a "mob chieftain's lawyer" and the like.

Only appropriate, as far as Slotnick was concerned. Besides his "o.c." clients—as he referred to the organized crime figures who made up much of his practice—Slotnick had represented celebrities and politicians, arms dealers and abortion doctors. He'd counseled Frank Sinatra and negotiated with John F. Kennedy. He liked to think of himself as the guy you called when you were up shit's creek. He was proud of his hard-won reputation for snatching victory from the jaws of defeat, racking up a remarkable twelve-year winning streak marked by unlikely acquittals and decisive courtroom victories. After every single one, he'd called Donna and uttered the same two words: "Not guilty." *The American Lawyer* had called him the best criminal lawyer in the United States.

Slotnick was an alchemist in his ability to transmute disaster. Leaving the hospital the night before, he had taken the time to field questions thrown at him by a throng of reporters and to pose for pictures. "I have no idea why this happened," he told the reporters. "I didn't see who did it...I was hit from behind. It could possibly have been a mistake...That's life in the big city...I would hope it was a random incident."

Yet Slotnick had to admit: the attack hadn't seemed like a mugging. The assailant hadn't asked for anything or even said anything. The papers suggested it might have something to do with the Goetz case. Maybe an angry New Yorker had targeted him. Slotnick couldn't rule out that possibility. The Goetz saga had been racially polarizing, and Slotnick was recognizable from his countless newspaper and television appearances.

The truth was that a lot of folks might want to hurt him. His job was to defend unpopular people and causes. Slotnick's whole career depended on helping unsavory characters, and he had to consider the possibility that he had finally angered the wrong client. But Slotnick could live with that. He saw himself as the foe of the all-powerful government. He was liberty's last champion.

PART ONE

CHAPTER 4

It was a Saturday afternoon in late December of 1984, three days before Christmas. In a subway tunnel on the West Side of Manhattan, a number 2 express train—covered inside and out with graffiti—hurtled southward from midtown to 14th Street. The train was packed with New Yorkers doing last-minute holiday shopping.

Except for the seventh carriage, which was, unusually, half empty. The only people at its north end were a group of four Black teenage boys who sat opposite one another and were talking and laughing loudly. They moved around a lot, changing positions in their seats, shooting looks at the other passengers, sometimes swinging from the straps on the ceiling, at other times shadowboxing.

The other passengers kept their distance from whatever was going on at the end of the car, clutching bags and purses and averting their eyes or burying their heads in newspapers. Mary Gant, an actress and temp worker on her way to the South

Street Seaport, glanced up once, saw the youths looking at her, and immediately returned her eyes to the book she was reading. Garth Reid, a Jamaican-born community college student in his early twenties, held his one-year-old baby tightly in his arms and snuck occasional glances at the kids.

At the 14th Street station, a white man in his thirties boarded the carriage at its north end and sat down near the kids. He was blond and thin and wore glasses and a blue jacket. Despite the cold weather, he wasn't wearing gloves. The next stop would be Chambers Street, a two-minute ride away. As soon as the doors closed, one of the kids, lying on a bench, turned to face the new passenger. The man stared back.

"How are you?" the kid said.

The man didn't answer but kept staring at him.

Most of the remaining passengers continued to look away as tensions rose at the other end of the car.

CHAPTER 5

Barry Slotnick poured another handful of tanning oil into his outstretched palm and slathered it on his last remaining patch of unglazed belly. Then he lay back on his beach chair, relaxing his lanky frame so that his feet dangled past the chair's end. Finally, he unfolded the three-panel metallic reflector that lay at his side, propping it on his chest at an angle that would yield the optimal concentration of the Caribbean sun on his face, which already sported a luxuriant tawny sheen.

Donna was always throwing the reflectors out, and Barry was always buying replacements. Tanning was one of the rare indulgences he allowed himself. Part of it was the physical pleasure of roasting under UV rays. And part of it was branding, his sun-kissed hue projecting ease and prosperity.

At home, he'd sunbathe in the backyard with a three-panel reflector. When it was too cold to lie outside, he'd park himself under a sunlamp in the basement, baking for hours as he read and annotated trial transcripts.

After hours perched on Barry's Coppertone-slicked torso, the stack of papers smelled like coconut. Beside his lounge chair rested a small hillock of binders full of legal filings and court transcripts awaiting his perusal. Absentmindedly, he reached over the side of the chair for the telephone before he remembered that there wasn't one there. He felt like some kind of amputee, grasping for a phantom limb.

For Barry, taking a vacation just meant working in a prettier place than usual. The family went to Florida every year, but even there, he would arrange for a phone line to be run to his poolside cabana and would have a receiver perpetually cradled to his ear. Finally, Donna had added an annual December trip to Sint Maarten, on the Dutch side of the island of St. Martin, at a hotel where Barry couldn't finagle a poolside phone (there was no pool). They'd been coming to Little Bay for a few years, but he still felt disoriented without a connection to his office and the daily churn of news and cases in New York. He loved his family dearly, but he felt bored and anxious not knowing what people were talking about back home.

On the beach, he watched as Donna played with their toddler, Chani, on the dazzling white sand. Beyond Donna and Chani, Slotnick saw their older kids—Stuart, Melissa, and Shoshana—splashing happily in the sparkling blue-green Caribbean water. He wasn't one to stop and smell the roses, but he let himself feel the moment: life was good.

Later on, when the Slotnick family returned to their hotel from dinner on the French side of the island, Barry and Donna left the kids together and went for a stroll by the water. As they walked down the sand, the faint melody of far-off music mingled with the sound of lapping surf.

The kids saw Barry so little during the rest of the year that the family tended to do everything together on these vacations, but now Donna had him alone.

"Hey, Slots," she said.

Barry looked over and smiled at his wife.

Donna reminded him how proud she was of him. Then, gently, she floated an idea she'd floated before. *What do you think about maybe...*

Giving a different kind of law a try? he interrupted.

Donna nodded. Wasn't he tired of criminal defense? Of the danger that went with it? Of the hassle of getting clients to pay their bills? Wouldn't it be nice to talk about his work without having to defend it?

Barry reminded her of his mantra: he was liberty's last champion. Everyone deserved a good defense. And he was *great* at this. It was how he'd made his name. It was how he took care of their family. It was how the family was able to vacation in places like this.

Donna heard her husband out. She knew that ultimately, only he could decide for himself. But she noticed that his arguments had less vigor than usual. For the first time, she thought he might be open to making a change.

CHAPTER 6

On the train, one of the Black teenagers stood and approached the white man and said something to him.

The man stood, turned away from the youth, unzipped his jacket, then turned back—holding a silver pistol.

The man extended his arms forward and gripped the gun with both hands, his right elbow bent. He looked angry.

Bang.

The kid clutched his chest and fell to the floor.

Bang. Bang. Bang. Bang.

Each of the three other kids collapsed, shot.

The man kneeled beside the first teen and studied his face. Then he stood up and sat back down on one of the benches. He put his head in his hands. Then he stood again and began pacing back and forth.

The other passengers were panicking. Some were running into the next car. Some were frozen in place. Others were on the floor of the car, cowering in fear.

* * *

Armando Soler, the subway conductor, was standing outside his cab, at the far end of the sixth car, when he heard several gunshots. Passengers started running into Soler's car. "Four people were shot," one of them said.

Soler pulled the emergency brake, then radioed the motorman over the public-address system, speaking in code to let him know there was a gunman on board and to alert police and ambulances.

Then Soler made his way through the onrush of people and entered the seventh carriage. It was a chaotic scene. More passengers ran past him. Another six people lay on the floor. He noticed one white man sitting on a bench on the right side of the car who seemed oddly calm.

Soler approached a Black woman who was lying facedown on the floor but uninjured. He helped her up, and she walked away. Soler next went to a white woman who was also lying facedown. She was in shock, and he helped her sit up.

Then the white man on the bench spoke: "I don't know why I did it. They tried to rob me."

The man was staring straight ahead, not directing his words to anyone in particular.

Soler went over to one of the teenagers, also facedown on the floor. Soler took his pulse, looked him in the eyes, and said, "Hang on," then moved on to the others.

When paramedic John Filangeri, responding to a distress call at the Chambers Street subway station, entered around 2:10 p.m., he found four Black teenagers bleeding from gunshot wounds to their upper bodies.

Troy Canty and James Ramseur were lying on the floor facedown, not moving. Barry Allen was crawling around the car. Darrell Cabey was slumped in a seat next to the conductor's cab.

Stepping quickly among the four, Filangeri assessed their conditions. Canty seemed the worst; he had a bullet wound in his chest, close to his heart. His skin was cold and clammy, his blood pressure was very low, and his pulse was racing, indicating severe shock. Ramseur had two wounds from a single bullet, which had gone through his left arm and into his chest; he was in shock, too. Allen had been shot in the back, dangerously close to his spine. Cabey had been shot from the side, the bullet severing his spinal cord, and appeared paralyzed and also in severe shock.

Filangeri and his partner first sealed all the bullet wounds and started each of the victims on oxygen. Then they put a pair of pneumatic antishock trousers on Canty to try to force blood up into his torso and head. They hooked Cabey up to a fluid IV, and Filangeri rode with him in an ambulance to St. Vincent's Hospital in Greenwich Village.

Back in car 7657, as police officers began to arrive on the scene, Armando Soler told them that the gunman had been a thin, clean-shaven, middle-aged white man who, after shooting the youths, had calmly announced that they'd tried to rob him.

CHAPTER 7

It was Saturday, and John Miller wasn't on the clock, but the TV reporter was in the channel 5 newsroom anyway. He'd worked at the local news outlet since he was fourteen years old, and now he was leaving to go to channel 4, the NBC affiliate. He'd stopped by one last time to collect his belongings.

There was always a police radio playing in the newsroom, and, suddenly, Miller heard the words: "Four shot on subway." He turned to his assignment editor and said, "How many calls on this?"

"Like, one," the editor said.

Major news events typically generated an instant flood of calls to the newsroom.

Miller shrugged. "It's probably unfounded."

He picked up the box with his things and left.

That night, Miller saw that the news was all over TV. The next morning, both of the city tabloids ran cover stories about the "subway gunman" and the "subway vigilante." The morning radio call-in shows could talk about nothing else. It was clear to Miller that a nerve had been struck. "It was part *Death Wish,* part a city weary of rising crime...crack has just come along, we're starting to see the edges of the craziness."

Mayor Ed Koch decried the shooter's "animal behavior" and declared that "a vigilante is not a hero": the gunman would be prosecuted when he was caught. The New York City Police Department immediately formed an anti-vigilante task force and set up a hotline for tipsters to call. Detectives fanned out to interview eyewitnesses and canvass the neighborhood around the 14th Street station. Based on the first descriptions, a police artist sketched a rough portrait of the suspect, and TV stations broadcast the image.

In a city besieged by crime, however, the idea of a lone everyman fighting back against street thugs caught the imagination of many citizens. The four teenage victims all had arrest records, and at the time of the shooting, it was reported, three of them had been carrying sharpened screwdrivers in their pockets. The *New York Post,* a daily tabloid, turned the mysterious shooter into a folk hero. Hundreds of the tips coming in to the police hotline offered praise for the gunman. On the FDR Drive, someone graffitied POWER TO THE VIGILANTE; N.Y. LOVES YA!, and passing cars honked in salute.

But there was also a lot of political pressure to find the shooter. Finally, an anonymous caller said he recognized the man in the police sketch. The informant had seen the man loading a chrome-colored gun with copper-jacketed bullets. The gun fit the description of the weapon, and the bullets were consistent with the wounds sustained by the victims. The man's name, according to the tipster, was Bernhard Goetz, and he lived at 55 West 14th Street. The caller reported that Goetz had been mugged before and had said if it ever happened again, he'd "get the bastards."

For the police, the call was just another lead to check out among the hundreds they were receiving. They checked gun permits and found that Goetz had applied for one in 1981. A photo was attached to the application, and police took it to Goetz's building; the doorman said he recognized the tenant but that he'd gone away for a few days. Police left a note in Goetz's mailbox, and another one under his apartment door, asking him to call them when he returned. They also put the picture of Goetz in a photo lineup they showed to witnesses they'd interviewed.

But the witnesses suggested that he wasn't the man they'd seen shoot the four kids on the subway.

CHAPTER 8

Around three o'clock on the afternoon of the shooting, the shooter had rented a car, a blue American Motors Eagle with New York license plates, and started driving north. New England somehow seemed clean and friendly to him. There was snow on the ground. In Vermont, he checked into a motel under the name Fred Adams, then returned to his car and continued driving.

North of Bennington, he pulled over and walked into the woods. He smashed the chrome-plated .38 he'd used in the shooting on a rock, then buried the pieces in the snow. Although he was wearing only a blue Windbreaker, he burned the jacket. Then he became lost and wandered in the woods for two hours, worried that he'd freeze to death. Eventually, he somehow found his way back to the car.

On Christmas Eve, he checked into the Mount Sunapee Motel, in Sunapee, New Hampshire, then drove around with no particular destination in mind. Outside the town of Warner,

New Hampshire, he stopped at a bookstore named Old Paper World and browsed some of the science books for sale. The owner made small talk, then asked, "How's it going down in New York?"

The man seemed to flinch. "How'd you know I was from New York?"

The owner told him not to worry; he'd just seen the plates on his car.

A few nights later, the man checked into the Ramada Inn in Keene, New Hampshire. This time he used his own name, Bernhard Goetz, but gave a Florida address.

At ten minutes past noon on New Year's Eve, Goetz walked into the police headquarters in Concord, New Hampshire, wearing a leather bomber jacket. He approached the front desk and said, "I am the person they are seeking in New York."

More than a dozen cars sped down the interstate. The first two cars were police cruisers from Concord. Their dome lights flashed red and blue, and their sirens screamed. The cars trailing them were full of reporters.

It was Thursday morning, January 3, 1985, and in one of the police cars sat Bernhard Goetz, in handcuffs. He was being returned to New York.

Goetz was thirty-seven years old. Twelve days had passed since the shooting, and the morning before he turned himself in, he'd spent hours driving aimlessly through the New England countryside. After turning himself in, Goetz had spent the next several hours providing three confessions. The first had been in writing, and Goetz had signed it. The second had been recorded as audio. The third, which lasted two hours, was videotaped.

He'd told the police that before he shot the teenagers, they had asked him for five dollars, which he had interpreted as the start of a mugging. He'd been mugged three years earlier, he said, and felt ill-treated by New York's criminal justice system.

Now the convoy drove for five hours, returning Goetz to that very system. The cars arrived at One Police Plaza in Manhattan in the early afternoon, and there, Goetz was charged with four counts of attempted murder.

Everyone suddenly knew his name. A little more than a week after the shooting, and three days after turning himself in, the *New York Times* was already describing him as "an overnight household celebrity."

CHAPTER 9

The phone was ringing as Barry Slotnick unlocked the front door to his house in Scarsdale, his family trailing behind him. It was a Saturday in early January, and they'd just flown in from the Caribbean.

Slotnick picked up the phone, and instantly his ear filled with the voice of Harry Ryttenberg, a former *Daily News* copyboy who'd started his own tabloid-style news service. He would listen to police scanners and hasten to crime and accident scenes with a video camera, then sell the footage to local TV stations.

Ryttenberg had told his reporter friend John Miller that "I know [Bernhard Goetz] like I know you," and Miller had suggested he call Slotnick, a mutual friend.

Miller's relationship with Slotnick went beyond the usual transactional alliance between reporter and source. Slotnick had taken a shine to Miller, who was twenty years younger, and they often had lunch or dinner together.

"Barry, I've got a case for you," Ryttenberg said now. "A guy shot some Black kids in a subway car."

"I don't represent people who shoot Black kids in subway cars," Slotnick replied.

"You may want this one."

Ryttenberg gave Slotnick the rundown on Goetz, explaining that he had gotten to know him because Goetz was a self-employed electrical engineer, and Ryttenberg sometimes took his broken police radios to him to be repaired.

"Where are you going to be tomorrow?" Miller, who was also on the line, asked.

"My office," Slotnick said. Even though it would be Sunday, he had work to do.

Slotnick agreed to at least meet with Goetz at the guy's apartment en route to his office, in lower Manhattan.

The next morning, Slotnick eased his Cadillac out into traffic. He enjoyed piloting the Fleetwood—which he called the Batmobile—though he only drove it on the weekends. During the week, he had a driver bring him to and from the city, and he'd use the time to get work done and make calls on his gigantic, clunky car phone.

The Cadillac was a boat—a huge black car with a wide body and long tail. It had big leather seats and felt like riding in a living room on wheels. When Roberto was driving, Slotnick kept the passenger seat moved all the way forward to give him maximum legroom. He had a small round mirror hung over the back of the seat so he could see himself as he knotted his tie before appointments.

The commute was nearly a straight shot south, and as Slotnick drove in on this Sunday morning, it was a tour of his life in reverse. Down past New Rochelle, where he and Donna had lived after first leaving the city. Then through the Bronx he'd left behind so long ago but never stopped missing. Then the Upper West Side, where he and Donna had lived before making the move to the 'burbs.

Driving backward through his own migration out of the city, he was reminded of the reasons he'd left it. The crime. The grime. The scary subway.

Just thinking about the case he was on his way to discuss, Slotnick felt his muscles relaxing. The island had been nice, but the truth was, he felt most comfortable while working.

He wasn't sure about the facts of this matter, but he trusted John Miller, and Slotnick had picked up some sense of how big a deal the Goetz story had become. He turned left onto 14th Street and started looking at building numbers. Up ahead, he saw a commotion on the sidewalk and a snarl of vehicles.

Then he realized: they were all in front of Courtney House, Goetz's apartment building, near Union Square. Slotnick was stunned at the sheer number of TV vans, paparazzi, and reporters hoping for a glimpse of the city's man of the moment. It was an army of journalists, more press than he'd ever seen in one place.

As Slotnick parked, he thought: *This* is *for me*.

CHAPTER 10

Bernhard Goetz opened his door and let Barry Slotnick into his one-bedroom apartment.

Goetz lived on the ninth floor, at the back of the building, away from the noise of 14th Street. He didn't have a lot of furniture, but there was a leather couch and a big mahogany chest in his living room, and he had put stained glass over his windows, giving the apartment a New Age feel. The space was clean, but Slotnick could see piles of electronic equipment as well as a lamp Goetz had made out of circuit boards.

Slotnick saw that he was the last to arrive. John Miller and Harry Ryttenberg were already there, as was Joseph Kelner, an eminent older attorney best known for having represented the victims of the National Guard shootings at Kent State University.

"I heard you're a big-shot criminal lawyer," Kelner said.

Slotnick agreed that he was.

Kelner said he was happy about that, because he was not

a criminal lawyer. He was mainly a civil attorney, representing plaintiffs who sought monetary damages.

Goetz had been charged with crimes ranging from possessing a weapon with the intention of using it to four counts of attempted murder, and a grand jury was weighing whether to indict him. The more serious charges could potentially send Goetz to prison for half a century. Darrell Cabey, one of the boys Goetz had shot, was in particularly bad shape: in addition to his having been paralyzed, subsequent complications at the hospital had left him with brain damage. Goetz's court-appointed lawyer had suggested that Goetz plead guilty and argue "extreme emotional disturbance"—essentially temporary insanity—but Goetz was reluctant to go along with that plan. Encouraged by the hero treatment he was receiving in the *New York Post,* Goetz increasingly felt that he had been standing up against criminals for an important principle.

But Goetz was twitchy and clearly overwhelmed by events. He paced as he spoke. There were some details about the shooting that concerned Slotnick, including reports that Goetz had shot two of the victims in the back. But as Goetz told his story, Slotnick's interest perked up. Beyond the robust media focus on the case, he related to Goetz's experience of the city as a place that was out of control and not doing right by its citizens.

Though he was a forty-five-year-old suburbanite with four children, Slotnick easily remembered what it was like to live in Manhattan.

Years earlier, when the Slotnicks were still living in the city, he'd been on his way to meet Donna and their young son, Stuart, to see the giant Christmas tree at Rockefeller Center. Slotnick had been carrying a suitcase filled with important papers and a lot of money: tens of thousands of dollars in small bills. His clients weren't always the kinds of people who had FDIC-backed checking accounts, so he was used to receiving cash retainers, but they made him vulnerable at times.

When a voice behind him said, "Give me your money," Slotnick turned to see a man in a suit and tie.

"What did you say?"

"Give me your money."

Slotnick wasn't reckless, and if he had just been carrying his wallet, he probably would have handed it over. But he wasn't about to give away tens of thousands of dollars.

Instead, Slotnick slugged the man in the jaw, hearing it crack.

Then, not wanting to deal with the police, Slotnick hurried away to meet his wife and child. He was very late, and Donna was worried, and his hand hurt, but they went to see the Christmas tree as planned.

"It was the Wild West out there," Donna remembers about New York at that time, when hustlers would wash your windshield without asking, then demand payment. "Squeegee guys on every corner, some of them deranged. Criminals would bite women's earlobes to get their earrings."

When they first married, she and Barry had lived in his bachelor apartment on the Upper West Side, but then they'd moved to Schwab House to make room for their growing family. At first, it had seemed glorious. Schwab House was a red-brick, nineteen-story rental building that filled the block from 73rd to 74th Streets. The Slotnicks' third-floor apartment overlooked Riverside Drive, alongside which a green park ran for several blocks. The view was of trees and grass and pedestrians and, beyond, the Hudson River.

Through all the dangerous moments of her husband's work, Donna had come to terms with the occupational hazards. At least, she understood that her husband wasn't going to suddenly give up his high-stakes criminal work for, say, a sedate trusts-and-estates legal practice. But a few months after Barry's encounter with the would-be mugger, Donna reached the limits of her tolerance. Recently, she'd been pushing Stuart in a stroller in the park, and a creep had flashed her. Much worse, though, was what had happened on one particular afternoon. When she'd first heard the sirens, she'd tuned them out. Just another song in the sound track of big-city life. But the piercing wail became impossible to ignore. The sirens were maybe a block away. Then they were almost in front of Schwab House. Donna watched from the window as several police cars pulled up, followed by an ambulance.

Men in uniforms rushed into the building next door.

Soon, a gurney was being wheeled out of the building. A woman was on it, and she appeared dead.

Police began roping off the area with yellow tape.

Another murder in Gotham.

But Donna, pregnant with a second child, had had enough. She wasn't willing to live in fear for her family's safety.

When Barry walked in that evening, Donna said: "We're moving out of the city."

CHAPTER 11

After leaving Goetz, Slotnick continued to his office down-town. He had other work to catch up on, but he couldn't stop thinking about this case. A stack of newspapers that had arrived while he was on vacation awaited him, and he began flipping through them, studying the coverage.

What Goetz had done seemed to have channeled the city's deep frustrations, and his popularity was remarkable. But Slotnick also saw that support for Goetz was hardly unanimous, and he had only to start reading Jimmy Breslin's columns to understand why.

Sometimes, Slotnick thought that he and Breslin really weren't so different. Both had grown up in ethnic families in the working-class outer boroughs. Both had a grudge against the government. Both saw themselves as David taking on Goliath. And both saw themselves as characters in the great drama of a great city. Breslin loved playing Breslin. Slotnick loved playing Slotnick.

In other ways, they were like oil and water. Breslin thought the government was too impersonal. Slotnick thought the government was too powerful. Breslin had a blue-collar sensibility, elevating the stories of everymen and everywomen above the anonymous masses. Slotnick was white-collar: his opposition to the government was theoretical, about the individual versus the state. Whereas Slotnick was tall and thin and a meticulous dresser, with a diplomatic manner, Breslin was beefy and disheveled and reveled in making enemies. Breslin was a bleeding heart. Slotnick was a conservative Republican. For Breslin, the world was black and white, full of heroes and villains. Slotnick was more sympathetic to those dwelling in the gray areas.

But Slotnick knew that a lot of people picked up the *Daily News* to see what Breslin thought about something—and therefore what they should think about it. "As lawlessness was applauded, we in New York arrived at that sourest of all moments: When people become what they hate," Breslin wrote in his first column about the shooting. "Would the gunman have fired, and would people now be so jubilant, if the four had been white? Almost nobody wants to hear that question."

While the rest of the press described the teenagers as all carrying sharpened screwdrivers, Breslin pointed out that only two of the four had screwdrivers, and none of them was sharpened. They were most likely not meant to be weapons but rather what the youths claimed they were: tools for prying open the video games they'd intended to burgle. Police had finally corrected their original misstatement on this point in response to Breslin's pressure.

He reminded his readers that Darrell Cabey was paralyzed.

"The bottom line," Breslin lamented, "is that people are

rejoicing over a nineteen-year-old kid who will be in a wheel-chair for a lifetime. I'm sorry, include me out."

Barry Slotnick certainly wasn't rejoicing about what had happened to Cabey, but he also wasn't condemning the man he'd met earlier in the day. The dim outlines of a defense strategy for Goetz had already begun to take shape in his mind.

Slotnick's goal was always the same—to establish reasonable doubt in the minds of a jury. There were a number of ways to accomplish this: Try to get as much evidence thrown out as possible. Try to discredit whatever evidence or witnesses remained. Point up inconsistencies in testimony. Sometimes the best a defense lawyer could hope for was to ding up the prosecution's case just enough to plant doubt among jurors. But the gold standard was to present an alternative theory of the case, a story that a jury could sink its teeth into, one that was persuasive enough to displace whatever tale the prosecution was telling.

Slotnick thought he could make a compelling, if topsy-turvy, argument in Goetz's defense.

It would be controversial, but Slotnick felt optimistic about his chances.

He was going to represent the subway gunman.

PART TWO

PART TWO

CHAPTER 12

Barry Slotnick wasn't wearing pants. The pale, sticklike legs that descended from his boxer shorts contrasted jarringly with the opulent tan of his face.

Above the waist, Slotnick wore a button-down shirt and tie and a dark suit jacket busy with silver draper's pins and tracks of white stitching. He held his arms out, angled away from his body, while a shorter man with thinning, backswept hair stood behind Slotnick and fussed over him.

William Fioravanti, whose studio was a block from the Plaza Hotel in midtown Manhattan, was a master tailor, a maker of bespoke men's suits. The small, wood-paneled room smelled like wealth. There were bolts of worsted wool and cashmere and gabardine and luxurious fabrics Slotnick didn't even know the names of. He loved coming here. In one hand, Fioravanti held a cloth measuring tape, and in the other he gripped a piece of tailor's chalk while his palms rested on Slotnick's waist.

"This suit has a power look to it, Barry," Fioravanti said in his soft Neapolitan accent. "See the way that back fits."

Power looks were Fioravanti's specialty. His clients included billionaires such as Steve Wynn and Ron Perelman as well as celebrities such as Frank Sinatra—and Barry Slotnick. Slotnick relished sharing a tailor with Wynn, who was also a client of his; it gave them something to talk about.

On this day, a writer from a men's fashion magazine was tagging along to Slotnick's fitting. Every year, he bought a half dozen suits from Fioravanti at twenty-five hundred dollars a pop, most of them pin-striped, and they required several fittings. Slotnick suggested to the writer that he only wore these suits for practical reasons. "You know what the importance is? The impression that you make on a jury. The prosecutor, in his rumpled seersucker, comes across as the poor civil servant who's doing this for the love of justice. But if I come in decked out in my polyester special, the jury will know it's a ploy. The worst thing you can do is lie to a jury—verbally, emotionally, or visually. If you do that, you're gone."

Slotnick looked at himself in the mirror. He was just back from two weeks at Canyon Ranch spa in Arizona, where he'd lost twenty pounds, and he liked what he saw. He looked like a million bucks. Correction: he looked like *ten* million bucks. Slotnick was the best criminal lawyer in America. *The American Lawyer* had said so. It was only fitting that he should wear the best suits worn by the best people. They made him feel omnipotent.

How far he'd come from Bronx Park East off Allerton Avenue.

CHAPTER 13

The Italian kids were getting rowdy. Barry Slotnick, eleven, was watching from his seat at the back of the subway car and wondering if he was going to have a problem. It wouldn't be the first time.

Until this year, he'd been able to walk to school, which was a couple of blocks from home. But Barry was a quick study. He'd already skipped two grades of elementary school, competed on the *Quiz Kids* radio show, and was attending a junior high school for intellectually gifted children. It was part of New York City's "rapid advance" program, which let kids who scored particularly high on the Stanford-Binet IQ test compress seventh and eighth grades into a single year.

The school where Slotnick had been assigned, JHS 113, was too far away from home for him to walk there. He now began his mornings by walking to the Allerton Avenue station of the el, the elevated, aboveground portion of the New York City subway system. There, he boarded the 2 train on the White

Plains Road line. He only had to travel three stops, but it was a perilous journey, because the Italian kids were often starting trouble with the Jewish kids. Slotnick was very familiar with anti-Semitism—his family's weekend home upstate had been vandalized, the windows broken, and swastikas painted on the walls. He tried to stay away from these clashes, but sometimes they were unavoidable.

"Kike!"

"Christ killer!"

This was one of those times. Slotnick wouldn't let anyone call him those things.

He stood and approached the kid who'd said them. Sometimes Slotnick got beaten up in these situations, but today the kid had only one friend as backup, and Slotnick punched the slur-slinger squarely in the face.

The kid stumbled backward, and Slotnick stood his ground while the kid's friend edged away. Then the conductor called out, "219th Street," Slotnick's stop, and he got off the train with his honor upheld.

That evening, as Barry entered his family's third-floor apartment, he tried holding his right hand close to his side. It was a small two-bedroom apartment where Barry lived with his parents, his older sister, Florence, and his grandfather; Barry slept on the couch. His mother, Rose, had a sixth sense, and she immediately zeroed in on his bruised knuckles. She shook her head. Barry's father, Meyer, just nodded respectfully at his son. Standing up for yourself was a good thing.

Meyer Slotnick had been born Meir Zlotnick in Poland in a time of pogroms against Jews and had fled to America when he was sixteen. Eventually he brought his whole family over, with the exception of his older sister, Shayna, who perished at Auschwitz with her husband and children. In the Bronx, Meyer had fed his family by working for a caterer and in a hat factory, but he was also involved in the community, serving as a Democratic captain and air-raid warden and organizing food drop-offs for needy families in the neighborhood. "They'd ring the doorbell, put the package down, and run away," Slotnick recalls, "so as not to embarrass the people." His father had been Barry's North Star, the man who instilled in him a sense of justice. "I'm not worried about you," he'd said. "You can take care of yourself."

Similarly tough was Harry Hurwitz, Rose Slotnick's brother. Uncle Harry was an influential man, a *macher* in New York's Jewish community. He was a rabbi who ran the union for the kosher catering business in the Bronx, and because the caterers' meat came from mobbed-up butchers who would sometimes try to pass off nonkosher meat as kosher, a certain amount of graft was involved. Harry had to be able to defend himself, so he always carried a handgun, earning the moniker "pistol-packing Yudel." Barry grew up feeling that he could handle himself, and he didn't want to waste time.

He was only twenty when he graduated from New York University School of Law, but he had to wait half a year before he was eligible to take the bar exam, at twenty-one.

As soon as he was sworn in, at the courthouse on the Grand Concourse in the Bronx, Slotnick immediately hailed a taxi. His first order of business was to go downtown to a storefront near the Manhattan courthouse, where he was going to pay ten dollars a month for a phone number, an answering service, and a mail drop at the Westinghouse Building, on lower Broadway.

As the car sped down the FDR Drive, on the eastern edge of Manhattan, he stared out the window, watching the ships plying the East River, framed by the jagged rooflines of Queens and Brooklyn. Slotnick made small talk with the driver. He felt like he was on the threshold of a great adventure.

When the cab reached its destination, Slotnick paid the fare and started to get out. Then he had an idea. He didn't have a business card yet, but he dug a scrap of paper out of his pocket and jotted down his mother's phone number. "If you ever need a lawyer," the virgin attorney said, passing it to the driver before stepping out of the car.

CHAPTER 14

implore you, Your Honor, do not ruin a life."

Not bad, Barry Slotnick thought, watching himself in the mirror.

He tried saying it a little differently.

"Your Honor, I implore you to save a life."

He liked that one, too. Maybe he'd use both.

Slotnick was in his one-bedroom rental apartment in Riverdale, a leafy neighborhood in the Bronx—cheaper than Manhattan and still close to his parents. The apartment was on a high enough floor to offer pretty views of a nearby park and the Hudson River.

"Your Honor, I am pleading for a life."

In the mirror, Slotnick tried to look humble as he said this.

"Let us not diminish his future. Your Honor, please—you have this boy's future in your hands."

Slotnick pursed his lips in a way that he thought looked appropriately solemn.

"It is the function of a court to help and rehabilitate. Not to punish and foster the philosophy of the medieval star-chamber."

Too over the top? Too many "Your Honors" and "I implores" and formal "let us nots"? Nah.

This was Slotnick's first client, and it was going to be his first trial and his first opening statement. He could hardly wait.

On April 21, 1962, soon after he'd given his phone number to the taxi driver, the gesture had paid off. The driver had called Slotnick and recounted a harrowing story.

At two o'clock that morning, a couple of police detectives had come to his Brooklyn home, barged past his wife after she answered the doorbell, and pounded upstairs, where their son Mickey was asleep. They'd arrested Mickey and taken him away, along with the taxi driver's red-and-cream Buick sedan, which was parked out front. The cops said that an hour earlier, around two blocks away, Mickey had hit a woman and her dog with the car, killing the animal and knocking the woman unconscious. They were charging Mickey with DWI, vehicular assault, and leaving the scene of an accident.

The driver was desperate. Could Slotnick help? He could. Slotnick scribbled out a retainer agreement for one thousand dollars in longhand, arranged for Mickey's release on his own recognizance, then set out to conduct a thorough investigation.

He paid an illustrator to draw forensic surveys of the accident site and paid a legal photographer to shoot pictures of it from various angles. He gathered car paint swatches. He subpoenaed the hospital records of the thirty-nine-year-old alleged victim. He demanded that the DA turn over the results of Mickey's "drunkometer" test as well as the notes taken by the police officers who'd arrested him. Slotnick also corralled character witnesses (a priest, a rabbi, a doctor) who knew the family. And he demanded a suppression hearing, in which he challenged the legality of the initial police search of the family home, arguing that the police had no probable cause.

Slotnick planned to attack the government's case from several directions. He was going to suggest the possibility of mistaken identity. He was going to challenge the idea that Mickey had been drunk. Slotnick was going to argue that even if Mickey *had* hit the woman, he wasn't responsible: what was she doing walking the dog at 1:00 a.m. in dark clothing, anyway?

On the vehicular assault charge, Slotnick was going to swing really big, arguing that there was no evidence the woman had even been struck by the car. The curvature of the street had prevented the two eyewitnesses from seeing what happened, and the rest of their testimony couldn't be relied on, either, given the poor light conditions. Police had recovered dog hair from the chassis of Mickey's car, but the only dent in the front fender was in its center: if that dent was caused by hitting someone, she'd have been run over. Though the victim had left the hospital wearing a giant cervical collar around her neck, there was no medical evidence of impact injuries.

Slotnick was, in short, going to treat this relatively minor legal problem as if he were Clarence Darrow arguing a death penalty case, and as he stood in front of the mirror, trying out phrases he might use in his opening, he felt like he was doing what he'd been put on earth to do.

And then, in early 1963, with the case soon to come to trial in state court in Brooklyn, a cop who'd be a key prosecution witness told Slotnick to pay him five hundred dollars to make the case go away.

"I'm not doing that," Slotnick said, though bribing cops and judges wasn't unusual at the time.

Whether or not Mickey felt differently, he replaced Slotnick with another lawyer, and the case was soon dismissed.

CHAPTER 15

Twenty-four-year-old Barry Slotnick glanced at the long black Lincoln parked outside the entrance, attended by serious-looking men in suits, and at the phalanx of newspeople behind a police barricade, holding cameras and giant flashbulbs. He passed under the cream-colored awning with the gold letters reading THE CARLYLE, noticing that the autumnal chill gave way to a cozy warmth generated by heaters parked outside the entrance. He went inside and took in the art deco lobby, which was large and stylish. He'd never been in a hotel this grand.

The Carlyle, in the heart of Manhattan's Upper East Side, was the height of elegant sophistication. He'd heard that every guest's pillowcase was personally monogrammed in gold stitching. This was where President Kennedy and his wife, Jacqueline, stayed whenever they came to New York, which they did so often that the hotel was nicknamed the New York White House. JFK was there now, on Friday, November 15, 1963, and the lobby was crawling with New York City policemen in blue and with more serious-looking men in suits with watchful expressions on their faces.

Kennedy was in town to give a couple of speeches, and Barry Slotnick had managed to score an appointment with the president of the United States to discuss a matter of concern to one of Slotnick's clients.

Slotnick represented Gaston Espinal, who until recently had served as the Dominican Republic's consul general to the United States under the Dominican president, Juan Bosch. Two years earlier, after the assassination of longtime military dictator Rafael Trujillo, Bosch had returned to the island after twenty-three years as a dissident in exile, and he had recently been elected president in what were considered the country's first democratic elections. But two months ago, after only seven months in office, Bosch had been overthrown by a military coup. The following month, Slotnick's client Espinal and a group of followers had broken into Espinal's former third-floor offices in Rockefeller Center and barricaded themselves inside. Espinal then telegrammed President Kennedy, asking that the US government "continue its policy of nonrecognition of the unlawful de facto government that is presently destroying the freedom and civil liberties of the Dominican people." Slotnick's charge was to get the United States to recognize Bosch as the island nation's legitimate ruler.

When Slotnick stepped out of the elevator on the thirty-fourth floor of the Carlyle, he saw Secret Service agents lining the hallway. There was a glamour to this world, far removed from the bustle of his shared office down near the courthouses or anything he'd known growing up, but Slotnick felt alive here, approaching the inner sanctum of power.

A staffer opened the door and ushered Slotnick into room

34A, informally called the presidential suite. It was a penthouse duplex, and Slotnick found himself in a living room, empty except for himself and the staffer. Slotnick looked out the huge picture windows, with their breathtaking views south toward midtown and west over Central Park. He noticed a charcoal drawing of three ballet dancers hung over a sofa. On a table, there was a copy of *Time* and a book titled *Flanders in the Fifteenth Century*. He saw a box of Cuban cigars next to a white telephone that had an image of the White House printed on the dial.

Twenty minutes passed, and Slotnick began to wonder whether the meeting was going to happen. Then: "Mr. Slotnick."

That familiar Boston honk. Slotnick looked up, toward the sound. The president of the United States was coming down the staircase from the upper floor and walking toward him—twenty-four-year-old Barry from the Bronx. And calling him *Mr.* Slotnick.

The US government, alarmed by the recent ascension of Fidel Castro in Cuba, was wary of another Latin American government with even a hint of leftism. But in their ten-minute meeting, Kennedy told Slotnick that as long as he was president, the United States would never recognize the three-man junta that had overthrown Juan Bosch.

As Slotnick left the Carlyle, he flattered himself that just as Kennedy represented the dawn of a hopeful new age, he was himself on the verge of a dazzling career.

A week later, John F. Kennedy was assassinated in Dallas.

Three days after that, Slotnick received a telegram from Dean Rusk, Kennedy's secretary of state, refusing to recognize Bosch's presidency.

CHAPTER 16

Slotnick paced the well of the majestic old courtroom, with its oak-coffered ceiling and oil paintings of judges past, and channeled the high purpose and passion he tried to bring to all his cases. Each case was the most important one he had ever tried. Each case, he deeply believed, was winnable. Each case was an all-out battle of the humble individual against the overpowering state.

"Your Honor," Slotnick said now, steepling his hands and speaking in the most grave tone he could muster. "I stand before you today to prevent a great injustice."

The judge nodded indulgently. Slotnick was only twenty-five, and he looked even younger.

Sitting behind Slotnick in the courtroom was Vincent "Chin" Gigante.

Gigante was a beefy guy with a dark, pomaded pompadour and sleepy-looking eyes. He was an ex-boxer and a soldier in the Genovese crime family. Supposedly, he'd made his bones trying to assassinate Frank Costello, the legendary Mafia boss whom tabloids dubbed the Prime Minister of the Underworld.

Slotnick had gotten to know Chin's brother Ralphie back when he lived in Greenwich Village, close to a luncheonette. It hadn't taken Slotnick long to realize that this wasn't any old luncheonette. There were often stacks of cash lying around. There was a phone no one was allowed to use. There were always knockabout neighborhood wiseguys in the place. Their base was a nearby social club, the Triangle Civic Improvement Association, but they seemed to run their bookie business out of the luncheonette. Slotnick felt comfortable around them and sometimes put money on Yankees games with Ralphie. Slotnick was devoted to the Bronx Bombers. Growing up, he and his friends would hang outside Yankee Stadium all the time and try to sneak into home games. When the team lost the American League pennant to the Cleveland Indians in 1954, he'd been too upset to eat dinner.

A few days ago, now that Slotnick was a practicing lawyer, Ralphie's brother Chin had come to him about an urgent personal matter, which was what had brought the two men to court today.

Right after uttering the words "prevent a great injustice," Slotnick paused dramatically, letting a pregnant silence fill the air and casting a doleful gaze at the accused, who, it was being claimed, possessed "a known vicious propensity."

Then Slotnick turned back toward the judge and resumed his grand oration. "I am here," Slotnick said, "to make sure that a tragic wrong does not occur."

Standing beside Slotnick, Bullets—Gigante's German shepherd—wagged his tail.

* * *

Vincent Gigante had undoubtedly done some terrible things in his life, but when it came to Bullets, "he loved that dog," Slotnick remembers. Bullets would sit all day at the Triangle Civic Improvement Association, on Sullivan Street, where Gigante and his buddies sat collecting bets and playing pinochle. Bullets had a nose for undercover police and would start barking like a maniac if he sensed one nearby. Plainclothes cops weren't the only group to whom Bullets took exception. Chin was "as racist as Archie Bunker," his daughter Rita would later recall, prone to throwing around epithets such as *moulinyan*—derived from *melanzane,* the Italian word for "eggplant"—and Bullets took after his owner. If a Black person made the mistake of walking down Sullivan Street, the snarling dog would give chase.

Whenever the police received reports that Bullets was at it again, they'd come to the Triangle and ignore the mobsters in search of the troublesome canine. If Gigante knew a police visit was imminent, he'd say, "Go, Bullets!" and Bullets would tear off down the street to hide in a neighbor's apartment until his master whistled to let him know it was safe to come out.

But a week earlier, Bullets had sunk his teeth into a woman he deemed a neighborhood interloper, and a police officer had come and taken the dog away. If the complainant could show that Bullets had not merely attacked her but also possessed "a known vicious propensity," the judge could order that the animal be euthanized. Gigante, desperate not to lose his canine sidekick, turned to Slotnick for help, and the lawyer had demanded a hearing.

Slotnick knew that this case wasn't going to be easy. Despite the attorney's youthful conviction that he could solve any legal problem if he just thought long and hard enough, he had—until yesterday—been stumped about how he could possibly save Bullets from being put down. Slotnick might argue that there were mitigating circumstances—that Bullets had had an under-privileged puppyhood on the mean streets of New York City, say, or that Bullets had been acting in self-defense—but he could not deny that the dog had a rap sheet. This was his third biting incident (or "*alleged* biting incident," as Slotnick emphatically described it), and Slotnick had turned the problem over and over until his head hurt, hoping for a bolt of inspiration.

Now, in the courtroom, as Chin glowered in his seat nearby, the victim and a series of police officers who'd had to deal with Bullets in the past took the witness stand. One by one, describing a succession of incidents, they painted a portrait of Bullets as some kind of foaming hellhound. As Gigante listened to the mounting evidence, his customary air of menace became increasingly tinged with what looked like genuine fear.

But when Slotnick stood to present a defense, all the at-torney's earlier worries had vanished. He felt and looked like he was in command, and he asked the judge to excuse him for a moment. Then he walked out of the courtroom, Bullets trotting along beside him. A minute later, Slotnick came back in. This time he was holding three leashes. Attached to each of them was a German shepherd. The three dogs looked identical.

When Slotnick reached the front of the chamber with the four-legged trio (two of whom he'd borrowed from an accom-modating neighbor in Greenwich Village), he turned to the woman who'd brought the complaint against Bullets.

"Miss," he said, "can you please tell us which of these dogs bit you?"

"Um..."

The woman couldn't ID the guilty dog. Nor could the police officers who'd confidently testified about prior bitings point out which dog had been responsible.

"This case is dismissed," the judge said, gaveling the proceeding to an end.

Slotnick turned to his client and smiled.

Chin, with his beloved Bullets returned to him, hugged Slotnick a little too hard.

Slotnick named the case *The People v. Bullets* and dubbed it his first death-penalty case.

CHAPTER 17

When Slotnick arrived at the courthouse, he was wearing his game face.

It was May of 1966. The day before, he had received a call from Jacob Kossman, a gruff lawyer in Philadelphia whose clients included Teamsters boss Jimmy Hoffa and several organized crime figures and who was regarded as so brilliant that Supreme Court justice William Brennan sometimes called to ask his opinion on legal issues. Kossman said he needed someone in New York to help with a matter there. A colleague had told him that Slotnick, not even twenty-seven years old, was a brilliant young appellate attorney already well versed in local statutes and case law.

Now, in the hallway outside the courtroom where Slotnick was supposed to meet the client, he saw a short man in a business suit standing by himself.

Slotnick asked, "Where's Joe Colombo?"

"That's me," the man said.

"I'm Barry Slotnick."

"You're my lawyer."

Slotnick had certainly heard of Joe Colombo, who was the reputed leader of an organization that had until recently been known as the Profaci crime family. Colombo was in his early forties, young for a crime boss. His father, Tony, had been a mafioso until he was found garroted in the back seat of a car. Allegedly, Joe had started out running craps games, then become a hit man, then a capo, and finally a boss after he double-crossed Profaci godfather Joe Magliocco and was installed in his place by rival families.

The man Slotnick met in Brooklyn, though, was quiet and less rough around the edges than the wiseguys Slotnick was used to.

Colombo had been subpoenaed to testify before a grand jury. For most clients, this wouldn't have presented a problem. Anyone subpoenaed to testify before a grand jury was granted immunity from being prosecuted for anything revealed in that testimony. But organized crime clients were different. Prosecutors exploited all possible loopholes to get convictions against mafiosi, who were maddeningly adept at slipping through the legal net. One of the most helpful loopholes was the Mafia's own code of silence. A witness who refused to testify after being granted immunity could be held in contempt of court and sent to prison. Yet mobsters would refuse to answer even the simplest questions on principle.

It became a ritual trap for prosecutors to set.

"How'd you get to court today?"

When the gangsters inevitably said, "I refuse to answer," they'd go to jail for six months.

This was the situation confronting Slotnick, but he saw an angle.

"That's ridiculous," he chided Colombo after the mobster explained that he wouldn't be answering any questions. "They're offering you immunity. How does it affect you to answer questions?"

"We don't want to give information."

"They're not asking you who you killed. They don't want you to have immunity for anything serious. You're a big gangster. This is a game they're playing."

"I'll try it your way," Colombo agreed.

This was a highly unusual move, and "all his guys were very pissed off," Slotnick remembers.

Even the prosecutor seemed startled when Colombo started responding to his banal queries. "He's answering questions."

"Ask him about the people he's killed," Slotnick said tartly.

Instead, the prosecutor sent Colombo home.

It was a groundbreaking tactic and the beginning of the end of that particular prosecutorial gambit.

From then on, Barry Slotnick was Joe Colombo's lawyer.

Soon he would be one of the small fraternity of go-to attorneys for a whole gamut of jammed-up wiseguys.

CHAPTER 18

It was late summer of 1966, and nineteen-year-old Donna Auerbach, blond and good-looking and without a care in the world, was strolling down a sidewalk one Saturday afternoon on the Upper East Side with her roommate, Hallie. Donna was a sheltered young woman from northern Ohio, a well-to-do real estate developer's daughter who'd grown up with horses, and she was enjoying her last few days of a summer in Manhattan. She'd spent the past couple of months living in a penthouse apartment at 77th Street near First Avenue, seeing Broadway shows and getting a taste of the big city. Soon she'd be heading home to Sandusky to continue her studies at Ohio State.

Donna noticed that she and Hallie had company behind them on the sidewalk.

"Let's get out of here," Donna said. "There are two guys following us."

"No," Hallie said. "Let's see what they want." Hallie, who was older than Donna, worked for an executive at Screen Gems and was what some would call a tough broad.

Barry Slotnick and his friend Stanley, who lived in this neighborhood and clerked for a judge, caught up with Donna and Hallie and talked them into joining them for a drink.

The dive bar on the corner of 74th Street and Second Avenue had a green-and-white-striped awning and a red neon sign announcing its name: Tinker's. Inside, it was dark and smoky; there was a long mahogany bar and a jukebox and sawdust on the floor. Hallie thought Stanley was neurotic but funny. Donna thought Barry was smart and sweet and sometimes silly.

When the men found out Donna was from Ohio, they insisted on showing her around the city in Barry's big Cadillac convertible. It was kind of a clunker, but still impressive, and Donna was charmed by the obvious pride Barry took in his car.

He drove the group down to Greenwich Village. Then they all rode the ferry to Staten Island and back. Then Barry drove the girls back uptown and dropped them at their building, but not before coaxing a phone number out of Donna.

When he called the next day, she couldn't remember his name. But something clicked.

Instead of returning to Ohio, Donna stayed in New York, renting a studio apartment and getting a job with an executive-recruiting firm. Soon, she and Barry were inseparable. He was her everything, and his world became hers.

If Donna needed to reach Barry in the evening, she knew to call the Copacabana, the legendary nightclub on East 60th Street patronized by celebrities and run by gangsters. That's where her boyfriend's clients tended to spend their time, so that's where their lawyer tended to spend his time. It was also where Barry took Donna on dates. They'd be whisked through the downstairs kitchen into the club and seated at a front-and-center table, where Barry would rub elbows with Frank Sinatra and Sammy Davis Jr. and various "colleagues" of Colombo while Donna smiled shyly.

Her mother had taken an instant dislike to her daughter's suitor, who soon became her fiancé. "How does he know they're not going to hurt him?" she'd ask about his clients.

The mobsters wouldn't harm Barry, Donna would assure her mother. Why would they? "He's helping them."

The night before Donna and Barry were to wed, on July 12, 1968, in Baltimore, Colombo called from the Thirtieth Precinct station, in Harlem. He'd been arrested in a roundup that also included Carlo Gambino, and he needed Slotnick's help. Only the sympathy of a friendly judge, who kept the courthouse open late so Slotnick could arrange Colombo's bail, allowed Slotnick to keep his two most important relationships from coming irreconcilably into conflict. Slotnick's desk would come to feature a paperweight that read: A GOOD LAWYER KNOWS THE LAW; A GREAT LAWYER KNOWS THE JUDGE.

Beyond all those nights at the Copa, Slotnick generally didn't socialize with his clients or necessarily even like them. But Joe Colombo had a genteel manner that was rare in the wiseguy business. Every September, he would escort Barry and Donna through the Feast of San Gennaro, a street fair in Little Italy where thousands of people squeezed into a few blocks of Mulberry Street to eat sausages and fried dough. "He happened to be a very sweet man," Donna says. "I don't know what he did in his professional life, but he was sweet to us."

One summer day in 1970, Barry and Donna and a new member of the family, their one-year-old son, Stuart, visited Joe Colombo at his five-acre horse farm in Blooming Grove, west of the Hudson River north of New York City. "It was a nice house, not crazy, a modest ranch house on a lot of property," Donna remembers, "and I guess we went up on a Sunday for a big, beautiful Italian lunch. His family was there."

The group was outside, and Slotnick commented on Colombo's youngest son, Christopher, a toddler.

"I want to know why your kid's walking," Slotnick said. His own boy was still a crawler.

"Give him to me," Colombo said. "He'll be walking before the afternoon is done."

The Mafia boss took little Stuart by the hands and started marching him back and forth.

Soon Slotnick was telling anyone who'd listen that Joe Colombo had taught his son to walk.

CHAPTER 19

On the morning of July 30, 1970, more than a hundred protesters who'd arrived on chartered buses held hands in a chain on West End Avenue. The group had been marching for five and a half hours, blocking trucks from coming and going by standing in front of a line of trucking bays at the Upper West Side printing plant of the *New York Times*.

In an era of long-haired protesters, this group looked very different. It included old women and men in suits as well as Joe Colombo and his twenty-three-year-old son, Joe Colombo Jr. Barry Slotnick was with them.

This had all begun when the younger Colombo was arrested and charged with conspiring with a coin dealer to melt down two hundred thousand dollars' worth of silver dollars in order to recast them as more valuable silver ingots.

Colombo, who already felt persecuted by the FBI, was enraged by his son's arrest. Convinced that he was being harassed because he was Italian American (and not because his father was boss of one of New York's five big crime families), Colombo Senior showed up with his family and a group of supporters in a dozen cars at the FBI office at Third Avenue and East 69th Street. As supporters stood behind him with homemade protest signs, he began kicking the front doors and yelling, "Here I am! You want me? You want my family? Come on down here and open the door!" The next day, in an era that was birthing many civil rights groups, Colombo founded the Italian-American Civil Rights League. Slotnick, as Colombo's lawyer, became the league's lawyer, too.

In the months since, the group had stood behind barricades almost daily, wielding pickets (FBI IS ANTI-ITALIAN), handing out leaflets, likening the Bureau to the Gestapo, and chanting, "Hi-dee, hi-dee, hi-dee, ho—the FBI has got to go!" as ice and eggs rained down on them from the windows of a nearby building. The group was growing at a rapid pace, with the protesters numbering as high as 4,500 people. A month earlier, the group had held the first Italian Unity Day, which drew fifty thousand people.

Today, as fifty police officers got ready to break up the picketers who were protesting the paper's use of Italian "labels" in its coverage of organized crime, Slotnick persuaded the group to stop blocking the New York Times printing plant's driveway and secured a meeting with the newspaper's leaders. The next day, Slotnick and a few league representatives met with the Times's managing editor, A. M. Rosenthal, and other executives. In the meeting, which lasted two hours, Slotnick, and Colombo's eldest son, Anthony, twenty-five, aired a number of grievances, such as the paper's inattention to the discrimination faced by Italian Americans.

"Unless you do something to solve this," Anthony Colombo said, "your trucks will not roll."

Finally, Rosenthal agreed to consider the matter while stating that the *Times* would not be strong-armed into changing its policy.

"We asked them not to use the terms *Mafia* and *Cosa Nostra*," Slotnick recalls.

The paper's mob beat reporter asked Arthur Gelb, then the metropolitan editor, about *Mafia*: "If we can't use that word, what's the point of my being here?" Gelb agreed with him.

"They told us to go screw ourselves," Slotnick recalls. "They were the *New York Times,* and they'd use any terms they wanted to."

Improbably, the league had more success persuading the US Department of Justice, which did stop using *Mafia* and *Cosa Nostra* in its racketeering indictments.

Joe Colombo's concerns about anti-Italian language continued. As far as Colombo and many Italian Americans were concerned, Mario Puzo's recent bestselling novel, *The Godfather,* was part of the problem. When he heard that a *Godfather* movie was going into production, to be directed by Francis Ford Coppola, Colombo had called the head of Paramount Pictures, Robert Evans, and, according to Evans, threatened him. After Evans disclaimed direct involvement, saying that Al Ruddy was producing the film, Colombo allegedly responded: "When we kill a snake, we chop its fucking head off."

The production had encountered one setback after another. Cameras were mysteriously broken. A Cinemobile truck with more than one million dollars' worth of equipment, parked in New York City's Little Italy neighborhood, vanished. Paramount's New York offices were evacuated twice over bomb scares. Ruddy found his car being tailed. Evans received threats against his wife, Ali MacGraw, and their baby son, Joshua. Finally, a young hustler named Gianni Russo, who'd sold a lot of one-dollar buttons to raise funds for the league and who also had Hollywood ambitions, went to Slotnick, who, he knew, could get Colombo to the table.

Now, in a conference room at the Gulf and Western Building, overlooking Central Park (later the Trump International Hotel and Tower), Ruddy agreed that anything in the script that Colombo deemed anti–Italian American, including all references to "the Mafia," would be removed. Slotnick said he'd mark up the script. He assured the producers that in return for their cooperation, their production problems would disappear.

Ruddy also indulged a "suggestion" by Colombo. Gianni Russo was trying to be an actor, and he wondered aloud in the meeting whether he could play Carlo Rizzi, Don Corleone's wife-beating son-in-law, whose role hadn't been cast yet. As Ruddy paused to answer, Colombo himself weighed in: "He plays Carlo." And so the previously unknown Gianni Russo made his acting debut in a supporting role in one of the greatest films of the twentieth century.

Russo credits Slotnick with launching his acting career and with facilitating the making of *The Godfather*. "If Barry wasn't there, there'd be no legitimacy to the meeting. Paramount would have run away." From then on, production went seamlessly. When Slotnick tried throwing in a script note of his own, though, he was less successful. In the screenplay, Vito Corleone referred to "a Jew congressman," and Slotnick asked for it to be deleted.

"Oh, no," Ruddy said. "We're only taking out Italian stuff, not what offends you; that wasn't the deal."

Colombo's involvement garnered him further attention in the press. But his increasingly public profile was at odds with his cloistered criminal life. Every time he did something that got him mentioned in the newspapers, the ill will toward him among his colleagues grew.

CHAPTER 20

It sounded like a thunderclap, as if the thunder were right next to him in suite 1510, on the fifteenth floor.

Barry Slotnick was sitting at his desk beside an open window at 3:45 on an August afternoon in 1970.

Then, all at once, Slotnick felt a push of displaced air. He heard a *boom*. His ears were ringing. There was a chemical smell of smoke. His mouth had dust in it.

It was strange, though. Nothing in his office looked different.

Then he ran to his door and opened it to see that the explosion had blown his suite's door in, demolishing the waiting-room furniture.

He rushed out to the hallway. The blast had thrown other doors along the hallway off their hinges and smashed the floor's drop ceiling to rubble, exposing pipes and wiring.

People were walking around, some dazed and crying, some chattering, some silent. Slotnick first assured himself that, miraculously, no one had been hurt. Then he thought quickly.

He was sure this wasn't an accident and that it had been meant for him. Of all the lawyers in the suite, he was the one with the most dangerous clients. He was angry and—not that he'd ever show it—terrified. Less than an hour before the explosion, Donna had visited with one-year-old Stuart in tow. What if they'd left later? Or the bomb had gone off sooner?

Slotnick called Donna right away at their apartment, near Lincoln Center, and said, without any explanation, "Go to the wall."

Donna knew just what to do. Her husband's occupation and notorious clientele had instilled in him a degree of paranoia, so he had established a contingency plan in the event of an emergency. This surely qualified as one, so he'd used their pre-arranged code phrase. "Go to the wall" meant that Donna was to immediately spirit Stuart to the Bronx, to the small third-floor two-bedroom apartment at 2504 Bronx Park East where Slotnick's mother, Rose, lived. It was across the street from a park with a huge stone wall.

Later, as Slotnick's offices were being cordoned off as a crime scene, police found fragments of a pipe bomb. They also found a note taped to his blown-in door that read: *"YOU HELP THE MAFIA. WE DON'T LIKE THEM."*

Donna later told Barry and the police that when she'd left the office shortly before the bombing, she had noticed a man in the hallway holding a knapsack and standing near the service elevator. An agent from the FBI would tell Slotnick that they believed the bomb to have been planted by an enemy of Joe Colombo. "The FBI, taking the onus off of them, believed it was rival mobsters," Slotnick would later recall.

But the Bureau didn't like Slotnick—"They considered me to

be part of the mob"—and he believed they'd been keeping tabs on him. "Barry felt we were under surveillance because he won so many cases that it left egg on the face of the government," Donna says. Slotnick wasn't prepared to rule out the possibility that the FBI itself had tried to bomb him to oblivion.

CHAPTER 21

On May 13, 1971, Slotnick was about to drive over from his office to Brooklyn to have dinner with Colombo when Meir Kahane called to say that he and six other members of the Jewish Defense League had been arrested.

A year earlier, Slotnick's uncle Harry, the "pistol-packing Yudel" rabbi, had called and asked his nephew to visit. When Slotnick arrived at his uncle's office, in the Bronx, Harry introduced him to Rabbi Meir Kahane. "This is my friend," Uncle Harry said of Kahane. "He gets into trouble. If he needs legal help, I want you to help him."

Kahane had already made a name for himself as a militant Zionist, popularizing the phrases "Never again," referring to the murder in the Holocaust of six million Jews, and "Every Jew a .22." He also founded the JDL, which used a Black Panthers–like logo of a fist superimposed on a Star of David.

Slotnick was sympathetic to Kahane's worldview—that

anti-Semitism was rampant and that Jews weren't in good shape in America—but he wasn't sure that he was the best person to give him legal advice. Kahane routinely did things like break the car windows of Russian diplomats, which he intended as a protest against the treatment of Soviet Jewry.

"Okay," Slotnick said, "but I don't do disorderly conduct cases. I do federal criminal cases."

"Okay," Uncle Harry said. "If he has a federal criminal problem, you'll represent him."

In 1971, Kahane did have a federal criminal problem. He and his associates had been arrested for making bombs and conspiring to carry guns across state lines.

Slotnick called Joe Colombo to cancel their dinner plans, explaining that he had to get Kahane and his people out of jail. It wasn't going to be easy, because they couldn't afford to post bail.

Colombo said he understood.

When Slotnick arrived at the Brooklyn federal courthouse, Colombo was already there, together with a bail bondsman. Colombo liked the fact that Kahane fought for his people; he saw himself as doing the same. Colombo paid twenty-five thousand dollars to bail out Kahane and another ten thousand dollars to bail out each of his associates. "Rabbi Kahane is a man of God, and his cause is just," Colombo said at a joint news conference speedily arranged by Slotnick.

Kahane and Colombo pledged to stand together, and the next day there they were, on the front page of the *New York Times*. The headline KAHANE AND COLOMBO JOIN FORCES TO FIGHT REPORTED U.S. HARASSMENT ran with a large photo of the leaders of the Jewish Defense League and the Italian-American Civil

Rights League, with Slotnick at their side. Slotnick was pleased to see that he was mentioned in the article. Barry Slotnick, fosterer of intergroup harmony.

Once again, though, Colombo's appearance in the media added to the growing discontent surrounding him and his activities.

Beneath a scorching sun, on June 28, 1971, thousands of people milled around Columbus Circle, at the southwest corner of Manhattan's Central Park, wearing red-white-and-green straw hats and quenching their thirst with plastic cups of orange juice and grape juice. They were waiting for the start of the second annual Unity Day rally, organized by Colombo's Italian-American Civil Rights League.

There was a ripple of turned heads as Joe Colombo himself, wearing green slacks and a white polo shirt, moved through the crowd, shaking hands and pausing to pose for pictures in front of a man with a camera and a press badge. Colombo was scheduled to speak, and Slotnick was at his most prized client's side.

Slotnick was defending Colombo in half a dozen cases, including those involving contempt of court, tax evasion, a seven-hundred-and-fifty-thousand-dollar jewelry theft, a five-million-dollar-a-year gambling operation, and perjury—the latter for understating his criminal record on an application for a state real estate broker's license.

In the year leading up to the second Unity Day, Colombo had become a media phenomenon, appearing on the cover of *Time* and on *The Dick Cavett Show*. This year, the organizers were projecting five hundred thousand attendees at the event, headlined by a variety of politicians and entertainers, and the New York City Police Department had sent more than one thousand cops to watch over it. Donna had brought Stuart in a stroller and stayed awhile, but she was pregnant with their second child, and as her feet grew tired, she left to return to their apartment, at the nearby Schwab House, on Riverside Drive.

But the reality was plain to Slotnick: there were maybe ten thousand people here, tops. All Colombo's media activity had antagonized his many underworld colleagues, who believed in the code of *omerta,* and they had put out word in the Italian American community discouraging people from attending.

Around 11:45 a.m., forty-five minutes before the program was to begin, Colombo turned away from the photographer he'd stopped for and—

Pop. Pop. Pop.

Deafeningly loud. Right in Slotnick's ears. Was it firecrackers?

But Colombo was lunging forward, reaching out to grab a police barricade but hitting the ground first. Blood seemed to splash from his head.

Everything was blurring together. The man who'd been taking the pictures a minute ago was standing over Colombo, holding a Luger. Now Colombo's son Joe Junior was tackling him. The man was still shooting as he went down. Now a cop was hitting Slotnick with his nightstick, protectively, to bring him to the ground.

The world was sideways. Slotnick focused on Colombo, who lay a few feet away from him. Colombo had rolled from his side onto his back. There was blood in his hair. Blood on his face. Blood pooling on the ground around him. His horn-rimmed glasses lay askew beside him.

Then the cries began.

"It's Joe!"

"They got Joe! They got Joe!"

"No, not Joe!"

Colombo's wife, Lucille, and their children were crying nearby. The crowd was panicking, screaming and scrambling and stampeding north toward 61st Street.

More gunshots. Now the shooter (a man later identified as Jerome A. Johnson) had been killed, shot twice in the back by an unidentified man assumed to be a Colombo soldier.

Slotnick snapped from his daze as fear began to surge through him. Whoever had come for Colombo might be coming for his lawyer next—or, worse, his lawyer's family. Slotnick rushed to a pay phone to call Donna, dropping coins in his haste to put money in the slot. When Donna answered, Slotnick exhaled with relief. Then, for the second time in a year, he told her, "Go to the wall."

One of Colombo's soldiers drove Slotnick the three blocks to Roosevelt Hospital, where a private ambulance adorned with Italian and American flags had already rushed an unconscious Colombo. It was chaos there, doctors and nurses weaving among the throngs of police and mobsters and reporters and photographers. Slotnick went up to the second floor to visit members of the Colombo family, who were weeping and praying in a private room they'd been given.

Outside the hospital, on Ninth Avenue, dozens of friends and supporters held a prayer vigil with candles and rosaries while Colombo underwent five hours of surgery. Two bullets were removed from his midbrain and neck, and a third was left where it had lodged in his jaw.

A surgeon told Slotnick that Colombo wouldn't live through the night. "Please don't commit to that," Slotnick said, "because there will be a lot of angry people."

Colombo lived, but his crime-boss days were over. For the first six months after the shooting, he was in a wheelchair and couldn't speak but was responsive. When Slotnick visited him, the gangster would squeeze his lawyer's thumb once for yes and twice for no. After that, he "checked out," Slotnick says, falling into a years-long coma.

Police snatched up several Colombo rivals, including Joseph "Crazy Joe" Gallo and Carlo Gambino, for questioning. Though Gambino was understood to be furious about Colombo's yen for publicity, Colombo's allies blamed Gallo, the leader of a dissident faction within the Colombo organization, for the shooting.

The following April 7, 1972, at 5:15 one morning, Colombo loyalists found Gallo celebrating his forty-third birthday at Umbertos Clam House, in Little Italy. Gallo, seeing the gunmen, rose and shouted, "You son of a bitch." Then the bullets started flying. Gallo died on the sidewalk out front.

Decades later, Meir Kahane, the JDL leader, was also felled by an assassin's bullet.

On the evening of November 5, 1990, in the conference room of a Marriott hotel on the East Side of Manhattan, Kahane, then fifty-eight, was giving a talk to a crowd of Orthodox Jews when a man approached him and fired a .357 revolver twice, hitting Kahane in the neck and chest. As the shooter—El Sayyid Nosair, an Egyptian-born American citizen who lived in New

Jersey—fled the hotel, he exchanged gunfire with a United States Postal Service police officer and was arrested.

John Miller was having dinner with a bunch of homicide detectives at Campagnola, a restaurant on the Upper East Side, when they got word of the shooting.

Miller immediately called Slotnick with the news.

"Meir Kahane is dead," Miller said. "He's at Bellevue."

For a moment, Slotnick was speechless.

Then he said, "I'm on my way."

At Bellevue hospital, a crowd of angry JDL members was gathering, but Slotnick spoke to them, helping avert a violent demonstration.

Slotnick was able to negotiate with the city's mayor, David Dinkins, and the NYPD to get Kahane's body released by the coroner so that it could be flown to Israel and buried within twenty-four hours of his death, as prescribed by Orthodox law.

Nosair was charged with Kahane's murder, but although convicted of assaulting the postal service police officer, he was acquitted of the murder.

Reuben Mattus, the founder of Häagen-Dazs ice cream and a major patron of the JDL, commissioned Slotnick to undertake an independent investigation into the Kahane assassination. According to Slotnick, he received information from the Israeli government that led him to conclude that the murder had been a conspiracy—even possibly the first death caused by Al Qaeda on US soil.

CHAPTER 22

On Wednesday, February 23, 1972, Slotnick awoke in New Rochelle, where he and Donna now lived with their two children—two-year-old Stuart and newborn Melissa—and went straight outside to pick up that morning's *New York Times*.

Standing in his bathrobe in the driveway, he started flipping through the A section. Finally, on page 24, he saw it. On the lower left corner of the page. Two columns. The headline: SUPREME COURT'S ACTIONS.

Slotnick quickly scanned the article until he found what he was looking for.

"The Supreme Court took the following actions today...Held 7 to 1, that Joseph Colombo, the Mafia figure, was punished for criminal contempt in 1966 when he was given a 30-day civil contempt sentence for refusing to testify before a Kings County grand jury and that the courts of New York must now decide if they have committed double jeopardy by subsequently indicting him on criminal contempt charges for the same refusal to talk (No. 71-352, Colombo v. New York). Dissenting: Douglas."

What the article wasn't saying was that the day before, Slotnick had won in the United States Supreme Court. Most lawyers never even had a case *reach* the highest court in the land. And Slotnick had just scored a *victory.*

Even as Joe Colombo lay incapacitated, a contempt case from 1965, before they'd met, still shadowed the crime boss. In that earlier case, Colombo had refused to answer questions put to him by a Brooklyn grand jury, despite a grant of immunity. A judge ordered him to answer, and he refused. The judge gave him a week to reconsider, and Colombo still refused. At that point, the judge found him guilty of criminal contempt and sentenced him to thirty days in jail and a two-hundred-and-fifty-dollar fine, which he served and paid.

Ten months later, he was indicted again for the same instance of contempt. A trial court threw out the charges, seeing them as a case of double jeopardy, but the appellate court reversed the lower court, arguing that each indictment was for a separate act of contempt: the first being contempt of a grand jury, the second contempt of a judge.

In the fall of 1970, Slotnick had petitioned the United States Supreme Court on the matter. The country's highest court agreed that the lower court's finding violated the Constitution's double-jeopardy clause, vacated the judgment, and sent it back to the appeals court in Albany for rehearing. The appeals court again rejected the double-jeopardy argument. Finally, on February 22, 1972, Slotnick won a second ruling from the US Supreme Court, a ruling that vacated the appeals court's decision and sent the case back to that court with an order to rule differently.

It was a bittersweet turning point for Slotnick. The Supreme Court decision came too late to benefit Colombo, whom the Slotnicks would continue to visit at his home in upstate New York until his death, at age fifty-four, in 1978. But as a legal matter, the decision was vindicating and gratifying. The *Times* mention was the cherry on top. Every lawyer in the country followed Supreme Court decisions.

Slotnick made his way back into the house and plunked the paper down in front of Donna. "Not guilty," he said with a smile. It didn't make sense in this instance, but Donna knew what he meant.

She gave her husband a kiss.

Though Slotnick was as good a lawyer the day before the decision as he was the day after, overnight it elevated him to another echelon of the legal profession.

A much broader range of clients began knocking on his door.

PART THREE

CHAPTER 23

Three days into the Dioguardi trial, Barry Slotnick approached the prosecutor, Jim Druker, in the hallway and said, "I have the guy who actually did it."

"C'mon, Barry," Druker said. "I'm not buying it."

"No," Slotnick said. "This is for real. This guy's name is Michael Laino. He's a taxi driver. He read about the case in the papers and didn't want someone else to pay for his crime."

Druker cocked an eyebrow.

It was late November of 1972, and Slotnick was representing Philip Dioguardi, a twenty-four-year-old former Colombo bodyguard who weighed more than three hundred pounds, in a federal trial. Fat Philly, as everyone called him, had been charged with bank fraud and was facing the possibility of serious prison time. He had pleaded not guilty, but halfway through the trial, things weren't looking good for him. Three reputable witnesses, all bank employees, had picked him out of a police lineup, fingering him as the man who'd come into their branch and filled out a fraudulent mortgage application.

From the beginning, Slotnick had insisted that Fat Philly was innocent. Druker had ignored Slotnick's protestations as rote defense-lawyer posturing. But the day after their hallway conversation, Slotnick produced Laino in court, and Laino said he was guilty.

Druker had to admit that the taxi driver was a dead ringer for Dioguardi, but he was still skeptical. He wouldn't put it past a mobster to bribe or pressure an innocent man to be a fall guy.

"I want to make a deal with you," Slotnick said. "I'll let my client take a polygraph if you agree to give Laino a polygraph. If they both fail, I'll get Phil to plead guilty."

Druker's boss gave him permission to make the deal, and Druker hired a polygrapher who wasn't known to be generous to defendants.

Dioguardi passed his polygraph, and Laino passed his polygraph.

On December 1, the judge declared a mistrial.

"I believed our case was a mistake," Druker recalls, "and Fat Phil was innocent." Druker kept his word and moved to dismiss the indictment.

Slotnick called Donna: "Not guilty."

Afterward, the three bank officers who'd been ready to testify against Dioguardi came to Druker's office. "They were angry," Druker says. "It's human nature: where people misidentify someone, they won't want to admit their mistake, and they dig in deeper."

The bank manager said, "I don't care what you say or the

polygraph says. I'll swear to my dying day Dioguardi was the one who filled out the loan application."

"It left me wondering," Druker recalled later. "Was this a case of digging in, or did I and Barry get snookered?"

Either way, Slotnick was developing a reputation for tactical brilliance and for handling cases journalists loved writing about. The media attention, in turn, was drawing more business, allowing Slotnick to expand his practice and build a staff of employees who were far from the typical plain-vanilla office drones.

Joanne Eboli, then called Joanne Cea, was one of those staff members. She worked as Slotnick's assistant and loved the job.

No day was the same as the last. Clients would send her gifts—a Persian rug, a thirty-foot palm tree. Benny "Uncle Benny" Ong, the Godfather of Chinatown, would send giant bags of Chinese food to the office three days a week, and she'd join Slotnick in attending Uncle Benny's annual New Year's banquet. "Barry was a such a baby with the food," she recalls. "He'd say, 'Make believe you're tasting it.'" As a waiter approached, wheeling a cart laden with platters of pigeon parts, "I'd say, 'He loves the beaks.' He'd say, 'She loves the feet.'" There was always laughter amid the intensity of their work.

Years later, Eboli worked as fashion designer Ralph Lauren's assistant, but that job never felt as meaningful. "The fashion business, you can spend three weeks deciding which blue is better," she'd say. She reveled in the force of Slotnick's charisma. He'd light up any room, take command of any conversation.

She also was less intimidated than most by the rough world of the firm's clients. Her father, Pasquale "Patsy Ryan" Eboli, had been a Genovese-family capo before disappearing without a trace in the mid-1970s, and she had grown up sharing Sunday dinners with such men.

Over the years, Slotnick's office neighbors in the Woolworth Building had mostly gotten used to the characters going up and down in the elevator, but not entirely. Slotnick had represented Michael Chen, the leader of the Flying Dragons gang, who'd been indicted for opening fire and killing two people in a Chinatown movie theater. Whenever Chen came to the office, the other secretaries in the suite scrambled to leave. "As soon as Chen got off the elevator, they were gone; they were afraid that someone might try to kill him," Eboli remembers.

One time, Slotnick told her that a client of his, a Gambino-family capo named Joseph DeCicco, would be coming up to the office. As the clock approached seven, Slotnick had to leave, but he asked Eboli to stay to receive DeCicco. The gangster had a court appearance coming up, and he was supposed to come by with his overdue retainer payment.

"If he doesn't pay," Slotnick told her, "I'm not going to represent him."

Slotnick left, and around half an hour later, DeCicco and an associate arrived.

DeCicco handed Eboli a plastic bag, which he said contained eighty thousand dollars.

Eboli looked in the bag and was startled to see stacks of crumpled bills held together by rubber bands.

"I'm like, 'What?'" she remembers.

"You want to count it?" DeCicco asked.

What she didn't want to do was insult him. "No, no," she said. "I'm sure it's fine."

"Miss, here's what I want you to tell Barry," DeCicco said. "'You better fucking show up, you Jew bastard, or I'll get you.'"

"I got it, Joe. I'll tell him."

"Excuse me for my language, miss."

"Don't worry about it. I don't care."

"Tell that Jew bastard I'm going to choke him...I'm sorry, ma'am; I'm sorry for speaking like this, miss." Every time he cursed, it would be immediately followed by an apology.

"He must have repeated those exact words ten times. I kept saying, 'I got it, Joe, I promise you.'"

After DeCicco finally left, Eboli called Slotnick and said, "I'm coming directly to the house with the money."

"I knew you could do it," Slotnick said.

But to catch the Metro-North train to Slotnick's house in Scarsdale, Eboli first had to make her way from downtown to Grand Central Terminal, bag of cash in hand. She wasn't thrilled about her encounter with the cursing thugs, and worried the whole way to Scarsdale that DeCicco and his friend might be lying in wait with plans to hit her over the head and take back the money, and that Slotnick would think she'd stolen it.

As soon as Eboli got to Scarsdale and presented Slotnick with the cash, she told him exactly what DeCicco had said.

Slotnick started laughing.

"I didn't think it was so funny at the time," Eboli recalls.

Slotnick was defending Joe DeCicco against charges of conspiracy and attempted bribery for a scheme in which DeCicco raised one hundred thousand dollars from podiatrists, allegedly to influence planned legislation that threatened to prevent podiatrists from being reimbursed under Medicaid.

DeCicco, along with a fellow mobster and a dozen foot doctors, had been indicted after a fourteen-month police investigation. DeCicco was big and brusque, his codefendant a short, bald man with a raspy voice, and on wiretaps they sounded like stereotypical, not-very-bright wiseguys. In court, DeCicco regularly nodded off at the defense table. He and his codefendant were "literally out of a comic book," Slotnick's former associate Jay Breakstone recalls. "By the end of the trial, the jury was hysterically laughing."

But Slotnick thought the prosecutors had eyes bigger than their stomachs and that in their thirst to include the podiatrists as defendants, they had filed the wrong charges. "You think I liked sitting next to this guy?" Slotnick asked the jury in his summation, after an eleven-week trial. "You might think he's despicable, but that doesn't mean he's guilty." Yes, Slotnick told the jury, DeCicco and his colleague had collected the money from the podiatrists. "But they were pulling a scam. It was a real-life *Sting,* because they never intended to use the money to bribe anyone."

At the time, *The Sting,* starring Robert Redford and Paul Newman, was in movie theaters, and Slotnick repeated the title *The Sting* many times. "They may not be as handsome as the stars of the movie, but they're smarter. They intended to keep the money, and they did." DeCicco and his confederates had pulled off "the perfect crime," Slotnick said. In case the jurors felt that if they let his client off the hook DeCicco would be getting away with too much, Slotnick assured them that the prosecutors could always bring new, more appropriate charges against him.

The jury apparently agreed, finding DeCicco and his

codefendant not guilty. But then Slotnick successfully filed a motion to block a second trial on the grounds that it would violate the Constitution's double-jeopardy protection. After one of the jurors read this in the newspaper, he called Slotnick to complain that Slotnick had hoodwinked the jury.

On the other hand, the juror added, if he ever found himself in legal trouble, he was going to call Slotnick.

CHAPTER 24

In courtroom 10 in the federal courthouse in Brooklyn, Slotnick stood before the man whom, in his opening remarks, he had called "the scum of the earth" and "the lowest type of animal that one could ever see."

John McClean, forty, was tall and wore a leisure suit. Once, he had been a narcotics detective in the New York City Police Department's elite Special Investigative Unit. Now he was a convicted felon, facing a nine-year sentence and cooperating in the hope of shortening it. It was the first week of April in 1976, and he was testifying against Slotnick's client Frank King, a fellow detective in the unit who stood accused of shaking down narcotics suspects based on illegal wiretaps.

"You didn't have a friendship with Frank King, did you?" Slotnick asked softly. He had laryngitis, and jurors leaned forward to hear him.

"I didn't work with Frank King that long to have a friendship with him," McClean said, a tremor in his voice. He was sweating profusely and shaking, apparently from nerves.

They were in a cavernous, formidable room, with twenty-five-foot ceilings and dark fir-and-marble walls. Fluorescent lights glared overhead. The judge, Jack Weinstein, was known for his unconventional approach to courtroom formality. He wore a suit instead of a robe, made the prosecution and defense tables equidistant from the jury (normally the prosecution table was closer to the jury), and sat at the same table as a defendant when he sentenced him.

At the nearby defense table, Frank King, portly and red-faced, wore a brown suit, brown shirt, and tie. He looked like an Irish cop straight out of central casting. Under better circumstances, he often wore a big smile. Now he looked on without giving away what he might be thinking.

"As a matter of fact," Slotnick continued, "you didn't like him."

"That is not true."

McClean was the lead witness, and Slotnick was going to annihilate him.

"Did Frank King ever have an argument with you: yes or no?"

"I had words with Frank King; yes, I did."

"Many?"

"Not too many."

"Did Frank King ever give you a write-up or send you over a bar?"

"What? I didn't understand what you said."

"Did Frank King ever smack you in the face and send you over a bar?"

"No, that is not true. That is not what happened."

"Did you ever have a physical fight with Frank King?"

"We had a pushing and shoving match in a bar, yes, in a bar one night, that is correct."

"So if a witness came here to testify that Frank King punched you in the face and laid you out over a bar, he would be lying?"

"Frank King never punched me in the face and laid me over a bar. Frank King might have took a punch at me and I might have took a punch at Frank King, but I wouldn't say that he laid me over a bar."

McClean was red in the face and angry.

Slotnick just smiled.

He treated every case seriously, but this one was especially close to his heart. King worked for him.

As a detective with the narcotics bureau's notoriously corrupt Special Investigative Unit, King had been considered one of the best in the city. He was also the prime suspect in a famous heist. In 1962, a pair of NYPD cops made the biggest narcotics bust in history, seizing 112 pounds of heroin that the Lucchese crime family had tried smuggling into the United States from France. The incident was the basis for the film *The French Connection*.

Ten years later, it was discovered that forty-four kilos of the French Connection heroin had been checked out from a thirty-by-thirty-foot cage in the NYPD property clerk's office by one Detective Nunziata: this was the name of a real detective, but the signature on the sign-out sheet was in someone else's handwriting. When investigators opened the boxes where the heroin had been stored, they were teeming with red flour beetles. The heroin had been replaced with flour and cornstarch. They soon learned that over a period of three years, "Nunziata" and other detectives had checked a total of four hundred pounds of heroin and cocaine out of evidence. With a street value of seventy million dollars, that made it the biggest theft in US history.

A massive five-year investigation followed, led by a specially appointed state prosecutor named Maurice Nadjari. Eventually, a wiretap of a criminal-defense lawyer who was under investigation in a separate matter recorded a phone call from Frank King, implicating him in the drug heist. King's phones were bugged, and he was tailed by detectives. In one call, he was heard discussing Nunziata's forged signature.

Nadjari, the prosecutor, was a zealot, with a penchant for overly bold promises and premature self-congratulation. In 1973, he vowed that he'd bring indictments against police officers for stealing the French Connection heroin. As the indictments failed to materialize, Nadjari started indicting suspect cops for other reasons. King was indicted for providing a prisoner with fried shrimp from Vincent's Clam Bar. With Slotnick representing King, that case never made it to trial. Then Nadjari indicted King on a charge of conspiracy to hide two fugitive associates of Vincent Papa, a central figure in the heroin theft. Again, Slotnick was able to persuade a judge to dismiss the case before it went to trial. In October of 1975, King was indicted a third time, on the current charges, and this case had now come to trial.

But in the meantime, Slotnick had begun using King as his main investigator. He was a talented detective and especially good at deciphering wiretaps, which over the previous ten years had become a major factor in federal cases.

* * *

Cross-examining McClean, Slotnick next turned to the witness's history of perjury.

"There is no question, is there, that at times you went into a grand jury when you were an arresting officer and lied to the grand jury?"

"On some occasions I did, yes," McClean admitted.

"There is no question that you have been in courtrooms before and taken the same oath that you took today and openly lied in those cases?"

"Not all of them."

"But some of them?"

"Maybe a few."

Had McClean lied on the stand while sitting just as he was now, Slotnick asked, with his arms folded and legs crossed?

"That is not the way it was."

"So your arms were not folded?"

By the time McClean stepped down from the stand, he looked like a broken man.

The next morning, Slotnick appreciated how the *Daily News,* in its write-up of the prior day's proceedings, had singled out his description of McClean as "a disgusting, vile animal who is about to be caged and will do anything to stay out, including damaging a decent, hard-working man."

Six weeks later, after another forty-four witnesses had testified and received similar treatment from Slotnick, Frank King was acquitted. In the courtroom, people screamed. King jumped to his feet and blew a kiss in the direction of the jury box. The prosecutor, who'd given a seven-hour summation, looked devastated by the verdict.

The defense attorney and his client hugged each other. King said, "Now I can get back to work."

The next few years were hard on King. He was eventually convicted of tax evasion (while represented by a different lawyer) and spent some time in prison in Danbury, Connecticut. When he got out, he came back to work for Slotnick, but with an unshakable air of sadness about him. The indictments and investigations had also ensnared his wife, a fellow NYPD detective; she had attempted suicide and been institutionalized ever since.

But in Slotnick's world, Frank King was beloved. He lived near Scarsdale in a nicely furnished colonial-style house. He'd often come to the Slotnick home to drive Barry in to work. The Slotnick kids called him the Commissioner. Jay Breakstone, who worked with Slotnick and would go drinking with King, remembers the investigator fondly. The infamous Special Investigative Unit? "They were probably the greatest group of New York City police detectives in modern times. Amazing people. And yeah, they were probably corrupt. They all had boats. How does a cop have a boat? They all wore three-quarter-length brown leather jackets, including Frank."

CHAPTER 25

In the mid-1970s, Barry had a new client around the corner from the apartment he and Donna shared on the Upper West Side: the Continental Baths, a Colombo-protected gay bathhouse in the basement of the Ansonia Hotel, on Broadway. Owner Steve Ostrow, a bisexual opera singer introduced to Slotnick by his barber, Joe, told the lawyer he was being shaken down by a couple of mobsters. Slotnick gave him his business card and said to show it to them if they came back. Soon enough, the mobsters returned, and when Ostrow showed them Slotnick's card, they vanished.

Ostrow went back to Joe the barber. "What the fuck is this guy Barry?"

"Oh, he's Joe Colombo's lawyer; that's all."

Soon Slotnick had put Ostrow and Colombo in business together.

"My friends who I represent would like to do a little business with you," Ostrow would recall Slotnick saying. "They would like to take over the garbage removal, the cigarette machines, the jukebox, and any other vending machines in the place...whatever deal you got now, they'll give you 5 percent more, plus you'll get better service and newer machines...they're just good people to do business with, and not only that, you'll also have a friend as a bonus. See, they like nice clean cash operations like vending machines and things."

There was also a lot of work for Slotnick in the Continental's operation. During the bathhouse's six-year run, it was raided more than two hundred times by police. Each time, Slotnick came to the rescue.

Barry and Donna became great friends with Ostrow and his wife, Joanne, and would go to the Continental every weekend to see the incredible performers Ostrow brought in. "There'd be guys walking around with loincloths," Donna recalls. "They'd be going upstairs to the orgy room."

For a few years, the house chanteuse was a campy young singer named Bette Midler. When Midler complained about how little she was paid, Ostrow had Slotnick mediate, and the lawyer was able to mollify her by arranging for a better pianist to accompany her, a young man named Barry Manilow.

"Bette was always very involved in getting paid," Slotnick recalls.

One evening in July of 1976, Donna and Barry were having dinner at Sepret Tables, a small, dark Italian restaurant on Third Avenue near East 25th Street in Manhattan, when Donna suddenly kicked her husband under the table. A couple had come in the door: Frank Sinatra and his fourth wife, Barbara Marx. The blond former showgirl and the crooner had just married. Sinatra was a regular at Sepret Tables, which had oak walls festooned with celebrity head shots. The owner, Louis "Louie Domes" Pacella, was a close friend.

Pacella was a short fifty-something Genovese-family soldier who was embroiled in a famous trial involving the Westchester Premier Theater. The Genovese and Gambino families had opened the theater as a cash cow to be fraudulently milked into the ground. Pacella had arranged for Sinatra to perform at the theater for several weeks in return for a significant kickback to Pacella from the theater. During an ensuing trial, a photograph of Sinatra backstage with several Mafia notables, including Carlo Gambino, found its way into circulation, cementing the Sinatra-Mafia connection in the public mind. Slotnick represented Pacella in the trial. "He was a sweet guy," Donna recalls. "I mean, you know, to us."

There was always that asterisk.

In 1974, after the birth of their daughter Shoshana, the Slotnicks hosted a big party in New Rochelle. It was raining torrentially, and their two hundred guests crowded into a tent in the backyard. The group included friends from their temple, other lawyers, people from the Jewish Defense League, and members of Joe Colombo's crew. Somehow it all worked.

But otherwise, Donna never invited Barry's clients to the house. (The one time a mobster did show up, it was an unannounced visit by Anthony Colombo, Joe's son. And young Stuart found himself uneasily having to deflect an attempt by the beefy Colombo to con him out of ten dollars.) But Donna would often see the clients when she and Barry went out on the town. For every gentlemanly type like Joe Colombo and Louis Pacella there were uncouth goons like Vinnie Vingo, a Colombo bodyguard who had a smarmily ingratiating manner and the broken-nose look of a guy who'd been in too many brawls. Some of them could be charming or funny—Jimmy Breslin had even written a comedic novel that became a movie, *The Gang That Couldn't Shoot Straight,* which was a thinly veiled portrait of the Colombo family. But "it made me uncomfortable to be with people I knew committed serious crimes," Donna says.

The perks bothered her, too. From the early days of their courtship, when they'd cut the line at the Copa and get ushered straight to one of the best tables, she'd been nagged by the feeling that it was unfair. She and Barry would fight about it. Barry liked to rail against how the system was stacked against ordinary people, but how was this any different?

Tonight at Sepret Tables, Sinatra and his new bride had been seated with a group of friends at an adjacent table, where a big box of Italian pastries had been delivered. When a large man came over to greet Sinatra, Barbara, mistakenly thinking he was the sender, said, "Thank you so much for the pastries; they're so wonderful."

"Why don't you shut your mouth?" Sinatra told his new wife.

Donna Slotnick turned to Barry and said: "Did you hear how he spoke to her?"

"Why don't you shut *your* mouth?" Barry Slotnick told his wife with a wry smile.

Donna opened her mouth in mock offense but laughed quietly.

CHAPTER 26

Barry Slotnick believed in taking whatever case walked in the door. He in fact said he practiced "door law." He also believed his own mantras about everyone deserving a good lawyer, about the presumption of innocence, and about the state's burden to prove its case beyond a reasonable doubt.

But now a man sat across a conference table from Slotnick and haltingly explained that there were accusations about him.

Slotnick stared at the man, waiting for more.

He had touched a girl.

Slotnick began to fear where this was going.

She was...young.

Slotnick felt queasy.

When people at cocktail parties inevitably asked him, usually with a note of disdain, whether there was *any* case Barry Slotnick wouldn't take, he always cited two exceptions to his open-door policy.

The first was: a client had to be able to pay what Slotnick charged, so he would weed out fakers by insisting that every new client cut a fifty-thousand-dollar check to him.

The second was more specific: Slotnick would *never* represent a child molester.

"Did you do it?" he asked the man now.

"No."

Slotnick nodded, but everyone accused of pedophilia denied it. On the other hand, it was always possible that someone who was accused of it and who denied it was in fact innocent. How could Slotnick turn that person down?

His solution was simple.

He said he'd represent the man to the best of his ability, but if he found out the man had done what he was accused of, Slotnick would do everything in his power to make sure he went to prison.

The man stood up, gathered his things, and hastened to the elevator bank.

Slotnick never heard from him again.

Another time, a man showed up at Slotnick's office without an appointment. When Slotnick talked about being willing to represent whoever walked in the door, he didn't usually mean that literally. Typically someone made an appointment or came with a referral. But Slotnick happened to be in the office just then, and he listened to what the man had to say.

He'd been arrested for stockpiling a small arsenal of guns, he said. Would Slotnick represent him?

"If you give me a check and sign a retainer," Slotnick said, "I'm going to be your lawyer."

The man wrote out a check and signed the retainer, and Slotnick became his lawyer.

The next day, Slotnick's investigator Frank King came in and said, "You can't represent that guy; he's a Nazi." An actual Nazi. A member of the American Nazi Party.

Slotnick didn't know what to do. One of the reasons he did what he did was because of what had happened in Germany: the Nazis would just knock on your door and take you because there was no constitution to protect your rights. On the other hand, it was Slotnick's job to represent the unpopular, to defend the indefensible.

But was he really going to represent a Nazi? He didn't have to *like* a client. He didn't really think about clients in that way. He was more like an ER doctor saving the life of someone who might have just killed another person. But he had an aunt and other family members who'd died in the Holocaust. His parents had fled Eastern Europe because of the antisemitic pogroms there.

That night, Slotnick mentioned the new client to Donna. Donna was still made uneasy by some of the people her husband represented. But this enraged her. Barry *had* to fire the guy.

Slotnick called the man and said they needed to meet. The man came back in to the office.

"Look," Slotnick said, "I'm going to give you back your retainer. You obviously don't know that I'm Jewish."

"Yeah, I do know," the man said. "I was told by someone at the Library of Congress that you'd represent me fully, and you were the best lawyer, and you took my retainer check, and you're my lawyer."

Slotnick felt he had no choice but to continue to represent the guy.

Donna was angry for weeks.

Slotnick was able to get the guns suppressed from evidence, and eventually he got the whole case dismissed.

Then he told the client never to contact him again.

"It was very upsetting to me," Slotnick remembers.

Slotnick now charged three hundred and fifty dollars an hour. So when he chose to donate his very expensive services, he didn't donate them to just anyone. A candidate for pro bono representation by Barry Slotnick had to meet certain criteria. One of them was that Slotnick had to think he could win. Michael Holowzak was involved in one such case.

In July of 1979, Holowzak escaped through a hole in a wall of an upstate jail and made his way by stolen car to New York City. Holowzak was thirty, with dark hair and a prominent mustache. He was in the middle of a nine-year prison sentence for burglary and had recently been charged, on the basis of accusations by two fellow inmates, with committing a one-hundred-and-sixty-thousand-dollar armed robbery. It was a case that could keep him in prison for another twenty-five years, and just as the trial was about to start, he'd broken out of Orange County Jail, in Goshen, New York.

Three days later, Holowzak phoned newspaper columnist Jimmy Breslin, and the two men met at Queens Plaza under the elevated train tracks. This was the kind of thing that happened to Breslin. Back in 1977, the Son of Sam, one of the most notorious serial killers of the decade, had written letters to Breslin. In 1969, Breslin and Norman Mailer had been running mates in the New York City mayoral race, with Breslin tipped to be city council president. He lost, but his influence continued to grow.

Breslin took Holowzak to the Green Derby, a bar on Second Avenue in Manhattan, for a hamburger. There, the escapee told Breslin that he was going to turn himself in, but he first wanted Breslin to hear his story. He didn't want to run, he said, but he'd been framed by other inmates on the armed-robbery charges and just wanted a fair chance to prove his innocence.

Breslin didn't know what to make of Holowzak's story. What if the guy was innocent? Breslin agreed to put him in touch with Father Louis Gigante, a charismatic Catholic "street preacher," former city councilman, and brother to bookie Vincent "Chin" Gigante, owner of Bullets the dog.

Father Gigante came to the *Daily News* office. After speaking with Holowzak, Gigante announced, "I don't think the man committed this crime. He needs a good lawyer." Gigante called Slotnick, and Slotnick spoke to Holowzak and heard him out. That the case had come through Breslin, even indirectly, was also appealing. Before Slotnick would represent Holowzak, though, he'd told Holowzak he'd need to take a polygraph test, and he sent him to an examiner he often used named Nat Laurendi.

Slotnick polygraphed clients all the time. If the results didn't benefit them, Slotnick had no obligation to reveal that an exam had even been conducted. Under both New York and federal law, polygraphs were inadmissible as evidence. But if the results were helpful, Slotnick would always make a motion to introduce them anyway. If that didn't work, or if a witness slipped while testifying and said the defendant had passed a polygraph, then it would be stricken from the record but maybe not from the jurors' memories.

The next day, Slotnick arrived at Nat Laurendi's office, at 299

Broadway, half an hour after Holowzak had finished answering the examiner's questions. Holowzak had begun crying when Laurendi told him he'd passed the test. "Makes you wonder how many guys are in there on bum raps," Slotnick said to the *Daily News* reporter dutifully scribbling down every word, "because they couldn't afford a good lawyer."

Holowzak had less than two dollars in his pocket, but Slotnick solemnly turned to him and announced: "We're going to represent you." Slotnick's associate Larry Herrmann drove Holowzak back upstate to turn himself in and later represented him in court, with Slotnick running the defense remotely.

Ultimately, after just fifteen minutes of deliberations, a jury acquitted Holowzak of the armed-robbery charge. After Herrmann phoned in with the news, Slotnick called Donna. "Not guilty."

But Slotnick had won even before the verdict.

Jimmy Breslin wrote not one but two columns about the Holowzak case, including one in which he called Slotnick "one of the best criminal lawyers in the nation." And Breslin was moved by the seriousness with which Slotnick's associate seemed to take the case, despite working for free. The day before the court hearing, Herrmann stayed at the jail with Holowzak prepping for the next day's hearing until 10:00 p.m., then went outside to phone Slotnick and talk over strategy. "I suppose cynics would sneer," Breslin wrote, "but I do know that Herrmann, sitting in a stuffy jailhouse in Orange County, is performing perhaps the highest duty: defending a man he believes to be innocent."

Before leaving the polygrapher's office, Slotnick had mentioned to the *Daily News* reporter there that he might have another good story for him soon.

CHAPTER 27

I t was the height of summer in 1979, and the courtroom on the eleventh floor of the Manhattan criminal court building was soupy. Waiting anxiously near the back of the room, a twenty-nine-year-old Black man sat sweating through his white knit shirt, while at the front of the room, his lawyer addressed Judge Harold Rothwax.

"Release Kevin Michael Key from the prison of his past," Barry Slotnick was saying on this Friday in late July. "Release him so he will realize the promise of his future. Allow him into the book of redemption."

That morning, Key had woken up in his apartment on 135th Street, hoping today would be the day he could get on with the rest of his life. When Key was eleven, his family had moved from Connecticut to Harlem. Soon he was skipping school, turning on fire hydrants, throwing bricks through windows, learning about junkies, becoming a junkie himself, and eventually dealing heroin. He ended up getting arrested more than a dozen times, but in each instance he gave a different name; he'd get released without having to post bail and just never show up for trial. In time, a yellow sheet of paper listed fifteen bench warrants against him.

After witnessing a friendly-fire cop shooting, Key fled to Brooklyn, where he changed his life: he kicked drugs, got a sanitation job, started taking classes at a community college, enrolled in the urban legal studies program at City College, and decided he wanted to become a lawyer. One of his teachers was New York State Supreme Court justice John Carro, and one day Key asked him, "If you have bench warrants, will they ever lapse?"

Key then went to another professor, Haywood Burns, and told him about his warrants under various names. Burns put him in touch with Slotnick and Herrmann. He told them his story, and they were impressed. The normal Slotnick retainer was twenty thousand dollars, but they agreed to represent Key for fifty dollars.

By the spring of 1979, Slotnick and Herrmann had managed to knock fourteen of the fifteen warrants off his sheet, and Key had been admitted to Rutgers Law School and New York Law School. Today, Judge Rothwax was going to review the sole outstanding warrant against Key, from a purse-snatching arrest. It was the only remaining hurdle to Key's becoming at least eligible to be a lawyer once he graduated from law school.

After Slotnick made his argument, Rothwax spoke. "I think all the facts set forth in this motion mandate that this case should be dismissed in the interest of justice," he said. "Good luck, Michael."

Outside the courtroom, Key's mother stood in the hallway.

"It looks like he's going to be a lawyer," someone said.

"Yes," Mrs. Key said. "Me, I wanted to be a doctor. But that was in those days."

When Key and Slotnick got into the elevator, Key recognized another occupant, a man from his old neighborhood. The man was nodding off—clearly a junkie, as Key used to be.

"You lost your teeth and everything," Key said.

"I'm just making a living," the man said.

Key shook his hand. Soon Key would begin attending New York Law School.

Even though Slotnick felt strongly that he was doing God's work by upholding the Constitution, he didn't delude himself by thinking that most of his clients were good people. By the time they got to him, the best most of them could hope for was to stay out of prison or to go to prison for a shorter period of time.

This case was different. Here it felt like Slotnick was really making a difference in a young man's life. The press would eat this up. And he liked this new role: Barry Slotnick, dream maker.

CHAPTER 28

In their new offices at 233 Broadway, on a day in early 1980, Jay Breakstone sat watching Barry Slotnick. Breakstone was Slotnick's "law man," a recent law school graduate who spent his time drafting briefs and motions and burrowing through arcane legal texts in search of just the right precedent for every situation. Slotnick's desk was a large conference table, and Breakstone's desk was a smaller conference table inside Slotnick's office. This gave him a front-row seat from which to study his boss's paper clip–mutilating proclivities.

When Slotnick wasn't smoking cigarettes, paper clips were his preferred instruments for working out anxiety. Slotnick would unfold them. He would bite them. He would drop them on the floor. Breakstone could track his boss through a courthouse by following the trail of paper clips.

The move to the new offices, the hiring of staff, the overwhelming but always fascinating work that came in: Slotnick's law practice was booming. But success meant pressure, and

Slotnick was even more anxious than usual because he was about to test a risky trial gambit.

Breakstone saw Frank King out in the hallway and signaled him with a nod. They'd been plotting this moment.

"Barry," Breakstone said now in Slotnick's office as King watched.

Slotnick looked up.

Breakstone asked Slotnick whether he'd heard about the international paper clip shortage resulting from a trade embargo with China.

Breakstone and King sat watching, knowing that Slotnick was ruminating. "Barry can be exceedingly gullible about this stuff," Breakstone recalls.

Slotnick called in his assistant and asked her to order two cartons of paper clips.

Breakstone and King could barely stifle their laughter.

But Slotnick was too preoccupied to notice. Today, he was going to pull off what he felt might be his most brilliant trial tactic yet—or else fail in spectacular public fashion and let two young Orthodox Jewish men go to prison. The case had come to Slotnick when he took a call from Rabbi Jacob Hecht, a politically connected, homburg-hat-wearing leader in Brooklyn's Lubavitcher community; Slotnick, as the longtime lawyer for Meir Kahane, was a trusted figure.

In 1972, the office of Sol Hurok, a theater impresario, was firebombed. His twenty-seven-year-old secretary, Iris Kones, was killed. The bombers hadn't thought anyone was there and were blowing up the office to bring attention to the Russian Jewish problem, since Hurok was bringing Russian performers into the States. Three young members of Kahane's

Jewish Defense League were prosecuted, and Slotnick, along with Alan Dershowitz and another lawyer, defended them in the first federal death penalty case in New York since the execution of Julius and Ethel Rosenberg. Ultimately the case was thrown out because the prosecution had used illegal wiretaps.

After Kahane himself was arrested for making a firebomb in a separate incident, Slotnick also did well for him, negotiating a deal in which Kahane pleaded guilty and received a suspended sentence of five years. Later, in a precedent-setting case, after Kahane went on a hunger strike because the Federal Bureau of Prisons refused to provide him with kosher meals, Slotnick went to court and persuaded a judge to require the prison to build a kosher kitchen for the JDL leader.

As Rabbi Hecht explained it, around midnight on June 16, 1978, outside 1307 Union Street in the Crown Heights neighborhood, a sixteen-year-old Black boy named Victor Rhodes, the oldest of seven children, had been kicked and punched into a coma. When police arrived, witnesses described a mob of assailants wearing "Hasidic garb" and pointed to a 1978 Chevy that was just then driving down the street, carrying two Hasidic men. Louis Brenner, twenty-four, and Jonathan Hackner, twenty-five, were arrested and charged with assault and attempted murder, "acting in concert with 30 to 50 others not apprehended."

In the early days after the arrest, Black leaders in the community contended that the attackers were part of a local Hasidic patrol that had recently been harassing Black men in the neighborhood. They said that Victor Rhodes had been dropping off his girlfriend at her home when the mob descended. Rhodes, fearful for his life, had run two blocks before the mob caught up with him at Utica Avenue.

Lubavitcher leaders allowed that some yeshiva students on their way home from a wedding had "overreacted" after the boy, they alleged, intentionally knocked off an elderly Jewish man's hat. But they said that the two men in the car, who were visiting from England, had nothing to do with the incident.

It was immediately a political case. There was a long history of tension between Black residents, who made up more than 70 percent of the Crown Heights population, and the Lubavitchers, an Orthodox Jewish sect. A year before, a Hasidic man had hit a black kid over the head with a wrench in a dispute over an open fire hydrant. Just two days earlier, a Black civic leader named Arthur Miller had been choked to death in Crown Heights during a run-in with police. Mayor Ed Koch visited Victor Rhodes, who was in a coma in the hospital ICU, and publicly decried the "vicious assault" as a threat to "the fragile thread of intergroup harmony and tolerance." With the boy expected to die, Bruce Cutler, the top homicide prosecutor in the Brooklyn DA's office, was assigned to the case.

As the trial began, Slotnick had been worried about whether this, finally, was going to be the case that ended his winning streak. Brennan and Hackner were easily identified because both men had red hair and beards. His fears deepened during jury selection, when a high percentage of the jurors who made it onto the final panel were Black. Then Slotnick remembered the case of Vincent "Chin" Gigante and his dog, Bullets.

Just before the calling of the first eyewitness who fingered the young men seated at the defense table, Slotnick made an unusual request, asking the judge to allow his clients to sit in the gallery pews, among the trial's spectators, rather than in the conventional spot at the defense table. Maybe a different prosecutor would have caught on to what was happening, but Cutler did not. (The homicide prosecutor had stayed on the case even though Rhodes had, thankfully, awakened from his coma.)

With a twinkle in his eye, Slotnick left the courtroom. In the hallway outside were more than four dozen men Slotnick had had bused in from Ocean Parkway. The lawyer motioned for his decoys to follow him, and they streamed into the courtroom, filling the pews around the two defendants.

Like those of Slotnick's clients, each of these men's faces was framed by traditional Hasidic sidelocks. They all wore the standard ultra-Orthodox garb of rimmed black hats and satiny black frock coats. And every single one of them had red hair and a red beard.

When Slotnick approached the witness box and asked the witness to identify the men, the witness couldn't do it. This was repeated for each of the succeeding prosecution witnesses. Not one of them was able to point to the men they said they'd seen assault Victor Rhodes.

Slotnick, in his summation, argued that this was a tragic case of mistaken identity and shrewdly played to the mostly Black jury's sympathies when he quipped to them about the prosecution's case: "Because all Jews look alike, right?"

He also managed to introduce how the Lubavitchers had passed polygraph tests, despite those results being inadmissible. When prosecutor Cutler was cross-examining Slotnick investigator John McNally and asked why Slotnick had brought him into the case at the last minute, McNally testified, as he'd practiced with Slotnick: "Well, he told me he couldn't under-stand why his clients were being brought to trial. They'd both passed polygraphs."

"Bruce went nuts," McNally remembers. "He threw his pen down."

After a two-month trial and two days of deliberation, the jury acquitted Brenner and Hackner of all charges. Slotnick, admitting that he'd been skeptical about whether he could get a fair trial from the jury given its racial composition, apologized to them.

He called Donna: "Not guilty."

The headline in the *Daily News* was: LACK OF IDENTIFICATION FREES 2 IN BEATING.

CHAPTER 29

Mark Baker was sitting at his desk when Slotnick stuck a subpoena in his face. It was for a client of the firm, which was embroiled in a case involving Drum Pharmacy.

"File a motion to quash," Slotnick said.

Baker considered how to most gently inform his new boss that this was a fool's errand.

Until recently, when Slotnick hired him, Baker had been an anticorruption state prosecutor. He'd met Slotnick in a case involving Father Louis Gigante. A mobster had confessed to the priest, and Baker, as part of an investigation involving the Tombs (the city jail in downtown Manhattan), had subpoenaed Father Gigante to testify before a grand jury. Father Gigante had refused to say anything, citing priest-penitent privilege, and Baker had charged him with contempt of court. Slotnick had been impressed by the young prosecutor, and when Jay Breakstone left for another job, Slotnick hired Baker as his law man.

Like Slotnick, Baker came from an Orthodox Jewish family and didn't have an Ivy League background; he had grown up on Long Island, then attended Brooklyn Law School, and now lived with his family in an apartment in Riverdale with a view of the Hudson River. He was a detail guy, loath to delegate to others, to the point where he still washed, dried, and ironed his own shirts. But Baker reveled in his identity as a lawyer. He got vanity license plates that said I D FEND and liked to wear a T-shirt that read, above a shark's head, TRUST ME, I'M A LAWYER.

Now it was time for Baker to start earning his keep by dropping a little of his expertise on the older attorney. Not wanting to offend the man who signed his paychecks, he chose his words carefully. "I've been issuing these subpoenas for ten years," Baker said in a tolerant tone that suggested that anyone could fall prey to the naive assumption Slotnick was making. "We don't have a chance in hell."

Slotnick gave his associate a long look. Being a defense lawyer meant fighting even the smallest fight, letting no motion go unopposed, and attempting to quash every subpoena, impeach every witness, and suppress every piece of evidence. "We are gladiators," Slotnick always said. He tried to instill this lesson in each of his associates.

"Until you have a crystal ball and wear black robes," Slotnick said, "never say nothing will come from it. Just move to quash."

Baker grudgingly did as he was told.

"I gave Drum a run for the money," Baker remembered years later. "Ultimately we lost, but we had them tied up in court for the better part of a year." The delaying tactics helped force Drum to the negotiating table.

From then on, Baker says—"for as long as it took to get the prosecutorial starch out of my collar"—Slotnick would cite the Drum case as an example of the value of not giving in quickly, and as proof that a lawyer should always fight the good fight.

CHAPTER 30

"Not guilty."

"Not guilty."

"Not guilty."

By the early 1980s, Slotnick's professional life was a whirl of colorful clients and charismatic interactions with juries and thrilling verdicts and triumphant calls to Donna and bold-face mentions in the press, every one of which he clipped and saved.

He epitomized the high-priced criminal-defense lawyer. There were attorneys who thought that the best way to present themselves to juries was as regular folks, with the same problems and concerns they had. Slotnick had never felt that way. At six feet one, dressed in one of his custom three-piece suits, he didn't walk into a courtroom so much as *enter* it, his overcoat draped over his shoulders like a cape, as if he were a matador or a count or Superman. "Slotnick *arrivée*," Jay Breakstone liked to say.

He was a familiar figure at the city's courthouses, arriving in his chauffeured black Cadillac, his salt-and-pepper beard trimmed just so. At night, he might go to Elaine's, the see-and-be-seen Upper East Side watering hole, to mingle among the city's players. It was good for business. It was fun.

Over the past two decades, Barry's clients had included Joe Colombo's children, Vincent Gigante, who, the FBI now believed, headed the Genovese crime family, and Carmine "the Snake" Persico, who'd assumed leadership of the Colombo organization after its founder became a vegetable. Slotnick had also represented countless capos and soldiers who worked under these men: o.c., or organized crime, cases were still his bread and butter.

The money was pouring in. Crumpled bills in plastic bags were par for the course. One Chinese gang member paid his retainer using gold bars. Another client paid his bill with an inaccessible patch of land in the Adirondacks, enclosed on all sides by property owned by other people. Another client handed over his Rolls-Royce Silver Cloud. Mark Reiter—a heroin dealer and "house Jew for the Gambino family," in one lawyer's words—paid part of his bill with an "old and shitty" two-seat Mercedes convertible.

Slotnick loved it all. He was personally frugal, never living a life quite as high as he might have, but he still enjoyed the fruits of his success. He started going to Fioravanti for his half dozen suits each year. The guy who'd snuck into Yankees games as a kid could now score field-level tickets whenever he wanted. Donna bought a boat, which Frank King taught her how to pilot around Long Island Sound. The Slotnicks invested in racehorses, a pair of trotters named New Brett and Fire Exit, and joined a country club, Brae Burn.

It had been Donna's idea to join Brae Burn, a prestigious Jewish golf club in Westchester. For her, it was a social thing, a place to see friends and make new ones. She thought it would be good for Barry to take up a hobby. All the other husbands seemed to play tennis, but when Donna tried to get Barry to pick up a racket, he wasn't interested. Donna arranged for the two of them to take golf lessons instead.

Slotnick, in golf pants, a golf shirt, and a visor, hunched over the club in his hand, looked down the fairway toward a distant hole, and began his backswing—

"Barry!"

Slotnick looked up, the club poised over his head.

"That's a putter," Donna said.

Barry shrugged as his wife walked over. He reached into his bag for another club, and Donna put her hand on his wrist to gently guide it away from the nine iron he was about to retrieve and placed it instead on a wood.

Thus equipped with the correct club, Slotnick again sighted the hole beckoning in the distance, and he swung the club backwards. At the height of its arc, the club head paused, then Slotnick whipped it downward. There was a loud thwack as the driver hit the ball, and Slotnick looked up so he might behold its glorious flight toward the target.

He squinted, not seeing anything.

"Barry," Donna said. He looked at her.

"Over there." She was pointing toward a copse of trees, forty degrees to the right.

Slotnick focused just in time to see his ball dribbling to a stop in the rough.

He shrugged again, and Donna sighed.

He only played golf when Donna asked him to, but Barry actually loved coming to Brae Burn. Instead of providing him with a diversion from his nonstop work, as Donna had hoped, the club had become a fertile hunting ground for new clients.

On weekends, Slotnick had a very different routine from his weekday ritual of armoring himself in an impeccable three-piece suit. Instead he'd pull on a pair of sweatpants and a sweatshirt, one that he'd wear under a long fur coat made from dozens of tiny rabbit pelts. Between the sweatsuit and the patchwork fur coat, Slotnick's look mortified his children.

Slotnick didn't care. He'd smile and drive into town to Scarsdale Bagels, where he'd pick up a bunch of bagels for the family breakfast—including an onion bagel for himself. Slotnick was a lanky 165 pounds and was always careful to watch his weight. Every now and then, though, he needed something besides plain nonfat yogurt and unsweetened oatmeal.

There were four kids now, and they were the pride of Donna and Barry, who'd tell them: "You're a Slotnick, and don't you forget it."

Life was good.

PART FOUR

CHAPTER 31

On January 18, 1985, a friend called Barry Slotnick and said, "Turn on your TV."

It had been less than a week since Slotnick had agreed to represent Bernhard Goetz, the subway gunman. Since then, Slotnick's confidence that he could get his client off had only grown. But now, turning on his television set, Slotnick saw that New York news stations were citing a *Daily News* report, slated to come out the next day, that supposedly contained quotations from Bernhard Goetz's videotaped confession in New Hampshire.

"I know it's disgusting to say, but it was so easy. I can't believe it. God."

"I would have kept shooting had I not run out of bullets."

"I should have gouged his eyes out with my car keys."

This was just a tiny fraction of what Goetz was on tape as saying. Who knew what other choice nuggets had been captured for posterity? There was an adage among prosecutors:

Deny what you can't admit, and admit what you can't deny. A videotape was the ultimate in nondeniability.

Suddenly Slotnick's new case appeared to be anything but a sure thing.

Slotnick was gnawing on a paper clip again.

It was after 3:00 p.m. on January 25, 1985, and he was in his downtown office with Goetz, waiting for news about the grand jury. After weeks of hearing testimony, the group of twenty-three citizens was finally going to render a decision about whether, and on what charges, to indict the subway gunman.

Now, awaiting the grand jury's decision, Slotnick ran the curved end of the paper clip along his gums, tracing the outline of his teeth. For the past ten days, Slotnick had been representing Goetz jointly with Joseph Kelner, the civil lawyer. Slotnick, as the lawyer more experienced in criminal matters, had prevailed against Kelner's desire to let Goetz testify before the grand jury without immunity, which would have been a rookie mistake.

More than a month had passed since the shootings, and the case continued to be polarizing. What had begun as a New York City tabloid story had grown into a national public debate. The Senate Judiciary Committee had held hearings on vigilantism, with pro-Goetz testimony given by Kelner and Curtis Sliwa (founder of the Guardian Angels, New York's homegrown self-defense group); even a committee member, Senator Alfonse D'Amato, had volunteered to testify on Goetz's behalf if there were a trial. On the other side, snippets of Goetz's confession had been selectively leaked to the media by sources who evidently wanted to tilt the public against Goetz, leading to headlines such as COPS SAY GOETZ WAS SORRY THAT HE RAN OUT OF BULLETS.

Finally, at 3:45 p.m., the phone in Slotnick's office rang. It was the Manhattan DA's office calling. After seventy minutes of deliberation, the grand jury had decided to indict Goetz—but only on charges of criminal weapons possession. He was not being indicted on any of the more serious charges, including attempted murder.

Slotnick and Kelner were surprised. Goetz exhaled in relief. They all smiled and shook hands. Then Slotnick called Donna. This time he said: "Not indicted." Sure, there was the weapons charge, but Slotnick told reporters that Goetz would plead not guilty to that. This was, Slotnick said, "practically an exoneration of our client."

"It was the view of the grand jurors that Mr. Goetz was justified in taking the force that he did," the Manhattan DA, Robert Morgenthau, said at his news conference.

CHAPTER 32

To the untrained eye, it seemed like the Goetz saga was winding down. It was the gusty, gray morning of February 27, 1985, a month after the Goetz indictment had been all but dismissed, and Goetz was sitting in a courtroom in lower Manhattan for a hearing on the sole remaining count: the weapons charge. Slotnick's partner Mark Baker asked the judge to review the grand jury minutes, suggesting that if he did so the only conclusion he could possibly come to would be to dismiss the indictment outright.

Barry Slotnick had been publicly confident, declaring that the gun charge would be appealed, but privately he was deeply worried. The Goetz case had become a political mess as much as a legal problem.

Columnist Jimmy Breslin had ramped up his anti-Goetz campaign. He'd published a sarcasm-laden column referring to "Bernie Goetz of the Light Brigade" and seemingly advocating Goetz for mayor. The column included a "write-in for Goetz" coupon.

Slotnick was rankled that Breslin called Goetz "a bedbug," that he always referred to the kids Goetz had shot as "the four unarmed teenagers," and that he continued to insist that the shooting had been racially motivated.

On a *Donahue* special about vigilantism, Breslin had criticized Goetz for shooting kids in the back and called Goetz's supporters "the great unwashed," drawing boos from the studio audience.

"Mr. Breslin," one woman asked, "if someone were to attack you, would you just stand there with your arms out and not protect yourself?"

"I hope I'd fight back," Breslin said, "and I also hope I wouldn't shoot two people in the back and another one in the side because he didn't turn around quick enough that I could shoot him in the back."

"Mr. Breslin," Phil Donahue said, "you appear to be whistling a lonely tune."

"I don't care," Breslin said. "It's the law. It's in a book. Go look it up. You're not supposed to shoot people."

In another TV interview, Breslin asked, rhetorically, "What color were the four kids who got shot?"

"Black," the interviewer responded.

"What color was the gunman?"

"White."

"Thank you!"

"What are you saying—this was a racial murder?"

"No, it was over *geraniums*!"

It wasn't just Breslin. The backlash had been especially fierce among the kind of prominent liberal opinionators with whom highly voter-sensitive DA Robert Morgenthau socialized at up-town cocktail parties. "There's little to be pleased with," a *New York Times* editorial began, "in the fact that Bernhard Goetz has now been indicted only for possessing an illegal weapon." Martin Garbus, a famously left-leaning trial lawyer, wrote a newspaper opinion piece criticizing Morgenthau and arguing that total or partial immunity should have been granted to one of the four kids who'd been shot in order to get them to testify before the grand jury.

Slotnick feared that continued public exposure might force officials to take further action against Goetz. Goetz's neighbor Myra Friedman, who had recorded a couple of phone calls with Goetz while he was a fugitive, was going to be publishing excerpts from them in *New York* magazine, and Slotnick asked Baker to try to persuade her to publish only material that reflected well on Goetz.

The biggest threat came from Goetz himself. Goetz had fired his first lawyer in part because that lawyer favored a low-profile, avoid-the-media strategy. Slotnick was unusually skilled at using the media to advance his clients' interests, but now the best thing Goetz could do was to lie low and hope that the public moved on to a new cause. He was turning down interview requests—as many as eight in the past ten days, including those from *Face the Nation,* network morning shows, and Japanese and British TV. He'd also canceled a *Nightline* appearance.

Slotnick believed that the best public posture right now was humility, and he made a similar request of Kelner, his cocoun-sel, who wasn't helping things with quotes such as, "We are not trembling in our boots."

But if someone stuck a microphone or camera in Goetz's face, Slotnick could never predict what he'd say. Goetz had begun to style himself as a kind of ambassador for crime victims, attending the wake of a retired school principal who'd been killed in a robbery and the arraignment of a man who'd stabbed an alleged thief at a subway station newsstand. Goetz sought out reporters, tossing off opinions about the city ("sick from one end to another") and the need for combat-trained, pistol-packing citizen "volunteer peace officers": "You've got to teach them how to get the gun out quickly. You can't have a guy fumbling with the weapon, trying to get it out of his pocket and dropping it. Crimes happen too quickly for that."

Goetz stayed up until 5:30 one morning giving newspaper interviews, including a three-hour session at his apartment with the *New York Post,* which resulted in a cover story headlined GOETZ: I'M NOT AFRAID OF JAIL, accompanied by a sidebar titled I'D DO IT AGAIN, SAYS AVENGER.

By helping to keep the story alive, Goetz provoked officials, who continued to leak damning details to the media.

Now, in court on February 27, prosecutor Greg Waples was required to give the defense a discovery package—important documents relevant to the case. That night, Baker read through the file. It included Goetz's December 31 written confession in New Hampshire, including his account of firing four shots, then getting up, going over to Darrell Cabey, and saying, "You don't look so bad; here's another," and firing a fifth bullet, which paralyzed Cabey.

As soon as Baker read the statement, he understood that Goetz and his lawyers were in trouble. Baker knew that the original document had been simultaneously placed in the public court file, and reporters had lined up all day to read it. Meanwhile, that same afternoon, Goetz had given the *New York Times* a two-hour interview in which he confirmed that the New Hampshire police report was "essentially accurate."

CHAPTER 33

As part of the discovery package, Slotnick got his hands on the Goetz confession video for the first time.

He popped the tape into the VCR in his office suite's conference room and pressed Play. Then, with a legal pad in his lap and a Sharpie in hand, he sat back to watch the ninety-minute recording. Slotnick saw, from the time stamp on the screen, that Goetz's interview had begun at 9:42 p.m. on New Year's Eve. Goetz's shirt was remarkably unrumpled given that the man had been on the run for ten days.

Susan Braver, a Manhattan prosecutor who'd interrupted her ski vacation to help conduct the interview, introduced herself. "I'm an assistant district attorney from Manhattan. Um . . ."

"Congratulations," Goetz said, unable to hide his contempt. "I'm, I'm sorry. Excuse me."

As Goetz slouched in an office chair at the head of a conference table, he looked to be in physical agony, squirming merely at Braver's nasal, distinct New York accent.

As Slotnick watched, it dawned on him just how devastating this video was to his client. There Goetz was, on camera, saying things like "I turned into a vicious animal" and "If there's a God, God knows what was in my heart. And it was sadistic and savage." According to his own estimates, Goetz was a "cold-blooded murderer" and a "monster."

Every time Slotnick thought it couldn't get any worse, Goetz would outdo himself. He'd been provoked when Troy Canty had said "Give me five dollars" by "the gleam in his eye and the smile on his face...What happened here is I snapped." Goetz damaged his chances of pleading self-defense by stating he wasn't worried that the kids might be armed, it was the idea that Canty "was enjoying this...And it was at that point I decided I was going to kill them after all, murder them all."

Anything else? "I wanted to kill those guys; I wanted to maim those guys; I wanted to make them suffer in every way I could."

Slotnick's heart sank as he watched his client confess, in irrefutable specifics, not only to what he'd done but also to what he had intended to do. A defense of temporary insanity might be the only option, Slotnick thought. Could he argue that Goetz had just lost it and unknowingly fired his gun in a rapid, unpremeditated hail of bullets?

But then, on the tape, Goetz started speaking in depersonalized military lingo about the "pattern of fire" he had planned while still seated, and how "you just target images in your mind" and "you aim for the center of the mass" and "you sight your target."

Surely Goetz had at least feared that his life was in imminent danger, that the kids kept closing in on him, no matter what he did? Well, the third kid he'd shot "seemed as if he was trying to get through the steel wall of the subway car. But he couldn't. I let him have it."

Then, Goetz recalled in the video, he had gone back to make sure he hadn't missed any of the kids. Two, lying on the floor wounded, "were taken care of." A third was still seated, and Goetz recalled saying, "You seem to be doing all right; here's another," before firing again and severing the man's spine, instantly rendering him paraplegic. The fourth, Canty, who'd first spoken to Goetz, was also wounded on the floor, but "I was gonna gouge…the guy's eyes out with my keys." Goetz stopped only because "I saw his eyes twitching, and I saw the fear in his eyes."

As Slotnick watched Goetz's self-immolation, he became almost nauseated. What had seemed like a winnable case now seemed impossible to defend—an express ticket to the Hall of Legal Disasters. "There's nothing more painful," Slotnick would say years later, "than seeing a client of yours confess on videotape."

CHAPTER 34

On a Saturday night, reporter John Miller drove to Scarsdale. While on the run in New Hampshire, Bernhard Goetz had called his neighbor Myra Friedman and had spoken at length to her about what had happened. Friedman, a writer, had recorded her conversations with Goetz without his knowledge, and Slotnick had recently obtained those tapes.

John Miller was after them, too. Slotnick liked Miller—he had chutzpah—and had told the young reporter to come up to the house that weekend. "You can listen to the tapes," Slotnick told Miller, "but you can't have them."

Slotnick also felt like he needed to start playing a more active role in guiding the media narrative about Goetz. He had seen the tide turning in the evolving comments of Mayor Koch. Two weeks after the first grand jury came back with its Goetz-friendly indictment, Koch had said, "The grand jury did the right thing." Now, just three weeks later, Koch was calling

Goetz "a flake" and saying he had no objection to a second grand jury.

When Miller arrived at the Slotnick house, Slotnick was helping one of his kids with her homework. He told Miller to go to the basement.

The basement was finished but simple: painted white Sheet-rock, utilitarian carpet, fluorescent lights, no windows. There were toys piled everywhere. Along one wall was a cheap foldout chair and table heaped with pounds and pounds of paper, Post-it notes, trial transcripts, and highlighters. Next to the table, in the corner, stood a Donkey Kong Jr. console, which Barry had gotten for Stuart from a client who sold arcade games.

Slotnick had a pair of Sennheiser headphones attached to a tape player, and Miller clapped them on his head. Then he pressed Play as he sat down on the foldout chair to listen.

"The threats were numerous and subtle," he heard Goetz saying. "In a situation like this, your mind, you're in a combat situation...Myra, those guys, I'm almost sure, almost sure, were vicious and savage. What I did, I responded in a vicious and savage way...I saw what was going to happen, and I snapped."

This was dynamite stuff.

"Most people assume I did what's called the right thing. I'm not going to say that. I think what I did was appropriate, if you can believe that, or reasonable under the circumstances."

Slotnick came downstairs. Miller pulled the Sennheisers off.

"So I can *have* the tapes," Miller said, "but I can't say where I got them?"

"No, you can't have them," Slotnick said, "but I want you to understand what's on the tapes, in context."

"I can *use* what's on the tapes," Miller said, paraphrasing what he thought Slotnick was saying, "but I can't have them."

"Maybe, but not really. Your job is to get the tapes."

"Well, give me the tapes," Miller said. *Well, give me the* fucking *tapes,* he was thinking.

"No. You have to get them. You have to go to Myra Friedman and figure out a way to get them from her. But if you can get them from her, then you know what's on them."

Miller was frustrated, but even more motivated than before. He spent the next two days tracking down Friedman, who agreed to meet him for coffee. There, he explained why it was important for the tapes to get out. After a long conversation, she said she'd give him permission to have them.

"Well, they're your tapes," Miller said, "but can you call Barry Slotnick and tell him it's okay with you to give me a copy?"

When Miller called Slotnick later, the lawyer just laughed. Miller went to Slotnick's office to pick up the tapes, and then he played them on air on NBC News. It was the first time the public heard Goetz's voice and what he'd said, including his statements about people needing to have guns. It was a huge coup for Miller as a journalist. "I was getting the story of the century," Miller recalls.

Later, as Miller thought about the way Slotnick had managed him, he was fascinated by Slotnick's talent for understanding his audience, whether it was a jury, the public, or the media. A conventional defense lawyer would want to sit on evidence like this and save it for court. Slotnick liked to get everything into the public sphere sooner rather than later so that people wouldn't be shocked during the trial: if they responded to the evidence beforehand, he could have his counterarguments ready when the trial began.

Slotnick was shrewd about nudging the process along. "I think he understood that if I actually heard the tapes with my own ears, I would work very hard to get them," Miller recalls.

CHAPTER 35

A couple of weeks later, on Sunday, March 24, 1985, Bernhard Goetz was in a conference room at Barry Slotnick's law firm, sweat beading on his forehead as a short man with a sweep of hair grilled him while Mark Baker sat watching. Years later, Ben Brafman would become as famous as Slotnick was, but in early 1985 he was a young criminal-defense lawyer who'd only left the DA's office five years earlier. He had interned for Baker there: they were friends, and Baker knew him to be a very sharp trial attorney who could make mincemeat of a witness. Baker had asked Brafman to put Goetz through the ordeal of a mock cross-examination to see how Goetz would hold up under pressure.

"The mood has changed," the *Times* had intoned a few weeks earlier, dismissing "Mr. Slotnick's blather" and calling for a trial. The same day, in a desperate attempt to stall the building anti-Goetz momentum, Slotnick had leaked the Goetz confession video to his friend Steve Dunleavy, a pompadoured

Australian correspondent for *A Current Affair,* hoping that if people absorbed the full confession, with all its nuance and passion and contradiction, they would see what the first grand jury had seen and understand why it hadn't indicted Goetz for attempted murder.

Baker wrote a letter to the judge in the case, Stephen G. Crane, amplifying his most recent oral argument and asking him, in addition to inspecting the grand jury minutes, to consider the Goetz confession video and his audio conversations with police and with Myra Friedman. "It is our view that only through exposure to all these materials will the Court become fully aware both of the breadth and extent of the grand jury's presentations, as well as the state of mind which specifically dictated defendant's actions at the time of the alleged offenses." Baker also asked that, in the event that the district attorney resubmitted the Goetz case to a grand jury, Baker be given a chance to be heard in opposition.

But by then, it was too late. The morning after *Newsweek* published an article titled "A Goetz Backlash?," DA Robert Morgenthau announced that he would present the case to a second grand jury. Slotnick and Baker were pursuing every legal avenue to challenge its validity, suggesting that it was double jeopardy and that a new witness Morgenthau supposedly had was bogus—"old wine in a new bottle"—but Justice Crane wasn't having it.

Meanwhile, Slotnick had announced that Goetz wanted to speak to the grand jury; it was just a matter of scheduling. Somehow, though, whatever the prosecutor, Waples, offered, Slotnick asked for a bit more—more time, more immunity. It was all theater. Slotnick never seriously considered letting

Goetz testify. He very rarely had a client go before a grand jury. Putting a defendant in front of a grand jury was one of the riskiest things a defense lawyer could do. There was no judge, just a district attorney controlling everything, and anything a potential defendant told a grand jury could be used against them later. The exception to this was if the accused had been granted blanket immunity, which wasn't being offered in this case.

But Goetz was agitating for an opportunity to speak directly to the grand jury, and there was no easy way for Slotnick to tell his client that he'd make a terrible witness. Then Baker got an idea: *show* Goetz what a bad witness he'd be. So he'd called his old friend Ben Brafman. Normally, Slotnick wouldn't let a rival defense lawyer have access to his client, especially at such an early stage, but Goetz needed to be convinced.

For four hours, the defense attorney mock-interrogated Goetz, trying to trip him up with inconsistencies, trying to provoke him.

As expected, Brafman destroyed Goetz.

And Goetz became less insistent about speaking to the grand jury.

CHAPTER 36

At 8:30 a.m. on March 26, Barry Slotnick and Bernhard Goetz arrived at the Manhattan district attorney's office.

Robert Morgenthau was six feet tall, from an old New York family, and highly regarded in the city. Slotnick respected him and knew him to be sharper and wittier than his stoic persona suggested, but he thought Morgenthau was blowing with the winds of public opinion in this case. Normally, Morgenthau didn't get nearly so personally involved in the cases his office prosecuted.

This was the kind of meeting Slotnick excelled at. If a trial seemed inevitable, as John Miller recalled later, Slotnick would "[set] the field of play in the time leading up to the trial, through carefully managed publicity, by trying to shape public opinion, trying to change the pitch and tone of the discourse out there." Even people like Rudy Giuliani, the mob-busting US attorney, praised Slotnick, saying things like, "I respect him. He is a good lawyer and an honorable person. I have always seen him keep his word."

Morgenthau's office was divided on the question of whether to indict Goetz. Morgenthau himself didn't think Goetz should be let off the hook. He believed Goetz had been intent on revenge when he shot those kids.

Morgenthau preached a lot of high-minded rhetoric, but he was also a deeply political animal. He was aware that the city was rooting for Goetz by a margin of three to one. He was also aware that a vocal and politically influential contingent of the Black community viewed Goetz as racist. Morgenthau would be campaigning for reelection in the fall. If he let Goetz walk, he knew his potential challengers in the DA's race would bludgeon him with it on the campaign trail.

For this morning's meeting, Morgenthau was joined by prosecutors Greg Waples and Robert Pitler. The stated purpose of the gathering was to discuss the possibility of Goetz testifying before the grand jury. Slotnick had a different agenda. He began by announcing that Goetz wouldn't sign the usual immunity waiver. He would testify only on the condition that questions be limited to the events of just two days: December 22, when the shooting happened, and December 30, when Goetz, making a brief return trip to New York City, gave two guns to Myra Friedman to hold.

Morgenthau said he wouldn't agree to this.

In that case, Slotnick said, Goetz wouldn't testify.

Two hours later, when Slotnick emerged from the building into the January chill, though, these details were forgotten.

It was *showtime*.

"He offered to testify," Slotnick told the assembled mob of reporters carrying notepads and TV cameras. "The district attorney refused our testimony."

Slotnick basked in the moment, professing to be astonished that Morgenthau wouldn't agree to Goetz's terms.

"Who," Slotnick asked disingenuously, "would not want to listen to Bernhard Goetz's testimony from his own lips and in the flesh and cross-examine him about the issue at hand?"

Privately, Slotnick was happy. He'd run out the clock. Another bit of theater had played out as he'd hoped.

The next day, the grand jury returned an indictment charging Goetz with four counts of attempted murder, four counts of assault, one count of reckless endangerment, and one count of possessing a weapon with the intention of using it. If there was a silver lining for Goetz, it was this: the day before the indictment, one of the four victims, James Ramseur, had been arrested for falsely reporting a kidnapping. Prosecutor Waples had informed the grand jury of this after Baker asked him to do so. It hadn't stopped them from indicting Goetz, but it was one more bit of evidence that would help Slotnick make his eventual argument.

Overnight, the stakes had risen dramatically. With the first indictment, Goetz had faced a potential prison sentence of only seven years. Now he was looking at the possibility of more than fifty years. "The chief judge has said a grand jury will indict a ham sandwich if the district attorney wants it to," Slotnick said. "Bernie Goetz today turned out to be a ham sandwich."

CHAPTER 37

S hortly after 4:00 a.m. on March 28, 1985, most of Queens was asleep. Five hours later, Bernhard Goetz was scheduled to show up with his lawyers at the DA's office for his formal postindictment arrest. But at the Bergin Hunt and Fish Club, in Ozone Park, John Gotti, his brother Gene, and a Gambino crime family soldier named Wilfred "Willy Boy" Johnson were playing cards.

The Bergin, despite its name, was not a rustic retreat for sporting enthusiasts. Located on 101st Avenue behind a pair of nondescript brick storefronts, it contained a couple of sparsely decorated rooms upstairs and a basement below. A plaque on one wall saluted Gotti and was signed "from the boys at Green Haven," a prison where Gotti had spent some time. This was the headquarters of John Gotti's crew.

Suddenly, Drug Enforcement Administration agents and city detectives swarmed in. In the back room, they found the people they were looking for.

"What'd we do?" John Gotti asked.

"Don't worry; you already did it," one of the DEA agents said. "Your crimes have caught up with you."

The gangsters laughed as they were put in handcuffs.

An accompanying federal indictment, handed down in the eastern district of New York, targeted Gotti, eight of his associates, and the man they all reported to, Aniello Dellacroce, underboss of the Gambino family.

Slotnick was Dellacroce's lawyer. Then seventy-one, Dellacroce had begun his tenure as underboss working for the family founder, Carlo Gambino, and seemed to punctuate every sentence with the word *cocksucker*. He frightened even the most seasoned investigators. Looking into his ice-blue eyes was "like looking right through him," one NYPD officer recalled. Another detective described it as "the frigid glare of a killer." When Slotnick met with Dellacroce, it was usually on the mobster's turf, at the Ravenite Social Club, on Mulberry Street in New York City's Little Italy neighborhood.

Dellacroce was very sick. He'd had a stroke a couple of years earlier. He had diabetes, was undergoing chemotherapy for lung cancer, and was on bed rest, confined to his home on Staten Island. Before that, though, he'd begun meeting Slotnick at the lawyer's offices, usually accompanied by a bodyguard named John Gotti. "I'd say to the receptionist: 'There are people coming in: do not ask who they are; just let me know, and I'll get them,'" Slotnick assistant Joanne Eboli remembers. Gotti would call her Kid, throw a hundred-dollar bill on her desk, and say, "Buy everyone breakfast." When she attempted to return his change, Gotti asked, "Are you trying to insult me?" On his way out, he'd drop another fifty dollars on her desk.

As Slotnick perused the new indictment at the office later that morning, he quickly focused on the most serious charges, which concerned three murders.

On May 22, 1973, Jimmy McBratney, a thirty-year-old ex-con associated with the Irish American gang known as the Westies, was drinking at Snoope's Bar and Grill on Staten Island when a young Gambino crime family hoodlum named John Gotti and two other men entered the bar, impersonating police officers, and attempted to "arrest" McBratney, who had been involved in the kidnapping and murder of Carlo Gambino's nephew Manny. A patron intervened, one of Gotti's companions shot and killed McBratney, and Gotti, whose participation would earn him his "button"—official membership—in the Gambino organization, ended up serving a prison sentence for attempted manslaughter.

Three years later, in 1976, Albert Gelb, a court officer who was scheduled to testify a few days later against a Gambino associate named Charles Carneglia in a gun-possession case, was found slumped dead over his steering wheel on 109th Street in Queens. He had been shot four times in the head and face. At the time, the murder went unsolved.

In August of 1979, Anthony Plate, a Florida loan shark who had been charged alongside Dellacroce with crimes including the murder of a Yonkers bookie, and whose testimony could pose a threat to Dellacroce, walked out of the Tropicana Hotel in Miami and was never heard from again. John Gotti and several other members of his crew were seen in Queens shortly afterward with new tans. The next year, when Dellacroce went on trial, he got a hung jury and walked away a free man.

* * *

As Slotnick read the indictment, he saw that the murders of McBratney, Gelb, and Plate were just three of a litany of crimes brought together to establish a "pattern of criminal activity" by a "continuing enterprise"—the two key requirements for bringing a case under 1970's Racketeer Influenced and Corrupt Organization Act, or RICO. Other crimes in the indictment included armored car robberies that netted one million dollars, truck hijackings, loan-sharking, and gambling. Dellacroce, by far the best known of the defendants at that time, was charged with the highest number of counts (fifteen), and the case was called *United States v. Dellacroce*.

The judge in the case, Eugene Nickerson, agreed to arraign Slotnick's enfeebled client by telephone, and Dellacroce pleaded not guilty.

CHAPTER 38

Aniello Dellacroce's health aside, for Barry Slotnick the racketeering indictment presented a challenge at least as daunting as the one posed by the Goetz case, because in the previous few years, the government had been waging an all-out offensive against the Mafia.

A 1968 law, Title III of the Omnibus Crime Control and Safe Streets Act, had made it easier for law enforcement to use electronic wiretaps in their investigations, but bugging operations were lengthy and expensive, with no guaranteed results, and it was hard to get funding for them. The RICO Act was perfectly tailored to go after the hidden structures of the mob. But RICO cases were complex and hard to build and didn't yield the kinds of easy arrests and convictions that boosted cops' and prosecutors' statistics.

Only now, with organized crime suddenly a priority for the Reagan Justice Department, did federal agents and prosecutors at last have the resources and political impetus to use these laws to their full advantage. And the harsh prison sentences mandated by RICO had another effect: prosecutors were able to leverage the promise of leniency to coax previously mute mobsters into becoming turncoats. Finally, there was an ambitious new federal prosecutor in Manhattan, Rudolph Giuliani, who had made it his mission to destroy the Mafia.

In just the previous five years, federal prosecutors had brought dozens of indictments against organized crime. Slotnick was already representing Dellacroce in two other cases beyond the most recent one: a tax-evasion indictment from the year before and a groundbreaking prosecution, only one month old, of the leading members of the Commission, the Mafia's board of governors. Slotnick's heartfelt belief that *any* case was winnable had taken him a long way. But it was hard to ignore that, so far, the government had prevailed in every single one of the new wave of organized crime cases that had gone to trial.

Slotnick, like his peers in the defense bar, regarded RICO as grossly unfair. In allowing people to be prosecuted based on crimes for which they had already been tried, it amounted to nothing less than double jeopardy. But Slotnick, also like many of his peers, had the growing sense that organized crime had an expiration date. And he knew from firsthand experience that prosecutors were beginning to take a hard look at the attorneys who helped keep the goodfellas out of jail. When a grand jury was weighing a racketeering indictment a year earlier against Joe Colombo's son Anthony, Slotnick himself had been subpoenaed by the jury to testify about whether Anthony Colombo was paying legal fees for his codefendants in another case, which would establish whether he was part of an "enterprise" under the RICO statute.

The subpoena wasn't just a threat to Slotnick's fees; it was also an existential assault on his ability to represent these clients. If he could be forced to testify about a client, which would make him a witness, there was a real question about whether he'd still be permitted to serve as that client's lawyer. Slotnick would eventually challenge the subpoena all the way to the United States Supreme Court.

In the meantime, he had his work cut out for him.

CHAPTER 39

When Bruce Cutler got to the federal courthouse in Brooklyn, he felt like a knight without a horse. He'd never enjoyed trawling for business.

Cutler had come to work for Slotnick a few years after losing to him in the Hasidic-look-alikes trial, and since then he had tried several Chinese-gang cases for him. He'd grown up in Brooklyn, the son of a cop turned lawyer, and attended the elite Poly Prep school. He was a barrel-chested ex-wrestler, ex–football player, and weight lifter with an in-your-face courtroom style at odds with the suave approach favored by his boss.

Though Slotnick had no reason to attend the arraignment of Dellacroce's codefendants, he was thinking ahead. Well aware that his client was unlikely to still be alive when the trial began, he'd shrewdly dispatched his brash young associate Cutler to the hearing to see if one of Dellacroce's protégés might need a lawyer, too.

At the courthouse, as Slotnick had predicted, lawyer Mike

Coiro, who was representing John Gotti's brother Gene, told Cutler to stand up for John, then a Gambino soldier so obscure that Judge Nickerson had to ask the prosecutor for the spelling of Gotti's name.

Besides Dellacroce, two other defendants were absent: Charles Carneglia and Armond "Buddy" Dellacroce, Aniello's son, who were declared fugitives. At first, the arraignment proceeded without incident. All seven defendants who were present, including John Carneglia—Charles's brother—pleaded not guilty. Then there was a bail hearing in which, one by one, the lead prosecutor, Diane Giacalone, consented to the release of the defendants on a one-million-dollar unsecured bond.

Until she got to Willie Boy Johnson.

Johnson was a forty-nine-year-old ex-boxer who'd been a Gambino associate for more than twenty years, serving mainly as muscle against delinquent borrowers. When Giacalone objected to bail for Johnson, the courtroom went silent. Judge Nickerson asked why Johnson shouldn't be granted bail, too. Giacalone then made a shocking revelation: Johnson should be held in protective custody, she said, because for the past fifteen years he'd been a government informant.

"It ain't true!" Johnson shouted as John Gotti ruefully shook his head.

It was true. Johnson had been helping the FBI for years, under the code name Source Wahoo. The part-Cherokee Johnson had been embittered, in part, because only men of Italian ancestry were allowed to become full-fledged members of the Mafia. But the FBI had vehemently opposed revealing his secret identity. Giacalone, defying the FBI, had included Johnson as a codefendant because, for legal reasons, it would require the disclosure of his informant role; Giacalone was gambling that once outed, Johnson would have no choice but to cooperate. Though he had begged her not to do it, saying, "I'll be killed; my family will be slaughtered," and adding that he'd never testify against his friends, the prosecutor had gone ahead with her plan. Johnson was denied bail and placed in protective custody, but he would continue to refuse to help Giacalone.

On the afternoon of June 25, 1985, Judge Nickerson, prosecutors Giacalone and John Gleeson, plus defense attorneys Slotnick and Cutler, two lawyers for Willie Boy Johnson, a court reporter, a newspaper reporter, and a federal marshal, all converged on Todt Hill, a Staten Island neighborhood popular among members of organized crime.

Todt Hill was expensive and exclusive, but the reason mobsters felt safe there might have been its geography: it occupied the highest ground in the five boroughs, with sweeping views of Manhattan and the Verrazzano-Narrows Bridge, and it offered privacy, with large lots, large trees, and no sidewalks.

Paul Castellano, the Gambino boss, lived there, in a house modeled after the White House. The Corleone family compound in *The Godfather* had been filmed in the neighborhood. Aniello Dellacroce, Castellano's underboss, lived at 597 West Fingerboard Road, in a 6,500-square-foot house with seven bedrooms and five bathrooms.

For Slotnick's firm to represent both Dellacroce and Gotti—a potential conflict of interest—Dellacroce would have to take part in a so-called Curcio hearing, confirming that he was making an informed decision to continue to be represented by Slotnick. But since Dellacroce was too sick to travel, Judge

Nickerson had agreed to hold the hearing at the gangster's home. The FBI had had the house under surveillance for months, and the Bureau's Gambino squad, angry at Diane Giacalone, had briefly considered activating the bug during the hearing. But squad leader Bruce Mouw, wary of surreptitiously recording a federal judge, ordered it shut off.

Judge Nickerson, sixty-six, with white hair and a clipped way of speaking, looked a bit like Jimmy Stewart and had a reputation for being smart and fair. But he was part of a very different world from that of Slotnick and his clients. The judge was a descendant of President John Quincy Adams. He'd attended St. Mark's boarding school in New England, where he captained the hockey team and was football team quarterback, then had gone to Harvard for college. There, overcoming a polio-stricken right arm, he taught himself to play squash with his left arm and became the team captain. After that came Columbia Law School, a Supreme Court clerkship, and a stint as a Wall Street lawyer. He was also a Democrat and had been nominated as a federal judge eight years earlier by President Jimmy Carter. Slotnick wasn't overly enthusiastic about Nickerson, who was also the judge in the Anthony Colombo subpoena matter and who eight months earlier had thrown out Slotnick's motion to dismiss it.

Inside the house, Dellacroce, withered by chemotherapy, sat up against the headboard of his king-size bed, wearing embroidered white pajamas. As Judge Nickerson gently queried him, with Slotnick standing nearby, the Gambino underboss rasped, "I have been sick, and I have had three angina attacks, and whatever my lawyer . . . whatever he does is okay with me." Gotti similarly waived any conflict-of-interest claim regarding Cutler.

If the hearing was straightforward, the scene itself was remarkable, a rare collision of the straight world and the underworld in the innermost sanctum of a ruthless Mafia leader. When Nickerson said "Mr. Dellacroce," he fully enunciated it, adding a distinct fourth syllable that no one who knew Dellacroce ever used.

In a moment not captured by the court reporter but recalled by a participant, Dellacroce also assured the patrician federal judge: "Barry would never double-bang me."

The proceedings ended before 3:32 p.m., when the FBI noted in a log that its wiretap was turned back on.

CHAPTER 40

On November 25, 1985, Jimmy Breslin arrived at a Manhattan courthouse at 9:30 a.m., only to be told he was five hours early for the Goetz hearing. Instead of waiting, he made his way to St. Vincent's Hospital. He'd arranged to meet Shirley Cabey there to visit her son Darrell, who'd been at the hospital, paralyzed, for the past eleven months.

Breslin found Cabey sitting in a wheelchair, wearing striped pajamas, a yellow sweater, and gold-framed glasses. Plastic tubes snaked out from under his clothes. His voice, Breslin thought, was "a little thick."

Breslin was always on the lookout for article material, but he had been told by many people that Cabey had no memory of the shooting, so the columnist wasn't expecting to break any news with this visit. He asked how Cabey was doing. Fine, Cabey said; his favorite soap opera was *Loving*. Breslin asked Cabey if he remembered the shooting, and to Breslin's surprise, Cabey said, "Yes."

Breslin asked more questions. A few times Cabey seemed confused, and it appeared hard for him to speak, but mostly he gave clear answers. He had come a long way since the first weeks after the shooting, when he'd been in a coma. It had taken months just to be able to form short words.

"Do you remember Goetz?" Breslin asked.

"He had on glasses and a beige coat."

"What else do you recall?"

Cabey started talking about the three kids he'd been with.

"I shouldn't have talked to them. Goetz saw me talking to them. He was down with them. They goin' rob him."

"Who were they going to rob?"

"Goetz."

"Why were they going to rob Goetz?"

"They were goin' to rob him. They thought he looked like easy bait."

"That's why they went up to him?"

"He looked like he had money. They ask him for five dollars."

"How were they going to rob him?"

"Just scare him."

Breslin knew that Barry Slotnick would love this. One of the central points of contention in the Goetz case was the kids' intent—whether they'd been *asking* for five dollars or *telling* Goetz to give it to them. Just now, Slotnick and Mark Baker were arguing to dismiss the attempted murder charges. Prosecutor Greg Waples had also claimed that Cabey was not mentally competent to testify. Yet here, in one of the victims' own words, was an admission of criminal intent.

Breslin felt no warmth toward Goetz's defenders, but this was news, and he had a column to write.

CHAPTER 41

A few weeks earlier, on November 2, 1985, Barry Slotnick, Mark Baker, and Bruce Cutler drove together to Atlantic Beach on Long Island for a wedding. Father of the bride was Angelo "Fat Ange" Ruggiero, John Gotti's best friend and deputy as well as a client of Slotnick and Cutler in another case.

Though the Mafia was under siege, some of its members had made little effort to assume a lower profile. Slotnick had recently been among the 1,500 guests at another wedding, that of Gotti's daughter Victoria. For that event, Gotti had booked Marina Del Rey, a catering hall in the Bronx that overlooked the East River. In one room, Connie Francis crooned; in another, Jay Black, of Jay and the Americans, sang; a third room featured a rotating cast of comedians, including Irwin Corey, Pat Cooper, and George Kirby.

Today, Ruggiero's daughter Ann Marie, twenty, was marrying Angelo Gurino, whose brother John Gurino was also a client of the Slotnick firm, in a murder case. Fat Ange had brought that case to Slotnick, asking him to have his "junior homicide partner"—Cutler—serve as John's lawyer, and Cutler had won an acquittal. Two other brothers, Caesar and Anthony Gurino, ran Arc Plumbing and Heating and were John Gotti's employers, at least on paper.

As Slotnick walked toward the entrance to the Sands Beach Club, he saw the usual cluster of government cars with their telltale antennae and clean-shaven occupants watching the wedding guests. There was also a pair of surveillance vans with mirrored windows concealing men with video cameras and telephoto lenses. Slotnick approached one of them and stood in front of a window, pointedly adjusting his tie in the reflection.

Inside the building, he saw the familiar tables full of neckless three-hundred-pound men—unaccompanied by wives—who never would have made it through a metal detector. Then Slotnick saw the father of the bride approaching. Ruggiero was wearing his usual oversize tinted glasses but had put on a tuxedo with a boutonniere for the occasion. Slotnick could tell he was agitated.

"Barry, can you fuckin' believe this?" Fat Ange said. "My wife booked a kosher caterer. What does a guy have to do to get some fuckin' calamar?"

One month later, around 9:30 on the evening of Monday, December 2, a seventy-one-year-old patient registered as Timothy O'Neil died in his sleep at Mary Immaculate Hospital in Queens. O'Neil was an alias for Aniello Dellacroce; he'd chosen the name because in the past, while carrying out murder contracts, he had sometimes disguised himself in a priest's collar and gone by the name Father O'Neill [sic]. The death certificate gave Dellacroce's occupation as a "salesman" of "meat."

Slotnick's office told the *New York Times* that there would be no public funeral service. The organized crime community would honor Dellacroce in a more private fashion. On December 4, a chilly day with an overcast sky, there was a wake for Dellacroce at Guidetti Funeral Home, on Spring Street in Little Italy. A line of mourners snaked around the corner, waiting to pay their respects. Rosemary Connelly, Dellacroce's longtime girlfriend, came in a black stretch limousine with her daughter, Shannon "Sandy" Connelly Grillo, who was also reportedly John Gotti's mistress. John and Gene Gotti, John Carneglia, Angelo Ruggiero, and several of the other codefendants all came by that afternoon.

Nearby was a comical snarl of competing surveillance teams. An NYPD sedan with four antennae was double-parked across the street from the funeral parlor. Two cars from the state's Organized Crime Task Force kept circling the block, with telephoto-lens-brandishing cameramen openly shooting pictures through rolled-down windows. The Manhattan DA's office had a van parked in front of a fire hydrant directly in front of the mortuary. The FBI had its own Dodge van full of agents parked a block away.

When Slotnick arrived with Cutler, they walked down the few steps into the funeral parlor and paid their respects.

The next day, a Thursday, Dellacroce's funeral was held at Old St. Patrick's, a church on Mulberry Street. A ten-car cortege brought the casket to the church. "Death is part of life, but this life is not everything," the priest said as four altar boys stood nearby. "Nelson Rockefeller had everything, but he couldn't get the presidency." It was a reference to the view among Dellacroce loyalists that he had been wrongfully passed over when Carlo Gambino elevated Paul Castellano to boss of the family that bore his name.

In fact, there was a glaring absence amid the throng of mourners. Castellano had chosen not to attend, generating chatter among Gambino family members. Slotnick tried not to concern himself with Mafia intrigue, but even he couldn't help noticing that Castellano hadn't come. Two weeks later, at 5:26 p.m. on Monday, December 16, Castellano, who was free on two million dollars' bail while awaiting trial in a different case, left the midtown office of his lawyer, James LaRossa. A little while later, Castellano, along with his bodyguard and heir apparent, Tommy Bilotti, arrived at Sparks Steak House, on East 46th Street near Third Avenue. They were there to meet with two Gambino capos.

As Castellano and Bilotti stepped out of a black Lincoln Town Car, four men in matching trench coats and Russian fur hats materialized around them. Two of the men, handguns out, went for Castellano, hitting him five times in the head and once in the chest.

"Oh, my God! Oh, my God!" a woman shouted as pedestrians ran in all directions or dropped to the ground.

The other two shooters pumped eight bullets into Bilotti, four in the head and four in the chest. Then one of the shooters fired a final round directly into Castellano's skull. After that, all the shooters fled.

Castellano, bleeding from his nose, ears, and mouth, sat slumped against the car. Bilotti lay in the street on his back, bleeding. Both men were dead.

TV vans and police cars and gawkers began to gather. John Miller was one of the first on the scene, and as he stood over the bodies, a cop he knew gave him a tip: "Keep your eyes on Gotti. He's probably behind this."

Based on earlier wiretaps, the FBI also immediately suspected that John Gotti was responsible for the hit. Castellano favored white-collar crimes and had long disapproved of Gotti's more violent faction. With Gotti's patron, Dellacroce, no longer alive to protect him, the theory was that Gotti had preemptively taken out Castellano before the rival capo could marginalize him. Or worse.

That night, as soon as Miller called Slotnick with the news, the lawyer's mind reeled with the implications. The combination of Dellacroce's and Castellano's deaths would reconfigure not just the "so-called Gambino organization," as Slotnick continued to insist on calling it, but also the case against it.

"It could be the beginning of a major mob war," the leader of the federal Organized Crime Strike Force, Ed McDonald, predicted. Confirming the FBI's suspicions, Gotti vaulted to the head of the Gambino family almost overnight, and as the prime suspect in the Castellano hit, he also became the best-known mobster in the country.

CHAPTER 42

On a chilly day in January of 1986, John Miller arrived at Barry Slotnick's downtown offices for one of their regular lunches.

The waiting room was furnished with a large bright-blue floral-patterned carpet, antique-style furniture upholstered to match the carpet, and a grandfather clock, which seemed intended to project an aura of tradition and success.

Scanning the space, Miller marveled at its occupants. With Slotnick handling the two biggest cases of the decade, the small room (presided over by a secretary answering an incessantly ringing phone) was filled with a motley assortment of legally imperiled characters.

Seated against one wall were a couple of Chinese gangsters.

A Russian mobster and a couple of Hasidic men sat across from them.

Bernhard Goetz, who spent a lot of time at the firm working on his case, was playing some kind of game with John McNally, one of Slotnick's private investigators. McNally had been lawyer F. Lee Bailey's private investigator in the Patty Hearst case. While Frank King was the investigator Slotnick wanted sitting next to him in the courtroom, advising on trial strategy, McNally was the one Slotnick used to investigate and interview witnesses. Slotnick couldn't have King do that work, because then King would be subject to cross-examination, and his checkered history made him too easily impeachable as a witness. Now McNally was making Goetz sit on a couch and show him how fast he'd gotten up to shoot the four guys on the subway.

"Bernie, that was too slow," McNally said. "Do it again."

Looming largest of all in the waiting room was a thick-necked guy Miller recognized as John Gotti's driver, who was apparently there waiting for his boss. Gotti suddenly popped out of a door down the hall and said, "Hey, where the fuck is the men's room?"

Slotnick's reception area, Miller thought to himself, was "the Star Wars bar" of criminal-defense lawyer offices.

Gotti and his codefendants were seated around a long conference table with their lawyers. Though Slotnick no longer had a client in the case, Bruce Cutler did, so trial prep was still being run out of the Slotnick firm.

Lunch had arrived, and as usual it was a multicourse Italian feast. Pretty waitresses from the restaurant catering the meal uncomfortably endured the grabbing hands of some of the portly Italian gangsters. One of Gotti's crew opened his mouth while a waitress put a meatball directly into it. "There was a yuckiness about it," recalls a former Slotnick paralegal. Only in her early twenties at the time, she recalls deliberately placing herself between one of the men and a waitress who was even younger, "a baby."

Gotti called down the table to lawyer Jeffrey Hoffman, who was seated next to his client in the case, Gotti's younger brother Gene.

"We need to get some money back from Barry," Gotti said.

Gotti had recently been complaining to Cutler about the retainer Dellacroce had paid Slotnick.

"Listen, John," Hoffman said. "You're never going to get money back from Barry. You could kidnap his family. You could torture them. He's not going to give you a dime."

Hoffman moved over toward Gotti and, in a low voice, offered another suggestion. John Carneglia, one of Gotti's codefendants, wasn't happy with his lawyer. Why not have Slotnick take over that defense?

Gotti pushed back, but Hoffman persisted.

"Barry's a great lawyer," he said. "You'll be doing John [Carneglia] a favor."

Gotti finally agreed.

Slotnick privately considered Gotti a loudmouth, but as Cutler's boss, he'd be overseeing the trial strategy anyway, and he was happy to earn the money he'd already been paid.

CHAPTER 43

One morning, Bruce Cutler walked into Barry Slotnick's office with a more pronounced strut than usual.

"Berschel," Cutler said. That was what he called his boss.

Slotnick looked at his junior partner. In the time since they'd met—even since the younger lawyer had started working for the firm—Cutler's appearance had changed. His arms had thickened. His chest had broadened. His neck had become like a bull's. The way he dressed had changed, too. Today he was wearing a double-breasted silk suit. He looked, Slotnick thought, like a goombah.

"What are you doing?" Slotnick asked. "It's not Halloween."

"You don't like my suit?" Cutler said. "John bought it for me."

Gotti had enthusiastically taken to his new role as boss, trading in his generic mob schlubwear for natty suits and silk ties, leading to tabloids christening him the Dapper Don. And over the previous nine months, Cutler and Gotti had begun to spend a lot of time together.

Cutler started meeting Gotti at the Ravenite. They bet on sports, the loser having to do sets of a hundred push-ups; then, as Gotti became a clotheshorse, the stakes became articles of clothing. Gotti introduced Cutler to David Nadler Custom Shirts, in Brooklyn, which made the mob boss's shirts; Cutler started having all his shirts made there, too. Gotti had also arranged for a friend to take Cutler to DeLisi Clothing, on East 55th Street in Manhattan, to buy Cutler this, his first double-breasted Brioni suit.

Other lawyers had begun making comments about Cutler's growing resemblance to Gotti. Even Cutler's family remarked on the similarity. Cutler took it as a compliment. Slotnick thought that Cutler had always needed a father figure and that Gotti was replacing Slotnick in that role.

Slotnick was all for cordial attorney-client relations, but he'd always been careful to maintain a professional distance. If you got too close to o.c. clients, you could get burned. He'd seen it happen to other lawyers—those who ended up losing their licenses or going to prison or showing up in court with two broken arms and a clearly made-up story about falling off a ladder or even one who ended up dead in Sheepshead Bay with his penis in his mouth.

Cutler's growing closeness with Gotti had begun to create problems between the law partners. Gotti, who'd initially been been the fourth named defendant in the RICO case, had overnight become the lead defendant. The prosecutors were retailoring their case to focus on him, and Gotti thought his lawyer—Cutler—should be running the show.

Slotnick and the Gambino boss clashed. Donna put it more bluntly. "Barry and Gotti hated each other," she says.

With the Goetz trial supposed to begin soon, Gotti accused Slotnick—whom he sometimes referred to as "the bearded guy"—of having divided attention. Gotti also didn't feel that Slotnick showed him enough deference.

Slotnick scoffed at this. How many cases had John Gotti tried? Why would he listen to him about trial strategy?

But Cutler, too, began to chafe at Slotnick's authority. Cutler was angry that Slotnick was representing Goetz, who, he thought, was "an angry white nerd" whose case was beneath the firm's dignity. Cutler was developing what was arguably an inflated sense of his own importance. Speaking with a newspaper reporter, Cutler recalled what friends of Gotti had told him: "They joked, 'No wonder you're Barry Slotnick's partner. With you around, who needs Barry Slotnick?'"

CHAPTER 44

O n January 16, 1986, Barry Slotnick was in his office when he got word that Justice Crane would be issuing a ruling on the second Goetz indictment later that day. Slotnick and Mark Baker had been challenging the indictment on technical legal grounds for months, but they were honestly unsure what to expect.

Crane was forty-nine, with glasses and a comb-over. Slotnick felt relatively at ease with him. While Judge Nickerson showed an obvious distaste for the Gotti case, Crane openly reveled in the chance to take part in a historic trial. To Crane's scholarly mind, the Goetz case posed fascinating legal questions.

That afternoon, a courier delivered Justice Crane's decision to Slotnick and Baker. It was thirty-five pages long. Crane found that the grand jury testimony of Troy Canty and James Ramseur "strongly appeared" to have been perjured. Remarks by Ramseur and Canty indicating that they'd intended to rob Goetz cast doubt on the truthfulness of their previous testimony, in which they said that they'd merely asked Goetz for money. Justice Crane also agreed with the defense's argument that there was "prejudicial error" in prosecutor Greg Waples's instructions to the second grand jury "on the defense of justification."

In repeating the elements of the statute, Waples had "omitted the requirement that the defendant believe that unlawful physical force was about to be used against him. Then the prosecutor reiterated the duty to retreat without reference to the defendant's knowledge that he can retreat in safety."

Justice Crane was striking down nine of the thirteen counts in the second indictment but letting stand the reckless endangerment count because not all Goetz's bullets hit their targets.

Slotnick noted that in the written opinion Crane had partially credited Jimmy Breslin's column about his November visit with Cabey for his decision.

For once, Slotnick had Breslin to thank for something.

But Crane had also written that he would allow the DA to impanel a third grand jury, a highly unusual step.

Slotnick announced that he was "very satisfied" about the dismissal of nine counts but "somewhat disappointed that the judge did not dismiss the charge of reckless endangerment." Slotnick said he hoped that the DA would "reevaluate his decision and perhaps end this nightmare" but nevertheless staunchly declared, "We're ready to go to trial."

In reality, of course, he was far from ready to go to trial. He had more pressing matters to worry about at the time, all having to do with Gotti.

CHAPTER 45

With the John Gotti case set to begin in April of 1986, things started to get crazy.

From the moment Paul Castellano was assassinated, there'd been a burst of news stories, sourced to law enforcement officials, speculating that Gotti had engineered the hit to clear the way for his own ascent.

In March, an unrelated case against Gotti went to trial in Queens. A year and a half earlier, police had arrested him for allegedly assaulting a refrigerator repairman named Romual Piecyk. Piecyk, having no idea who Gotti was, complained to police that after he honked at a double-parked car, Gotti and another man, Frank Colletta, had slapped him around and stolen three hundred dollars from him.

John Santucci, the Queens DA, seized the opportunity to go after a man who had since become the most powerful mobster in America. But Piecyk's tune had changed. In February, he wrote a letter to Santucci, saying that having recently read that

Gotti was "next in line for Godfather, naturally, my idea of pursuing this matter dropped. I can't and will not live the rest of my life in fear."

Piecyk told prosecutors that he had been threatened and also that the brakes on his car had been tampered with. Interviewed by a New York tabloid, he said, "I'm not going to go against Mr. Gotti" and claimed that the only people harassing him were from the DA's office.

On the same day Piecyk made that statement, FBI agents revealed that William Battista, an informant scheduled to testify in the upcoming Gotti racketeering trial, had disappeared on January 22 after his role as an informant was disclosed.

Both incidents generated news stories speculating about Gotti's intimidation tactics, adding to Slotnick's fears that it would be impossible to get a fair, impartial jury in the case. Slotnick and the other defense attorneys filed a motion to postpone the trial, but Judge Nickerson was unmoved.

On the day Piecyk was scheduled to testify in Queens, he was a no-show. Police tracked him down at Mercy Hospital on Long Island, where he'd scheduled elective surgery simply to avoid having to testify. When Piecyk left the hospital, they arrested him as a material witness to ensure his appearance in court. But there was no way to force him to tell the truth. He called WCBS-TV to say he didn't remember "the names or the faces" of the men who'd assaulted him. On the witness stand on March 24, when asked to identify the men who'd attacked him—Gotti and Colletta sat at the defense table, alongside Cutler—Piecyk looked around the room slowly and said he could not. How was the assailant dressed? "To be perfectly honest, it was so long ago I don't remember." In fact, Piecyk said, he now didn't remember being robbed at all.

The judge declared Piecyk a "hostile witness" and, the next day, dismissed all the charges against Gotti and Colletta.

The cover of the *New York Post* blared: I FORGOTTI.

On March 31, Aniello Dellacroce's son Armond, a codefendant in the racketeering case, didn't show up for his sentencing, forfeiting a two-hundred-and-fifty-thousand-dollar bond. Judge Nickerson issued a bench warrant for his arrest. The disappearance of another person who'd been scheduled to play a role in the upcoming Gotti trial resulted in more headlines:

NATIONWIDE MANHUNT FOR ARMOND DELLACROCE.

SECOND PERSON IN GOTTI'S CASE IS NOW MISSING.

Still, Nickerson rebuffed defense motions to postpone the start of the trial, now only a week away. Slotnick had resigned himself to the idea that the trial wasn't going to be delayed. Jury selection would begin, and it would be a farce. People would either lie about having no preconceived opinions about Gotti or they'd tell the truth, which would mean they were total wack jobs who dwelled somewhere other than planet earth. The last thing Slotnick wanted, he said, was a jury of "the unknowing, the unwise, and the illiterate."

Meanwhile, Gotti continued to act like a guy who sought out the media glare. On Monday, April 7, as jury selection got under way, Gotti—newly tan from six days in Fort Lauderdale—came to court wearing a thousand-dollar suit, see-through monogrammed socks, and a diamond pinkie ring. He theatrically held a door open for a female prosecutor.

Every day seemed to yield another notoriety-enhancing news

story. On the second day of jury selection, prosecutor Diane Giacalone told Judge Nickerson that a government witness, Dennis Quirk, had been threatened: two men posing as detectives had gone to a home once occupied by Quirk, president of the New York State Court Officers Association, and asked where they could find him.

Just this morning, men in a black Mercedes-Benz had tailed Quirk, yelling that they wanted to talk with him about the 1976 slaying of Albert Gelb, whom Quirk had been friends with. John Gotti, Giacalone informed the judge, drove a black Mercedes. Nickerson instructed the defendants to steer clear of witnesses.

The next morning, a man who claimed to be John Gotti called 911 and said he was going to blow up the federal courthouse in Brooklyn "in about an hour." Hundreds of people were evacuated and the building was checked for bombs before US marshals traced the call to Alexander Galka, fifty-two, of Queens, a patient at the Creedmoor Psychiatric Center who was due at the courthouse later that day to face charges of making threatening phone calls to President Ronald Reagan.

Again, the defense team asked Judge Nickerson to postpone the trial until the media furor had died down. "Because of this publicity, you have maniacs like this using [Gotti's] name," Cutler said. The media coverage, the lawyers argued, had been "sensational" and "irresponsible." Nickerson denied the request.

Then the other lawyers asked that their clients be tried separately from the increasingly infamous lead defendant. "I doubt that he can get a fair trial now," Slotnick said of his client John

Carneglia. "Perhaps without Mr. Gotti, we can get a fairer trial." This request, too, was denied.

Adding to the defense team's sense of being under siege, later that same day, in the federal courthouse across the river in Manhattan, a judge handed down harsh sentences to five Gambino mobsters involved in a car-theft ring.

The New York *Daily News* published an editorial, "The Gotti Trial: Very High Stakes," arguing that what was on the line was nothing less than the rule of law itself—"the ability of the prosecution, the judiciary, the government to guarantee that the mob cannot run wild, leaving the laws of this land trampled in its wake." The paper noted that Judge Nickerson "has the power to revoke Gotti's $1 million bail. He shouldn't hesitate to use it."

Cutler griped that the press was "making my client into a monster," and the defense team spent an hour trying to persuade Nickerson to put a gag order on the media. The judge rebuffed this idea, too.

Around lunchtime on April 13, Gotti's underboss, Frank De-Cicco, attended a Gambino crew meeting at a social club in Bensonhurst, an Italian neighborhood in Brooklyn. Afterward, he walked to a gray Buick Electra parked nearby to fetch some business cards from the glove compartment for Frank Bellino, a member of the rival Lucchese crime family. As DeCicco sat in the front passenger seat and Bellino stood nearby, the car exploded in a ball of fire, a black mushroom cloud rising over the neighborhood. DeCicco was blown to bits. Bellino was seriously injured. Investigators suspected that the car bomb had been triggered by remote control.

Once again, the newspapers went crazy:

CAR BOMB KILLS THE NO. 2 MAN IN CRIME FAMILY.

WHO KILLED FRANK DECICCO?

FBI SUSPECTS REVENGE IN N.Y. MOB BOMBING.

Jimmy Breslin thought the bomb had been meant for Gotti, but Gotti had stayed in the social club longer than anticipated: "Gotti was supposed to come right out. He tarried. The bomb did not. Mr. DeCicco became dust."

Two weeks later, as Slotnick sat in court with the other lawyers and their clients, Judge Nickerson said that he had an announcement to make.

"The events of the past few weeks and the Court's observation during the examination of prospective jurors have convinced the Court that it has been using procedures to qualify jurors that under present circumstances are unsatisfactory...In the light of this decision and the extensive attention heretofore paid to the case by the media, the Court deems it unwise to recommence jury selection immediately; therefore, sets August 18, 1986, at 10 am as the date and time when the jury selection will begin."

Nickerson was postponing the trial's start by three months. He had finally come around to the defendants' argument that they couldn't get a fair and impartial jury because of all the publicity.

Slotnick was pleasantly surprised.

CHAPTER 46

"Your Honor," Barry Slotnick said, standing and facing Judge Nickerson, "those charges don't pertain to my client."

Slotnick was speaking at a bail hearing a few days after Nickerson's big decision. With the trial postponed until August, prosecutors Diane Giacalone and John Gleeson were asking that bail be revoked and that John Gotti, Gene Gotti, John Carneglia, and Anthony Rampino be held in jail until the trial was over. Their main arguments were that John Gotti, since the original indictment, had risen to become boss of the Gambino family, that he and the others were continuing to conduct criminal business as usual, and that they were interfering with the case by intimidating witnesses.

Slotnick was arguing that his client John Carneglia was not John Gotti and that consideration of their bail status should not be lumped together.

"Let the record show that that's Mr. Gotti they're talking about," Slotnick continued, "not Mr. Carneglia."

Gotti didn't care about high-minded legal principles or the lawyers' code of ethics. As far as he was concerned, any attempt to create daylight between himself and his codefendants was traitorous.

To outward appearances, at that moment, Gotti looked icy and dead serious, but inside he was fuming. As a hidden FBI bug would later record, he told his underboss, Sammy "the Bull" Gravano, that the whole time Slotnick spoke, Gotti was thinking, *Sit the fuck down or I'll knock you down, you cocksucker!*

Judge Nickerson decided that John Carneglia and Gene Gotti could remain free on bail, but he was sending John Gotti and Anthony Rampino back to jail.

Slotnick and his cocounsel immediately moved to sever their clients' cases from Gotti's. Nickerson denied the motion, but once again, Gotti was livid about the breaking of ranks.

As soon as the hearing ended, Gotti tore into one of the cocounsel: "If you make an application like that again, you'll be carried out of this fuckin' courthouse wrapped in that rug over there," he said.

The lawyer froze.

"You understand me?" Gotti said. "You see that elevator over there? You'll be taking it down without the elevator!"

A few days later, Slotnick's associate Mark Baker learned that John wasn't the only volatile Gotti. In a meeting room at the Slotnick offices, Baker passed along an offer to Gene Gotti in front of his codefendants: prosecutor Giacalone had called to say that she was prepared to offer him a plea deal with reduced charges in return for his cooperation.

"I know you won't take it," Baker added, "but it's my duty as your lawyer to make you aware of it."

Gotti got a hard look in his eyes. "You go tell her to go fuck herself," he said.

"Okay," Baker said. "I'll tell her you don't want to take the deal."

"No," Gotti said, the edge in his voice sharpening. "Like I told you, you go tell her to go fuck herself."

"That's not how we speak to prosecutors," Baker said.

Gotti seized Baker by the shoulders and shoved him into the wall.

"Angelo!" Baker called out. Fat Ange Ruggiero was in the next room, and Baker had established a rapport with him. "Is someone going to tell this guy to get his hands off me?"

Ruggiero poked his head in and sized up the situation.

"Hey, Gene," Ruggiero said, "take your fucking hands off my Jew lawyer."

CHAPTER 47

I n Scarsdale, Donna looked out the front window. Still no sign of Barry.

The children were getting hungry.

Donna was pissed.

She had long ago accepted the terms of their life. They were a team. Donna took care of the kids, the social life, the home, and all that came with it. Barry was the provider who brought home the (kosher) turkey bacon. He had a brilliant career doing important work. He worked very long hours. Most evenings, he didn't arrive home until after the children were in bed. Donna, with her more affluent upbringing, had helped smooth his rough edges, introducing him to fine wines and beautiful art, both of which they began collecting. Sometimes, Donna felt lonely, but she'd filled her life by raising four children and developing her own circle of friends.

There was one night a week, however, when the Slot-nicks were always together. Every Friday, they sat down for

Shabbat dinner. It was inviolate. The kids, two of them now in high school, weren't allowed to go out that night. And Donna expected Barry to leave work in time to be home for Shabbat.

Bogusha, the Slotnicks' housekeeper, pointed out that the chicken was getting cold.

Donna looked out the window one last time, then herded the kids into the dining room to begin without Barry.

She lit two candles as she said a prayer: "Baruch atah Adonai…" Then she and the kids kissed each other as Donna said, "Shabbat shalom."

Barry was supposed to say the blessings that came next, one for the girls, one for the boy, but tonight Donna said them instead.

Barry was supposed to bless the wine, too, but tonight Donna did it. She poured a few glugs of Yarden, a kosher wine considerably better than Manischewitz, into a silver kiddush cup. Then she poured a bottle of Kedem grape juice into a bigger silver contraption that funneled the juice into four little cups, which she handed to the kids. She was finishing saying the kiddush when she heard a car door shut, then the front door open.

Barry came into the room, looking meek. "Sorry," he said softly.

Bogusha served the chicken soup.

Donna stared daggers at Barry.

Barry found a parsley leaf floating in his soup bowl to be particularly fascinating.

Donna held her fire as the family ate roast chicken and salad and Barry tossed chunks of challah bread at the kids.

After the kids had eaten their Stella D'oro fudge cookies and moved to the living room to watch *Miami Vice,* Barry walked over and embraced Donna.

She was palpably tense.

"I'm sorry," he said. "These two cases. It won't be like this forever. I promise."

PART FIVE

CHAPTER 48

As Barry Slotnick stood at the sink in his office bathroom, washing his hands, Bernie Goetz wouldn't stop yapping. Slotnick found himself thinking, *Is this really so much better than actual physical threats from clients?*

Goetz was always going on about guns, among other pet topics. He had recently pressed upon Slotnick a book titled *How to Shoot a Gun: The Handbook for the Average Citizen.*

"Bernie is a nut," recalls Howard Varinsky, Slotnick's jury consultant. "He just jabbered and wouldn't shut up."

Slotnick began drying his hands on a paper towel.

"Bernie," Slotnick said, "I have only one regret—that I took you on as a client."

Goetz giggled.

For the first six months of 1986, while the Gotti case was producing one drama after another, the Goetz case had been in a state of suspended animation.

When Justice Crane dismissed most of the indictment against

Goetz in January, Slotnick wasn't under the illusion that his client's biggest troubles were over. The government had appealed to the state supreme court's appellate division, an intermediate-level court that upheld Justice Crane's decision in throwing out the attempted murder and assault charges. Then the government appealed again, this time to New York's highest court, the New York State Court of Appeals.

On a Wednesday in July, the high court, led by Chief Judge Sol Wachtler, reversed the lower court's decision, holding that the applicable self-defense standard should be what a "reasonable man" would do. The full Goetz case would proceed. It had finally crossed the threshold from "Should Goetz stand trial?" to "Will he be found guilty?"

Slotnick now faced another dilemma. Justice Crane had already scheduled the Goetz trial to begin on September 2 should his ruling get overturned. But that had been when the Gotti trial was expected to begin in April. Slotnick wrote to Crane explaining the situation: the start of the Gotti trial had been pushed back to August, and he expected the trial to run for four months; Goetz would have to wait.

Crane gave Baker and Slotnick a month to straighten things out. He suggested that Goetz be represented by Baker instead, but Baker said Goetz preferred Slotnick.

"A lawyer cannot permit himself to be tied up in multiple trials," Crane said, seemingly exasperated with Slotnick.

"It's a physical impossibility for him to be in two places at the same time," Slotnick's associate Gillian Coulter said.

"I'm not threatening," Crane added, but he felt that Slotnick should have a "healthy respect" for the need to get this case moving.

CHAPTER 49

He's such a ladies' man."

"He looks so different without his tan."

"This is the best show in town, and it's free."

Outside the courtroom, spectators were oohing and aahing about the trial to come.

The defense lawyers may have been exaggerating slightly when they called the Gotti trial "the biggest media event since World War II," but when Slotnick arrived at the six-story Emanuel Celler Federal Building, in Brooklyn, on August 18, 1986, for the opening of the Gotti trial, the place was crawling with journalists.

The courthouse, though showing its age of nearly a quarter century, was still impressive and designed to intimidate. The building bristled with federal marshals and other security measures. Inside, the atmosphere was quiet and professional. Only one case was heard at a time in each courtroom, and in most of them, only the handful of people directly concerned with that case tended to be present. Federal prosecutors had vast resources behind them and were always well prepared. When Slotnick tried cases in federal court, he had to fight off the feeling that everything was stacked against him.

Upstairs, in courtroom 11, John Gotti wore a dark-blue double-breasted suit with a white pocket square, black shoes, no tie, and no jewelry. After several months in prison, he had an indoor pallor and shaggy hair. But he still projected a charisma unlike that of any other mobster in memory, and fans and acolytes milled about in the hallway.

Slotnick and the other defense lawyers were full of gripes. They continued to complain about pretrial publicity. They accused Diane Giacalone, the lead prosecutor, of "judge shop-ping." They accused Nickerson of bias: "We can't have our day in court," Cutler said, with Nickerson on the bench; his rulings so far suggested that he believed prosecutor Giacalone "has already proven her case." They kvetched about the courtroom seating arrangements, which they said gave the prosecutors better eye contact with the jury. And they kvetched about exactly where John Gotti would be served lunch. Nickerson rejected a defense request for sandwiches to be brought to Gotti in court so that he and his codefendants and their lawyers could confer during the lunch break.

"Why don't we just not eat?" Gotti said. "Why should we even bother eatin'?"

Though in theory the government had more resources than the defense, in the courtroom the matchup looked lopsided in the other direction. Prosecutor Diane Frances Giacalone, thirty-six years old and wearing a blue silk dress, had grown up in a very different Ozone Park from John Gotti's. A nice Catholic girl who'd attended Our Lady of Wisdom Academy, across the street from the Bergin Hunt and Fish Club, she went on to get an undergraduate degree in political science, a law degree, and a master's degree in tax law, all from New York University. She had ramrod-straight posture and, according to a newspaper profile timed to the trial's kickoff, "resembles the actress-comedienne Lily Tomlin [and] is animated and quick to laugh." She was in the midst of restoring an old house upstate, which this trial was making it hard to find time for. The only other person with her at the prosecution table was John Gleeson, a bespectacled assistant US attorney.

The defense table, meanwhile, was a clown car, with seven defendants and at least as many lawyers wedged around two sides of it in an L shape. Even in the courtroom, Gotti acted like the boss. He was at first squeezed amid the other defendants and lawyers; then he moved to the head of the table after Cutler rearranged some furniture, prompting Nickerson to say, "Just leave a space for the government." Slotnick and Carneglia sat next to Cutler and Gotti. After codefendant Leonard DiMaria's lawyer Michael Santangelo said, "He has never committed a crime in his life regarding the quality of life"—suggesting that he was trying to distinguish his case from Gotti's—Gotti appeared to take DiMaria to task; Santangelo then explained to the Court, according to the *Daily News,* that "his client was not actually afraid of Gotti, but of the irresponsible reporters who follow him around."

The man who would serve as referee was comically WASP-y. Judge Nickerson's usual lunch was sardines on toast or Yankee bean soup, and he expected lawyers in his courtroom to wear white shirts. The Nickersonian version of saying "What's past is past" or "Why don't you let it go" was the nautical "Now it has drifted astern." When he overruled or denied something, he elongated the second vowel sound, so it came out like "over-ruuuuuuled" or "deniiiiied." One of his daughters had married an Italian man, and the judge was studying the language, so he insisted on calling Carneglia—who pronounced his own name with a silent g, so it rhymed with "Amelia"—"Mr. Car-nig-lia." Nickerson could be blunt—his most-used phrases in the court-room included "This isn't helpful" and "This isn't useful." But it wasn't clear whether his understated approach would be able to handle the garish personalities populating the Gotti case.

CHAPTER 50

Outside the courthouse, a pair of Russian journalists—a TV reporter and his cameraman—buttonholed Slotnick and asked a leading question: Did Slotnick think his client could get a fair trial?

For the past year, Slotnick had been arguing that he could not—that the pretrial publicity and anonymous jury had created a situation in which the jury would be biased against the defendants. But the Cold War was still raging, and Slotnick wasn't about to deliver a sound bite that could be repurposed as Russian propaganda.

"We've got a fair judge, and the government will have to prove its charges beyond a reasonable doubt," Slotnick said. He placed his hand over his heart, as if he were about to sing the national anthem: Gotti, he said, was living in the only country in the world that would give him a fair trial. "We have faith in the American system. We'll get a fair jury . . . Russia wouldn't give him a trial this fair."

The Russian journalist then told another American reporter that he found Slotnick "self-assured, arrogant, with an answer to everything. We have people like that in the Soviet Union."

Moments later, in the courthouse bathroom, Slotnick was singing a different tune. Jimmy Breslin had followed him in, seeking elaboration. "We would be better off in Leningrad than we are in this place," Slotnick told Breslin. "This is not justice. This is Fascism!"

The next morning, Slotnick opened the *Daily News* and turned to Breslin's column, wondering if he'd made it in.

Jimmy Breslin was thriving more than ever. Partly for his Goetz columns, he had been awarded the Pulitzer Prize for Commentary in April. Then, as if that weren't enough, in May he'd hosted *Saturday Night Live*. He'd even called himself "the fucking John Gotti of journalism."

Today, Breslin's column was titled "Moscow on the No. 5 train"; Breslin had spent the rest of the day with the Russians, riding around on the subway with them. Slotnick skimmed the text, looking for his name. Breslin had written: "I was not going to act like a child in a schoolyard the way Barry Slotnick did over in Brooklyn."

What was it with this guy?

Slotnick generally projected confidence, but Breslin's tone rankled him.

Barry's teenage son, Stuart Slotnick, sat in the back row of the courtroom beside Victor Borden, a TV reporter. It was a Wednesday in late August, and he was still on summer break.

After the courtroom crowd rose to acknowledge the judge's entrance, Nickerson announced that he'd been informed by his clerk that Romual Piecyk, the repairman who'd "forgotten" that Gotti assaulted him, was at the courthouse with a CBS reporter, apparently under the belief that he'd be heard by Nickerson on the spot. "Do you know anything about it? Any of you?"

"Apparently," Diane Giacalone said, "Mr. Slotnick called at least one TV station and advised them to be here today at eleven thirty because something was going to happen."

Slotnick responded that was inaccurate—he'd spoken with a TV person who'd informed *him* that Piecyk would be coming to the courthouse. What Slotnick didn't mention was that he had then tipped off his son, an amateur photographer who was photo editor of his high school yearbook, and told him to hang out with that reporter, Borden.

As soon as Piecyk walked into the courtroom, accompanied by his lawyer, Stuart rushed downstairs and went to his car to grab the 35mm Mamiya camera his dad had given him.

Upstairs, Piecyk sat in the front row, but he got no acknowledgment from Gotti, and Nickerson informed Piecyk that he wouldn't be permitted to address the Court. Instead, Piecyk held a news conference on the courthouse steps, where he complained that Gotti had been denied bail unfairly and that the media had turned Gotti into a "human monster."

"I honestly feel Mr. Gotti should be out on bail," he said.

Stuart, after snapping a picture of Piecyk exiting the courthouse, sprinted to the *New York Post* offices and made his first photo sale, for one hundred and twenty-five dollars. "It was the greatest thing on earth," Stuart remembers. "I was like, I'm going to be a professional photographer."

CHAPTER 51

Finally, jury selection began anew, with a starting panel of 450 prospects for a jury that would ultimately have twelve members and six alternates. All had filled out questionnaires in advance, aimed at sussing out biases. The process was a minefield, as Slotnick well knew.

He had once been hired to defend an ex-cop, indicted for felony extortion. Going into the trial, Slotnick was convinced that the government had a weak case, and every witness the prosecution put up, Slotnick destroyed on cross-examination. He knew when he was winning, and this was clearly one of those times. When the jury returned from deliberations, however, they found his client guilty. Slotnick was shocked and mystified: How could this have happened?

As he was nursing his wounds in the week after the verdict, he received a series of curious phone calls from jurors on the case. The first said that there had been one juror among the group, juror number 8, who seemed to have some kind of connection to Slotnick's client. This juror had dominated the deliberations, working the rest of the jury into a lather and swaying them toward a conviction. The next caller echoed the first: juror number 8 had had some kind of problem with the defendant and persuaded everyone else to find him guilty: now, the caller said, he was having second thoughts about the verdict. The third caller said much the same thing as the first two.

At that point, Slotnick went to his files, looked at the jury selection sheet, and called his client.

"Do you know a guy named John Smith?" he asked the ex-cop.

"I used to know one guy with that name."

"Who was he?"

"Ten years ago, a guy named John Smith accused me of sleeping with his wife."

"Did you know that John Smith was on the jury in your case?"

"I saw the name, but that wasn't the same John Smith. The one I knew was skinny and clean-shaven and had an afro. The John Smith on the jury was fat and bald and had facial hair and glasses."

It turned out that it was the same guy; he'd just become physically unrecognizable.

Ultimately, Slotnick got the conviction reversed.

The Gotti prosecutors were pressing for an anonymous jury to avoid the possibility of jury tampering. The defense was vigorously opposing this, arguing that anonymity would prejudice jurors by implying that the defendants were dangerous.

Slotnick was still very concerned about jurors being tainted by press coverage. Judge Nickerson asked each candidate what media they consumed. *Big Beautiful Woman,* one man responded. "Do you have any fear of serving on this jury?" Nickerson asked juror number 613. "Maybe I have some," the man answered. Nickerson dismissed him.

Slotnick knew it was unrealistic to expect jurors to be blank slates. On the twenty-page questionnaire, many prospects claimed not to have heard of Gotti or anything about the trial, but "Anyone who can see or hear and has half a brain has to know about my client," Cutler complained. The best Slotnick could realistically hope for was jurors who'd read about the case but seemed able to approach it in an unbiased, impartial way.

Yet Nickerson appeared to take the self-professed blank slates at face value while being skeptical of people who claimed to have open minds but admitted knowing of Gotti. At the same time, Nickerson said that even jurors' county of residency wouldn't be revealed. Slotnick argued that this was important information to know in order to understand their possible predilections.

Of eighty-eight people called the first day, Nickerson eliminated thirty-four because of written answers they'd given. Another fifty-two people were excused for other reasons. Two women, known only by the numbers 105 and 114, were selected for further questioning.

Slotnick observed that Gotti took a vain pleasure in hearing what the potential jurors had to say about him. One woman who made it to the next round of winnowing was a fifty-nine-year-old nurse who said she'd seen TV news reports describing Gotti as a "godfather." Asked if she knew what that meant, she said, "To me a godfather is someone who stands up when a child is baptized, but I don't think that is what they meant." Gotti laughed.

Another jury prospect said that she'd heard about the Mafia from her Italian American boyfriend, who'd said: "If you do anything wrong, I'll get the Mafia after you. You'll be wearing cement shoes." Gotti laughed at this, too, but Nickerson excused the woman from the jury.

Gotti also found funny the answer of number 149, a thirty-seven-year-old accountant who, when asked by Nickerson what he'd read about the case, said, "That he's a Dapper Dan" and "That he's a ladies' man." Gotti smiled when another woman, who ended up being disqualified, said that she understood Gotti to be "a numbers runner." One prospect, a forty-four-year-old telephone repairman, was excused after describing the Mafia as "the head of the Italian race."

On September 9, a prospective juror was asked if she'd ever been involved with a criminal court case. "Yes," she said.

What kind of case?

"Murder."

"And what," Nickerson asked, "was your role in the case?"

"Defendant."

Hearing this, Gotti, at the defense table, "was so happy that for a moment he appeared incapable of killing anybody," according to a later description by Jimmy Breslin.

The process was slow going. After two days, only five jurors, all women, had made it through the initial screening. Cutler complained about some of the cartoons in that day's *New York Post*: under the title "Mafia Fashion Styles," they depicted one person wearing cement shoes, another in the East River, another face-first in spaghetti, and another in the trunk of a car. "We are in worse shape in August than we were in April," Cutler lamented.

Slotnick asked for a gag order on prosecutors and prevailed on Judge Nickerson to caution prospective jurors to avoid media coverage of the case and not talk among themselves about it. "Just take up some other subject," Nickerson suggested. He advised them to talk about "what Mr. Qaddafi is doing or how the Yankees won last night on a Winfield home run."

It was agreed that once the trial began, marshals would clip newspapers delivered to jurors, excising trial-relevant articles.

"Would the Court admonish the jurors not to receive *GQ*?" asked Slotnick, who was the subject of a forthcoming profile in the magazine. The article, titled "The Godfather's Lawyer," described him as "the most successful criminal-defense lawyer of our time."

"I heard about that," Nickerson said.

"And *Esquire*," Slotnick added.

He was being profiled by that magazine, too.

Slotnick was genuinely concerned about the jury being exposed to news about the case, but he was also laying the groundwork for a possible mistrial or appeal, a tactic he'd used in the past.

In the Joe Colombo Jr. silver-melting case, the judge had asked the press not to cover the trial until there was a verdict, lest misreported facts taint the jury. Slotnick later asked the judge to question all the jurors about whether they'd followed his instructions to avoid news accounts of the trial. Five of the jurors admitted that they'd disregarded the instructions and had heard reports that Colombo's father was a reputed crime boss. Slotnick moved for a mistrial, and the judge granted the motion.

In the Gotti trial, jury selection ended on September 23, 1986. The final jurors—six men, six women—would be known only by their numbers. They ranged from a sixty-five-year-old Irish-born retired chauffeur who'd served in World War II and had three children to a single twenty-four-year-old Italian American Brooklyn woman who worked as an accountant. Two of the jurors were Black.

Slotnick was still grumbling. "Obviously," he said, "the jury is not satisfactory." Nickerson optimistically said that he hoped the Gotti trial would be over by January.

"Unbelievable," Gene Gotti was saying.

He was in a small conference room at the Slotnick firm, talking with Sammy "the Bull" Gravano. Jury selection was over, but the trial hadn't started. While John Gotti remained in the custody of the Federal Bureau of Prisons, his brother Gene spent most of his time here with the other defendants, conferring with their lawyers about the upcoming trial.

Gravano leaned forward and spoke in a low voice: he'd been approached by Bosko Radonjic, a Serbian who, improbably, had become the leader of the traditionally Irish Westies gang. Radonjic said a guy he'd worked with on a construction job the year before happened to be on the Gotti jury.

The man's name was George Pape. He was forty-eight, lived on Long Island with his wife and two kids, and had a drinking problem. He'd come to Radonjic, knowing that the Westies and the Gambinos sometimes did business together, and Radonjic had come to Gravano with the news that Pape could be bought.

The Gotti brothers would at the very least get a hung jury.

"Unbelievable that this fuckin' drops out of the sky like this," Gene Gotti said to Gravano now. "My fuckin' brother has nine lives."

"To get this goin'," Gravano said, "I just need an okay from John to tell Bosko to offer the guy money."

Two days later, Gene Gotti passed along a message from his brother: "John likes it, so you do what you have to do."

CHAPTER 52

Barry Slotnick was in the back of his Cadillac Fleetwood, en route to the city, balancing two fourteen-inch legal pads on his knees. Beside him on the tan leather seat was a small pile of office supplies—highlighters, Sharpies, Post-its—as well as a three-ring binder full of documents.

Slotnick scrawled a sentence on the right-hand pad, looked at it, considered it, then scrawled the same sentence on the left-hand pad. He was writing his opening argument—two of them, actually—for the Gotti trial.

In recent weeks, John Gotti had been pressuring him for a copy of the remarks. The mobster was used to being in charge and hadn't hesitated to try to dictate all the lawyers' approaches.

"I don't write openings," Slotnick told him. "I don't do dress rehearsals."

This was a fib. Slotnick liked to scrawl his openings out in longhand, then have them typed up and memorize them.

Gotti had kept insisting. It became a big issue. Finally, Carneglia told Slotnick, "Just write something up and give it to him."

Slotnick was annoyed that he had to go through this charade. Gotti thought he knew better than he did how to orchestrate this case? Slotnick scoffed at the thought. He saw Gotti essentially as a thug. But he wanted Gotti off his back, so he was manufacturing a fake opening-argument document to placate the Gambino boss.

On the pad on his right knee, Slotnick jotted down a few lines distinguishing John Carneglia's case from Gotti's, part of the argument he planned to make for the jury to consider his client separate from the lead defendant.

These sentences he did *not* copy onto the other pad.

Suddenly, the car pulled up short at a light, and the documents slid off the seat in all directions.

Just another annoyance.

Slotnick sighed and gathered together the scattered papers.

Then he picked up a Dictaphone and recorded some new thoughts. Later, he'd have his assistant type them up, and he'd fold them into at least one of these versions of his opening.

At the head of the defense table, John Gotti wore his navy suit with a pocket square and what looked like a hand-painted multicolored silk tie. After six weeks of jury selection and two and a half years of pretrial legal maneuvering, the Gotti trial was finally starting.

All one hundred seats in the sixth-floor courtroom were filled, a fourth of them by journalists and courtroom artists. Family and friends of the participants had come to observe the historic event. Diane Giacalone's mother, brother, sister-in-law, and aunt were there. Stuart Slotnick had brought the twenty-three fellow students in his criminal justice class at Scarsdale High, as well as their teacher, to watch. "Gotti was very shy," Stuart says. "My dad pretty much made him come over. He said, 'Hello,' very soft. You'd have thought he was very gentle and humble."

Judge Nickerson called the proceedings to order at 10:30 a.m., and then Giacalone, wearing a red two-piece suit, stood up to speak.

"Jimmy McBratney was a big man," she began. "He was over six feet tall, and he weighed over two hundred pounds." She told the story of McBratney's murder. "This was no simple barroom quarrel gone bad. It was part of a pattern of criminal activity." Gotti had taken part in the crime out of "ambition to advance himself in an organization known as the Gambino crime family."

Giacalone then walked to a green chalkboard in the back of the room and drew a diagram showing the triangular structure of the organization. Starting at the top and working her way down, she wrote out the various positions in the hierarchy—boss, consigliere, underboss; capos, lieutenants, soldiers. Then, below the soldiers, she drew a line from left to right, with only associates below it. That, she told the jury, was where Gotti and his peers ranked when McBratney was killed. The murder was Gotti's bid to "break through that line."

"What sort of organization is it," Giacalone asked the jury, "where murder is a means of advancement?"

As for her case's biggest weakness—its dependence on a series of lowlife informants—there was little for Giacalone to do other than acknowledge it. "They're just horrible people," she said.

After ninety minutes, she sat down. During her presentation, Gotti had appeared to listen carefully, smiling occasionally, and the courtroom had been marked by a respectful hush. But anyone assuming that a dignified tone had been set for the trial to come was about to learn otherwise.

Bruce Cutler, as counsel to the lead defendant, went next, and as soon as he spoke his opening words, it was clear that he was a very different lawyer from Giacalone—or Slotnick, for that matter.

Cutler, too, drew a chalkboard diagram, showing the same hierarchy as Giacalone did. But he did so solely in order to then flamboyantly erase and dismiss it as "a fantasy." If the prosecution's case promised a patchwork of meticulous evidence, Cutler's counterargument swung big: not only was Gotti *not* a Mafia boss, but the Mafia itself was a figment of the imagination. Cutler wasn't going to put on a defense. He was going to put on an offense.

Yes, Gotti "did get in trouble" when he was younger, but "there's no apology for that...He doesn't apologize for coming from a family that was poor, for being one of thirteen children, eleven who survived, and being on his own since he was twelve." Gotti was guilty of nothing more than associating with people the government didn't like. "When John Gotti got out of jail, he didn't have a dime. What did he do? He stayed with people he grew up with." Since then, he'd been an honest "success" who dressed well out of "pride" rather than boldness. Prosecutors simply didn't like his "lifestyle."

Cutler was getting worked up.

"The only family John Gotti knows is his wife and children

and grandchildren...The only godfather John Gotti is is god-father to his friends' children, and that's no crime." Organized crime was "a fantasy world that doesn't exist."

Giacalone had stood at a lectern in front of the jury box for most of her opening. Cutler paced back and forth like a hungry animal, radiating aggression. He made it clear that the defense strategy would not be limited to the usual discrediting of witnesses or even, broadly, the government. He was going to make it personal. He accused Giacalone of conjuring the Gambino family from her imagination in order to advance her career. He repeatedly referred to her as "the lady in red." He held the indictment over his head and called it "a rancid stew with rotten meat that makes you retch and *vomit*."

He was shouting now.

Then, pausing over a trash can, Cutler slam-dunked the indictment into it.

"It's *garbage*," Cutler bellowed as spectators gasped. "*That's* where it belongs."

After Cutler sat down, it was Slotnick's turn to give his opening.

Cops, prosecutors, and judges tended to see Slotnick as a breed apart from the typical mob lawyer. "Frankly," says George Gabriel, a member of the FBI's Gambino squad and present in the courtroom that day, speaking of Slotnick's reaction to Cutler's performance, "I bet that was embarrassing to him." Rudy Giuliani, despite being a zealous mob-targeting US attorney, called Slotnick a "professional, honest guy." When Slotnick discussed his job, he spoke of it as a high-minded calling. "I represent people who are accused of crimes," he'd say, "many of them unjustifiably." (Men universally regarded as mobsters were, in Slotnick's words, merely "so-called organized crime figures.")

But Slotnick also liked to say that a trial was a form of "mortal combat"—a phrase he used so often that at least one aspiring young lawyer who found the description inspirational received as a gift from his mother a pillow embroidered with the words A TRIAL IS MORTAL COMBAT. So Slotnick approved of Cutler's aggressive approach. "If something worked," he recalls, "we'd do it."

For the moment, he would play good cop to Cutler's bad cop. As Stuart Slotnick watched from the gallery, his father, one hand in his pocket, strolled casually across the room to the trash can where the government's indictment languished. Barry Slotnick peered in. Then he reached down and fished out the document. He calmly dusted it off and put it back on the defense table.

As Slotnick delivered his own opening, his words were nearly as caustic as his partner's. The government's case, Slotnick told the jury, was indeed "garbage": "The government is now serving it to you on soup plates and asking you to swallow it." He echoed some of Cutler's broad disdain for the case, calling it "a grade B movie," including the government's use of the word *Mafia*.

"So what?" Slotnick said. "What does it mean?"

It was a word used simply "to prejudice the jury against the defendants."

Slotnick hinted at the vulnerabilities of the government's witnesses. One, named James Cardinali, for example, had been "involved in a plot to kill an FBI agent and...there are government reports with regard to that."

Then Slotnick turned to the specifics of his own client. "In the past fifteen years John Carneglia has become a reputable, respected businessman," he said. Carneglia was "involved in finance, involved in real estate, and he's involved in scrap metal. A hardworking man. You'll see what John Carneglia is by the time this case is over."

It took a few more days for the rest of the lawyers to deliver their openings. All of them sounded the same general theme: this was a case not about wrongdoing by the defendants but about prosecutorial greed. One of the other lawyers told the jury not to be taken in by the prosecutors' "magic show," claiming that Diane Giacalone was "going to create a crime."

CHAPTER 53

John Carneglia liked lawyers who yelled at judges.

Barry Slotnick was standing next to Diane Giacalone at a sidebar with Judge Nickerson. Carneglia had been recorded talking about lawyer Mike Coiro, who'd previously represented both Carneglia and John Gotti and was later sentenced to fifteen years in prison for crimes including RICO Act violations, and Giacalone was seeking to have the wiretap transcript admitted into evidence. Nickerson read Carneglia's transcribed words aloud: "I like him, because he doesn't just say, 'Yes, Your Honor,' 'No, Your Honor.' He gets up and yells at the judge. That's the kind of lawyer I like."

Carneglia, like other mobsters, sneered at the collegiality of most trials, in which defense lawyers and prosecutors, during breaks in a day's proceedings, will banter and gossip with the same people they'd been attacking just moments before.

"We're beginning to understand the case a little better," Giacalone said sardonically.

The prosecutor had planned to lead off her case with one of her star witnesses, Sal Polisi. But the defense had successfully postponed his testimony, convincing Judge Nickerson that Giacalone had improperly withheld tapes of Polisi speaking with an author about a potential biography and that the defense lawyers needed time to listen to the tapes to properly prepare for Polisi's testimony. Slotnick was thrilled: this sort of early tactical victory in a trial could knock the prosecution off its game.

Instead of starting with a bang, Giacalone's case had begun tediously, with procedural skirmishes like this one and relatively unimportant witnesses testifying about comparatively unsexy components of the case—such as illegal cigarette dealing—involving the least known of the defendants. As a string of detectives and ex-detectives testified about these matters, the men at the defense table, sensing blood in the water, had become boisterous.

The mob was no-holds-barred when it came to legal proceedings. They would do anything to avoid prison, whether it meant fixing juries or killing witnesses or co-opting their lawyers. Some lawyers, such as Coiro, were pliable and willing to cross ethical and legal lines for their clients. Others weren't. So the Mafia ended up having two kinds of lawyers: strategic brains such as Slotnick and the kind of guys who were willing to claw it out in the trenches. (Many of the cocounsels in this case would run into disciplinary or legal trouble in later years.)

Now, at the sidebar, Slotnick said, "I really don't think it's important to know that Mr. Carneglia doesn't like high-priced sharpshooting lawyers and he likes a lawyer who yells at a judge."

"But that's a part of it," Nickerson said. "I mean also, that very thing is refuted by your presence in the case."

"I've become a witness in the case," Slotnick said.

"High-priced," Giacalone suggested Nickerson had meant.

"I mean the 'Yes, Your Honor, no, Your Honor,'" Slotnick said.

"I haven't heard you yell at a judge," Nickerson said.

"I just don't think it's relevant to this proceeding," Slotnick said. "I think it's idle gossip."

"Tell your client I'm very disappointed that you're not shouting," Nickerson said drily.

"He is, too, Your Honor," Slotnick said.

"Is he?" Nickerson asked.

He then ruled against Slotnick in the matter.

"Maybe I *should* be shouting," Slotnick said.

In fact, it was Slotnick's silky smoothness that seemed to chafe against Nickerson's Yankee broadcloth. Whenever Slotnick raised an objection, he almost always qualified it with "most respectfully." Once, while challenging Giacalone on a legal point, Slotnick began, "I also think, most respectfully, while we're here—"

"Please don't keep saying 'most respectfully,'" Nickerson interrupted. "I know you do it in good faith and with absolute honesty, but please don't: it makes me uneasy."

"I don't want to make the Court uneasy," Slotnick said.

CHAPTER 54

On October 2, 1986, Salvatore Polisi finally took the stand and was sworn in. He had curly brown hair and hooded eyes and a Brooklyn accent.

Polisi had been arrested for cocaine dealing in 1984. Facing a long prison sentence, he agreed to cooperate with the government. A year earlier, Polisi's testimony had helped convict a Queens Supreme Court judge accused of case fixing. For this trial, Polisi's value to the prosecutors was significant: he claimed to have spent a lot of time around Gotti's crew at the Bergin and to have had criminal dealings with them. He could testify about many of the major counts in the indictment involving key defendants, including John and Gene Gotti and John Carneglia.

Diane Giacalone and Gleeson had a large, complicated, disjointed case to present, based on thirty hours of wiretaps and ninety witnesses. There were seven defendants in the courtroom, and each was charged with a different configuration of crimes. It was going to be hard for the jury to keep track of it all, but the persuasive core of the government's case was a handful of star witnesses—people whom Giacalone and Gleeson were going to put forward as particularly knowledgeable mob insiders. Polisi was the first of these.

Polisi was also typical of the government's most important witnesses in his flimsy credibility. Now, anticipating his brutal interrogation by the defense lawyers, Giacalone methodically walked Polisi through his psychiatric history and criminal record.

Polisi said that he'd been discharged from the Marines in the 1960s after learning how to fake mental illness. He talked about his career as a professional thief, burglar, robber, and forger. He recalled how he had gotten into the illegal gambling business with his uncle in Ozone Park and later into loan-sharking and truck hijacking. Polisi acknowledged that his nickname on the street was Sally Ubatz aka Crazy Sal.

Polisi also spent a chunk of his time on the stand dutifully identifying people in surveillance photos taken outside the Bergin, which Giacalone presented to him one by one. As Polisi answered the prosecutor's questions, the defendants sat listening scornfully.

During a break, Gotti, wearing a red-striped tie, said to a reporter: "How come he ain't in any pictures if he was there every day!?"

After three days off, on Monday, October 6, Giacalone resumed examining Polisi. Slotnick had to pay particular attention, because his testimony covered several of the counts concerning Carneglia. Polisi had spent time with John Carneglia and Fat Ange Ruggiero when all three men were imprisoned in the

Lewisburg penitentiary from 1973 to 1974. Later, Polisi said, he met with Carneglia several times at the Fountain Auto Mall (Carneglia's business in Brooklyn) as well as at the Lindenwood Diner, on the Queens-Brooklyn border. He described agreeing to sell auto parts to Carneglia, who was running an illegal chop shop, reselling cheap stolen cars and car parts.

Slotnick sensed danger. Whether Carneglia was or wasn't engaged in that activity, nowhere in the indictment were chop shops mentioned, and Slotnick saw that the prosecutors were trying to paint a broad picture of Carneglia's criminality. Slotnick stood to object, but Nickerson overruled him. "I think you're wrong," Slotnick said.

Polisi testified that Carneglia was mainly interested in parts from GM cars and in particular front doors and front bumpers and said that at one point, Carneglia had offered to introduce Polisi to a few teenagers who could steal more cars for him.

Polisi also testified about selling some Brooklyn real estate to Carneglia (in return for a shopping bag full of twenty-dollar bills totaling eighty-five thousand dollars) and about later borrowing twenty-five thousand dollars from Carneglia. In a meeting at the Fountain Auto Mall, recorded by a body wire Polisi was wearing, they'd discussed the loan.

In what was potentially his most damaging testimony, Polisi also talked about the murder of court officer Arthur Gelb, who, the indictment alleged, had been killed by John Carneglia. Polisi testified that Carneglia's brother Charlie had told him they "whacked out" Gelb.

While Polisi was speaking, Slotnick panned his gaze across the jury box, studying each juror one by one. Were they buying this? He couldn't tell.

Then, as Polisi's direct examination drew to a close, Giacalone said there were some other witnesses whom she wanted to examine before turning over discovery material about them to the defense, out of concern for their safety. Given the prosecutors' fears about witness tampering, her wish was understandable. But so was Slotnick's indignation over being denied access to the material. It was "outrageous," he said. "What is this, Himmler and Adolf Hitler?"

CHAPTER 55

Despite his damaging testimony for the prosecution, Polisi was a defense lawyer's dream, an embarrassment of riches— or, more accurately, an embarrassment of embarrassments. There were so many ways to attack him as a witness that it was hard for Barry Slotnick and his cocounsels to winnow down the list. So they divvied up the work.

When Polisi's cross-examination began, on Tuesday, October 14, Slotnick suggested that Polisi wasn't merely crazy like a fox. There was a reason his street name was Sally Ubatz. He'd been discharged because he was "a menace and a bum."

"Would you tell the jury what a chronic undifferentiated schizophrenic with a passive dependent disorder with psychopathic dependency is?"

"A very sick person," Polisi said.

"How about someone who has delusional thinking?" Slotnick suggested.

When Polisi stuck to his story that he'd been fooling all

the shrinks, Slotnick started questioning him about the disability checks he still received from the Veterans Administration, illuminating his fraud not just on taxpayers but also on fellow veterans. Slotnick highlighted the fact that the prosecutors, despite knowing about Polisi's mental-illness fakery, were still using him as a witness and that, cravenly, they hadn't alerted the VA to the disability fraud. "As a matter of fact, didn't you tell [an investigator] that you were getting the fifteen hundred dollars a month for, in your words, 'being fuckin' wacky?'"

"I may have said that."

The jury had two Black members, and Slotnick hammered Polisi on a racial incident that had occurred while he was in prison. "You considered Black people the lowest form of life?"

"I might have said that."

One of Slotnick's weapons, in cross-examining Polisi, was a draft of a book manuscript in which Polisi had spoken boastfully and in great detail about his sordid life and career. Barely disguising them as questions for the witness, Slotnick made the jury aware of Polisi's most self-incriminating stories, such as the time he got a guy hooked on heroin and then mercilessly beat him, and Polisi's habit of using a device to fool pay phones into letting him make long-distance calls for free.

He cornered Polisi into acknowledging that it was a government investigator who'd told him that Charles Carneglia had said, of Gelb, "we whacked him out" rather than Polisi having been the one to hear it. He got Polisi to confirm that he once said, of the Queens DA's attempt to use him in a different trial: "They are going to take a fuckin' psychopath and make him into a credible witness."

Most damaging to the government's case, Slotnick proved that Polisi's supposedly incriminating wiretap of Carneglia talking about a loan actually made his client look great. The prosecutors had played only a limited sample of the recording. Slotnick showed that in fact Carneglia had told Polisi, who was behind in repaying Carneglia fifteen thousand dollars, that he needn't bother paying the interest due and even offered to connect Polisi with a legitimate Citibank mortgage broker for another loan Polisi was seeking. Slotnick made it look like the government had deliberately withheld exculpatory information.

The defense table was audibly enjoying the domination of the witness, so much so that at one point Giacalone asked the judge to admonish the defense against "comments coming from behind me." But Slotnick's cross-examination had been artful and devastating—locking Polisi into testimony that Slotnick would later be able to refute. It was a style that had won Slotnick a great many victories, and it was markedly different from the aggressive style favored by his junior partner.

Already, with some minor witnesses, Bruce Cutler's cross-examinations had been so savage that colleagues had begun calling them Bruce-ifications. When it was Cutler's turn to hold Polisi's feet to the fire, he bypassed subtle and went directly to bludgeoning. "Did you find out that [another judge] yesterday called you a lowlife and a liar?"

Giacalone objected.

"Stop, stop," Nickerson said. "Don't do that again, Mr. Cutler."

Cutler: "How many lies have you told in your life, Mr. Polisi?"

"Untold amount of lies."

"Thousands of lies, you think... How many drugs have you sold, if we piled them up in the witness stand, how high would it go?"

"I can't answer that question."

"About."

"A lot of drugs."

"How much? How high would it go on the floor of the witness stand if we piled up the heroin and the cocaine that you put out on the streets of New York? How high would it go?"

"A lot of drugs."

"How high would it go, sir?"

"I'm not sure."

"Could you approximate it for the jury, sir?"

"I'm not sure."

"Could you approximate it for the jury, sir?"

"I can't approximate it."

And on it went.

"How much money have you stolen in your life?" and "How many policemen have you corrupted in your adult life?" and "How many women have you abused in your adult life?"

"Many," Polisi said.

Giacalone again complained to the judge, asking that he "take sanctions against counsel if counsel continues to behave improperly in front of the jury, sir." The judge admonished Cutler, but as the lawyer returned to his questioning, there was no noticeable softening of his approach.

Had Polisi photographed his wife performing forcible sex acts on other men while he had sex with other men in the room?

"It's incorrect," Polisi replied.

"Do you remember a birthday party when your own son was,

what, a two-year-old baby, and you threw him into the pool, and you said in front of ten to twenty witnesses, quote, and I will use your words, no offense intended, 'Fuck him, he can swim'—do you recall that incident?"

"Absolutely not."

"Do you recall people had to save the young child?"

"Absolutely not."

Cutler asked about Polisi punching a Black fellow prisoner from behind when he was at Lewisburg "and running away and showing everybody around you the yellow dog that you were." The action was so provocative, Cutler added, "that a race riot began in the jail, sir, isn't that what happened, sir?"

"That's incorrect."

"John Carneglia treated you like the human being you shouldn't have been treated when you went to see him in person: Isn't that right, sir?"

"That's correct," Polisi said for a change.

As Slotnick watched his protégé at work, their differences had never been clearer. And behind the scenes, their relationship had become more fraught. In August, just before the trial began, Cutler had come to Slotnick and asked him for 10 percent of the firm's gross revenues. Slotnick had always been essentially a one-man band. He hired associates and retained more experienced lawyers to be "of counsel." On a handful of occasions, he'd given nominal equity stakes of 1 or 2 percent to particularly valued lawyers, including Cutler. (He also from time to time let other lawyers share billing in the firm name. Currently, he was operating as Slotnick & Cutler.) But Slotnick was the business-getting rainmaker, and he wasn't interested in having a true commercial partnership. He also had begun to question Cutler's judgment. He refused Cutler's request, and after that, he knew it was only a matter of time before Cutler left the firm. But Slotnick would never break ranks with him publicly.

After lunch, Giacalone tried to rehabilitate her battered witness, eliciting from him a statement of remorse for his past activities, which he now considered "completely un-American, and I'm ashamed of the way I lived my life." But Cutler had tasted blood, and when he recrossed Polisi, he seemed to exult in the process, as if he'd already knocked him down and was now viciously curb-stomping him.

"When did you get this new religion, this elixir? Tell us, Mr. Polisi, who gave you this elixir?" Cutler pointed at Giacalone. "This woman?"

Giacalone immediately objected, and the judge sustained her objection.

"Did you receive an elixir from the government to become a new man? Did someone give you some injection? Tell us, so we could free the jails, so we could free the jails of the lowlifes in there like you."

Giacalone objected again, but before the judge could rule, Cutler said, "I have no further questions."

Nonetheless, as Cutler took his seat, Nickerson turned to the jury box: "Members of the jury, comments of counsel and questions that are overruled, regardless how loudly stated, are not evidence."

After the jury left the room, Giacalone continued to complain to the judge about the way the defense lawyers, Cutler in particular, had questioned her and Gleeson's credibility. Cutler repeated that he had heard from witnesses who complained that the prosecutors were harassing and intimidating them.

"The accusations that have happened in this courtroom are extraordinary," Giacalone said, "and today I think they reached about as low as I have heard in quite a number of years here."

CHAPTER 56

The aroma of clams oreganata hung over the courtroom.

Judge Eugene Nickerson had changed his mind and decided that John Gotti could eat lunch with his co-defendants in a room off the courtroom, deeming it unfair to exclude him from working lunches with his attorneys. Every day at 1:00 p.m., a familiar ritual began: a massive feast would arrive for the defendants and their lawyers, delivered by US marshals to the room where they ate. And each day, the defendants seemed determined to outdo the previous day's meal. One day it was veal scaloppine from S.P.Q.R., a beloved restaurant in Little Italy. On another, it was dim sum from a Cantonese joint in Chinatown. One day it was steaks from Peter Luger. On one occasion, John Carneglia was glimpsed emerging shirtless from the lunch room, prompting speculation that he was trying not to stain his trial attire. Today's lunch had been catered by an Italian seafood restaurant in Sheepshead Bay.

When the jurors returned from their own lunches of

pedestrian courthouse grub, the courtroom air would be redo-lent of marinara sauce, say, or dill pickles. "This went on for weeks," recalls Michael Shapiro, who served as law man for Barry Slotnick and Bruce Cutler during the trial and estimates that he put on fifteen pounds. "I kept wondering, what does the jury think when they come back in and the whole courtroom smells from the aroma of lunch?"

There were weather problems and a commuter-rail strike. The courthouse elevator continued to break down. Judge Nick-erson constantly asked if anyone else felt cold. Defense and prosecution continued to skirmish over what was admissible and where the boundaries of cross-examination were. The two sides also traded insults. Slotnick described Giacalone as "not known for giving ice away in winter to defense counsel."

Gotti had terrible teeth. He'd already lost several of them and wore dentures, and when he developed a gum infection, Judge Nickerson granted a defense motion to permit a dentist to give him an examination in the lunch room. These were the most benign examples of the trial's departures from courtroom norms as the arrogance and brutality of the lead defendant infected all aspects of the proceedings. It was comparable to an unruly classroom: the defendants were the kids in the back row shoot-ing spitballs, their lawyers the brawlers who did their bidding, the prosecutors the front-row A students complaining about the others, and the judge the fair-minded teacher trying to retain some sense of order in the room. His task was becoming increasingly difficult.

Judge Nickerson found himself asking Gotti not to lean back in his chair because there was no money for a new one. When Cutler said that Gotti was only doing what he'd seen Nickerson do, Nickerson noted that his own chair had a swivel in it. Nickerson had to tell lawyer George Santangelo, brother of Michael, not to let the jury see him chewing gum.

The defendants regularly made faces at Diane Giacalone and her witnesses. A steady stream of threatening invective could be heard from the defense table, including, about one witness, "The rat is dead." A prosecution witness, an ex-cop, told the prosecutors that while he'd been on the stand, the defendants had been making "unequivocally threatening gestures" at him.

When one witness was asked by a defense lawyer where he currently worked, he refused to say, and in a sidebar Gleeson explained that the witness was worried about his safety because of who the defendants were. After asking for the jury to be excused, Giacalone said that she'd distinctly overheard Gotti saying to Cutler about the witness, "He is doing it because we threatened him, that is why."

"If I can hear him," Giacalone said, "there is a chance the [jury] could," too.

"It's not true, Your Honor," Gotti said.

Nickerson addressed him sharply: "Don't make comments."

"But it's not true," Gotti continued. "If anybody is making comments, it is her."

"Mr. Gotti," Nickerson said, "listen to your attorney."

"Is this really necessary?" Cutler now chimed in. "She cleared out the courtroom and does a little song and dance—we would like to try the case."

But as Cutler resumed his cross-examination, he continued to be loud and aggressive. "Stop it, Mr. Cutler. Please don't shout. It is not useful," the judge chastised him.

After a break, Nickerson told the lawyers that he'd also

received a note from the jury, saying, "Your Honor, please ask the lawyers to stand behind the podium and not have their backs to the jury. 'Yelling' toward the jurors is also not necessary. Thank you."

At this point, Slotnick realized they might have a problem on their hands—antagonizing a jury was never a good thing—and Cutler asked the judge to explain to the jurors that "at certain times there is nothing wrong or untoward with a lawyer getting excited."

Nickerson agreed, but added, "I do think shouting, which you did at Mr. Gleeson, was improper, as I stated. I don't like it."

"I don't like to have to do it," Cutler replied, "but sometimes you have to."

The judge disagreed. "Not under any circumstances," he said, ending the discussion.

Giacalone escalated the hostilities. She wanted Cutler held in contempt, she told Nickerson. "Mr. Cutler has made it obvious, in every examination that he has done, that he intends to introduce before this jury evidence that is improper," she said after one lunch break, before the jury came back in. "He intends to shout at the government and make comments about the government's behavior that are not evidence, and he intends to do it for a very clear purpose. He is attempting to take this courtroom and turn it into a music hall for Mr. Cutler. I believe, Your Honor, that the government cannot have a fair trial if Mr. Cutler continues to perform a vaudevillian act before this jury."

"I don't think I am going to hold him in contempt now," Nickerson said, "but the questions were plainly improper and have been with respect to several of the witnesses."

Cutler piped up. "Several of the witnesses?"

"I am very reluctant to hold anyone in contempt," Nickerson continued. "I have never held an attorney in contempt since I have been on the bench, which hasn't been that long, but I think your actions have been improper."

Cutler shot back, "Your Honor, you want to know what I think? Ms. Giacalone doesn't like the way I question people because I show the jury the scum that they are...the government doesn't like my style in questioning...Judge, witnesses call me and tell me what the government does to them. Witnesses call me and tell me how Ms. Giacalone threatens them, how Mr. Gleeson threatens them. And then they get up here in a nice little dress and a nice suit and say in front of the press, 'John Gotti is going to influence witnesses.' That's not the truth...Now she gets up and she doesn't like my questioning...I don't care, Your Honor...My questions are proper. Their case is sliding down the tubes."

Slotnick wasn't a fan of Cutler's tactics, but he still leaped to his partner's defense. "I would like to add something to the record, and I think it's important," he said. "We are all engaged in battle, and sometimes things are said during a trial which should not be. Most respectfully"—despite Nickerson's request that he stop using the phrase, Slotnick continued to use it liberally—"this case is made up...When I ask a question, I think it is on good faith; I know when Mr. Cutler asks a question, it is on good faith...With regard to the questioning of witnesses, the government has opened the door to bring up their conduct, and we will do it at the appropriate time. But on behalf of Mr. Cutler and [on] behalf of myself and all defense counsel here, I am somewhat offended, and I think the Court should be offended, for Ms. Giacalone to get up and posture."

CHAPTER 57

Barry Slotnick could feel John Gotti, who sat between him and Bruce Cutler at the defense table, getting angry. The mobster's leg was twitching, and his sighs of exasperation were increasingly audible as the man on the witness stand continued to talk about him.

James Cardinali, thirty-seven, was the government's second and most important star witness. He had first met Gotti in 1976, when both men were imprisoned at the Clinton Correctional Facility, in the upstate New York town of Dannemora. Cardinali had been convicted of armed robbery, and Gotti was still serving time for the McBratney killing. Cardinali had since also gotten to know Gotti's lieutenant Angelo Ruggiero as a fellow prisoner at Attica.

After Cardinali's release, in 1979, he moved back to his mother's house, in Ozone Park, and Gotti helped get him a no-show job at a trucking company in Queens and gave him a weekly allowance of between one hundred and two hundred dollars to hang around the Bergin and run errands. Unlike Sal Polisi, Cardinali had actually spent time with Gotti, and in the courtroom, as Cardinali's testimony began, the mob boss was clearly irked by his presence. This was a real betrayal.

As Giacalone had done with Polisi, she began by attempting to inoculate her witness against the coming assault on his credibility by the defense. Cardinali, wearing a sweatshirt, khaki pants, and sneakers, acknowledged that he was currently serving a five-to-ten-year prison sentence for manslaughter. He acknowledged, among other sins, that one time he had hurt a priest with a gun during a robbery. He acknowledged that in return for his cooperation, he'd been promised ten thousand dollars from the government and immunity from prosecution for any other crimes he divulged.

Cardinali was critical to the government's case because he could testify about most of the major counts involving nearly every defendant, and he could testify about the Gambino crime family as a whole. Cardinali recalled Gotti once telling someone who wanted to leave the organization: "You don't get released from John Gotti's crew—you live with John Gotti, you die with John Gotti." He spoke of Gotti's rules and ruthlessness, saying that Gotti had told him, in 1980, "No use of drugs; no selling of drugs. If I ever catch anybody in my crew, I'm going to kill them. I'm not going to let anyone embarrass me, and I'm going to make an example of the first one I catch."

He recalled Gotti telling him to congratulate John Carneglia on getting made. In fact, Cardinali could talk about many of Carneglia's activities. They'd first met, he said, at Carneglia's auto yard in 1979. At the Lindenwood Diner, Cardinali said, Carneglia just "roams around. Goes behind the counter when he wants. He is there very often. Does what he wants." He described a conversation at the Bergin in which Carneglia stopped hoodlums from shooting a guy, saying they needed to wait for Gotti to arrive. Later, he delivered a message from Gotti: "Don't kill him. Shoot him in the leg or something."

Most threatening to Slotnick and his client, Cardinali testified about the three murders in the indictment, including a conversation in which Carneglia had told him: "I whacked a court clerk."

As Cardinali spoke, never glancing over at the defendants, Gotti looked increasingly furious, and the steady background chatter at the defense table became disruptively loud.

"I can barely hear, Your Honor," Giacalone complained.

During a lunch recess, Gotti came to the railing separating the courtroom well from the spectators' section and spoke to reporters. "Not one thing he said was the truth," Gotti said of Cardinali, "except his rat name."

Finally, as Cardinali talked about Gotti's role in the McBratney murder, Gotti grabbed a pen and a scrap of paper, scrawled a note, and handed it to Cutler, ordering him to pass it around to all the other lawyers. Cutler handed it to Slotnick first, who unfolded the note and silently read Gotti's words: *I WANT THIS GUY MOTHERFUCKED!!*

"Meanwhile," recalls fellow attorney Jeffrey Hoffman, "we're trying to say he's not the head of anything."

Giacalone questioned Cardinali for three days. The defense would keep him on the stand for two weeks.

As with Polisi, there was no shortage of ammo with which to discredit the witness. Cardinali acknowledged that he and an accomplice had once killed a man on a boat and, before tossing him overboard, kicked an anchor down his throat to make sure he sank. He acknowledged that he had carried out that murder for ten thousand dollars and some cocaine and that "at the time I had no qualms" about it.

"Would you have no qualms," Jeffrey Hoffman asked, "about simply telling a lie for ten thousand dollars and complete immunity from all your acts?"

Some of the ammunition had been provided to the defense team directly by the witness. Back in May, Cardinali had called the Slotnick offices from prison and spoken to Bruce Cutler and later to a Slotnick investigator, Victor Juliano. The conversations gave Slotnick and the others a diagram for disemboweling Cardinali.

"Would it be accurate to say," Hoffman began, "that you have one primary reason for testifying?"

"Correct."

"And have you described that primary reason as to save your own ass?"

"Exactly."

Would Cardinali "lie, cheat, and steal" to get what he wanted?

"Absolutely."

Cardinali said that he'd tried to back out of his deal with Giacalone "numerous times" but was "locked in": she had threatened him with a racketeering indictment, Cardinali said, which could have gotten him sentenced to twenty more years in prison.

"The reason she yelled at you," Hoffman continued, "is because you said, 'I'm not going to go into that court and tell those stories that you want me to tell.' Correct?"

"Correct."

"Did Miss Giacalone ever lie to you?"

"In my opinion, yes."

"Did she ever tell you about any things that went on between she and the court and the judge, how he treated her?"

"Objection," Giacalone said, jumping to her feet. "Objection."

But Judge Nickerson said Cardinali could answer the question. Hoffman carefully led Cardinali up to the point where he asked, "Did you ever say that [Giacalone] said that [Judge Nickerson] treats her like a daughter?"

"She told me that."

"And that she gets whatever she wants from him but the defense gets nothing? Did she tell you that?"

"I've heard her say something like that."

Again, Giacalone angrily objected.

"He's lying!" she said.

"About her own witness," Hoffman recalls, marveling at the memory. "This was incredible. Here's a witness they're trying to use to make a case, and they're calling him a liar."

Despite the sharpness of Hoffman's attack, he was the lawyer most similar to Slotnick, in that he favored a deft but leisurely style of cross-examination as opposed to the sledgehammer approach preferred by Cutler and their clients. As Hoffman's questioning spiraled on, Gotti began to get bored and lose patience.

Once again, he took pen to paper and passed a note to Cutler. This time, Cutler stood and approached Hoffman and handed him the note. Hoffman paused his cross-examination of Cardinali and read it to himself.

It said: *SIT DOWN OR YOU'RE DEAD*.

Hoffman coolly balled the note up. He put it in his mouth. He chewed it. Then he swallowed it.

"Everyone saw it," Hoffman recalls. "The jurors kind of got a kick out of it."

Slotnick began his cross-examination by asking whether Cardinali knew his name.

"Mr. Barry Slotnick."

In fact, Cardinali knew all the lawyers' names, didn't he?

"Just listening to talk in the US attorney's office."

"You knew Mr. Hoffman because he was described as—what?—a tall, good-looking, affable gentleman, kind?"

"No objection to that," Hoffman offered.

"Yes," Cardinali said.

"And they told you Slotnick's the guy with the beard, is that correct?"

"No—they don't have to. I've seen your picture."

"Not in the post office, I hope," Slotnick joked before coming around to his point: "So you've been a long study in the making, is that correct?"

He meant that *everything* Cardinali had said was practiced. *All* his testimony had been tailored to Giacalone' and Gleeson's specifications. The jury should trust *none* of it.

Cardinali was a liar, Slotnick emphasized through his questioning, who'd say anything to get what the government had promised him: ten thousand dollars, immunity from prosecution for five slayings (two in Florida, where he'd face the death penalty), a sentence reduction, and a new identity and relocation after he was released from prison. "Did you tell [another inmate] that you chopped a guy up in a bathtub and you put his limbs in a bag and you dumped it into the Florida sea and then you had a pizza right afterwards?"

"Never. I didn't say that."

"Did you tell [him] that you had killed over twenty people?"

"Never."

"Did you tell [him] that you were going to end up doing about three months per killing?"

"Never."

When Slotnick grilled Cardinali about inconsistencies in his testimony, Cardinali replied, "Mr. Slotnick, I lie a lot."

"Yes?"

"Yes."

"I'm sorry; I missed that. You lie a lot?"

"Everyone does."

"On that, I guess, I am going to conclude my cross-examination."

The following week, the intramural sniping among the lawyers became more frequent. Giacalone accused Cutler of harassing her in front of the jury and at sidebars, "the most extraordinary harassment that the observers in the courtroom have ever seen in either a federal or state court."

"Your Honor," she said on another day, "this is such baloney that all they need is two slices of bread to make the sandwich complete."

At another point, not captured in the official trial record but recalled by some participants, one of the Santangelo brothers, feeling that Giacalone was wagging a finger in his face, told her to "stick your finger up your ass."

Slotnick, for his part, felt that Nickerson was overly deferential toward the government. Plus, Slotnick was feeling pressure from all sides.

The Gotti trial was taking longer than anyone had anticipated, and the Goetz trial couldn't be put off indefinitely. At the same time, Slotnick had to reckon with an opposing, equally certain fact: he could hardly pull the rip cord on the Gotti case, even if he wanted to. As a client of the firm, John Gotti was the hotel you could check into but never leave. He had to be constantly appeased—reassured that Slotnick's attention to his case was undivided. Slotnick wasn't exactly afraid of the Gambino boss, but Gotti was still not someone he wanted to cross. Gotti was, after all, a man whose civilian neighbor, after accidentally killing Gotti's twelve-year-old son, Frank, with his car, had mysteriously vanished and was said to have been dismembered with a chain saw and dissolved in a fifty-five-gallon drum of acid.

CHAPTER 58

S o now, some twenty-four years later, you sit here accused of... sexually abusing a fifteen-year-old girl; is
that correct?"

"Yes."

Barry Slotnick was cross-examining the next in the prosecution's parade of dirtbags. On direct, Gerard Curro, thirty-seven,
had testified that his brother Andrew, who'd been convicted in
the armored car heists the defendants were accused of, had told
him about the robberies and implicated Carneglia in them.

On cross, Slotnick had already asked Curro about having
twice been admitted to the Creedmoor psychiatric hospital between the ages of nine and twelve. Now he was asking Curro
about current charges he was facing.

Slotnick proceeded to ask Curro whether he'd stolen from his
mother, strangled his aunt after she pressed his mother to turn
him in to the police, thrown his brother through a window,
stolen from his brother, been a heroin addict, taken part in the

armed robbery of a drug dealer, a crime in which an accomplice had shot the dealer in the head, and been fired from his job as an elevator operator for drunkenness.

"How about when you committed sodomy on the fifteen-year-old girl—were you sober?"

"Yes."

Gleeson objected and was sustained, and Giacalone pointed out that "sodomy" wasn't part of the evidence, but Slotnick was confident the jury wouldn't remember that distinction.

"And when Kim Valenti [Curro's then girlfriend and now wife] told you about your child, your first child, did you tell her that you didn't want to see her or the child?"

"Yes, I did."

"Did you also tell her that if she came over to the house you'd take the baby and bang the baby's head on the concrete?"

"No, I didn't say that."

Slotnick moved on to an incident in which Curro had repeatedly hit a police officer in the head with a lead bar. "Are you aware of the fact or aren't you aware of the fact that the police officer whose head you broke with the stick was unable to return to work as a police officer as a result of that beating you gave him?"

After lunch, over Slotnick's objections, the government called William J. Herrman, a former NYPD detective who testified that he had observed Carneglia, in the pens of the courthouse, see a mob associate named Joey Cavalcante and scream at him, "Keep your fucking mouth shut" and that Carneglia would get him a lawyer. All Slotnick could do, in cross-examining the ex-detective, was to try to cast doubt on the story, asking how many other people were around when the incident happened and whether the detective had made any notes of the encounter at the time.

By January 14, 1987, when the prosecution rested, Slotnick was deeply uncertain about which way the jury might be leaning. However obvious it was to him that the government's witnesses had been left bleeding in the gutter, and however questionable he felt the RICO statute to be, he never underestimated the brute power of the federal government. The sheer number of witnesses and exhibits could be overwhelming, he knew, and he worried that the dark cloud of publicity that had shadowed the case from the beginning had tainted the jurors, no matter what they might claim or even believe.

On January 21, there was snow on the ground in Scarsdale. "It's a winter wonderland," Slotnick told Nickerson, who agreed they could start half an hour late.

Just as Slotnick hadn't been required to make an opening statement, he didn't have to put on a defense at all. A beautiful thing about the American legal system, he liked to say, was that the government, and the government alone, had the burden of proof. A person charged with a crime came to trial cloaked with the presumption of innocence. Slotnick could, in theory, sit silently through an entire trial saying *nothing:* no opening statement, no objections, no cross-examinations, no motions, no pleadings, no witnesses, no closing.

One time, he had done just that. He was representing one of fifteen defendants in a federal drug case in New York. Throughout the long trial, Slotnick made sure his client, who was one of the low-ranking defendants, sat at the far end of the defense table, physically separated from his codefendants. After months of this, when it was time for summations, Slotnick rose to his feet and said: "Ladies and gentlemen of the jury, I'm Barry Ivan Slotnick. I haven't said anything during this trial, and the reason is there's been no evidence presented about my client, so I have nothing to add." Then he sat down. Slotnick's client was acquitted. The prosecutor in the case, Jim Druker, was so inspired by Slotnick's tactic that when he later became a defense attorney, he used it in one of his own cases, speaking for less than one minute. "He was innovative," Druker recalls admiringly.

But cases like that were rare. Usually, it verged on legal malpractice to not present an aggressive defense. It was almost always better to go beyond just dinging up a prosecution's case through cross-examination, though Slotnick was concerned that Bruce Cutler's theatrics may have gone too far. And Gotti would never tolerate a passive approach.

This was the first day of the defense case, and the lawyers began by entering into evidence a chart titled "Criminal Activity of Government Informants," which they put on an easel for everyone in the courtroom to see.

The left-hand column listed twenty-seven different crimes, ranging from murder and heroin dealing to pistol-whipping a priest and sexual assault on a minor.

The top row listed seven of the key prosecution witnesses.

Under each witness, an X marked every crime the witness had been convicted of.

The winner was Sal Polisi, with eighteen X's.

The chart would stay on its easel, in plain view of the jurors, for the duration of the case. Slotnick wanted to make sure that the jury continued to be reminded of the sordid collection of witnesses who'd testified on the government's behalf.

CHAPTER 59

Should he eat the pastrami sandwich, or should he not eat the pastrami sandwich?

Today's over-the-top lunch had been catered by the Second Avenue Deli, and the table was buried in butcher paper piled with mountainous sandwiches of pastrami and rye alongside dill pickles.

Slotnick had not long ago come back from Canyon Ranch in Arizona, where he and Donna had eaten spa food. More recently, a nutritionist had put him on the Pritikin diet, furnishing him with a thousand-calorie-per-day menu plan. It was a grim typed document prescribing unadorned, boringly healthful food doled out in ridiculously tiny portions. Half a cup of shredded wheat. Two tablespoons of raisins. One cup of raw jicama sticks.

Jicama sticks!

Everyone else in the room, lawyers and clients alike, was tucking into the sandwiches. Was Slotnick really supposed to abstain? It was bad business to make his client feel judged. It was not collegial to hold himself above his cocounsels. Eating the pastrami sandwich, he told himself, would be the right thing to do, really. Just this once, he would allow himself the indulgence.

Anyway, he had a more consequential decision to make.

Four months earlier, when the trial was already under way, the Slotnick firm had received a call from a man named Matthew Traynor, a forty-year-old career criminal. Traynor had said he was in the Witness Security Program (also known as WITSEC) and was slated to testify for the prosecution in the Gotti trial. A few weeks later, on a Friday, Bruce Cutler and Jeff Hoffman met with Traynor at the Nassau County jail and spoke with him for three hours.

Traynor told a long and unsavory story about his relationship with Diane Giacalone, who, he said, had courted him to be a witness against Gotti. The methods he claimed she had employed to induce him to cooperate were shocking. Traynor said that he had asked Giacalone to get him a prostitute; she had said that she couldn't do that, but that she was a recreational jogger, and he claimed she gave him a pair of her sweaty underwear. She also arranged for him to be taken to a hospital and given narcotics he had been denied by the jail's medical staff. Traynor said he now wanted to help Gotti and damage Giacalone.

The question for Slotnick and his cocounsels then became whether to call Traynor as a witness for the defense. Traynor's accusations about the unethical and distasteful lengths to which the prosecutors had been willing to go to make a case against Gotti and company could potentially be very damaging to the government. Perhaps his claim about the trip to the hospital for

Valium could be corroborated, even if he was lying about the rest. Traynor had a well-documented history of making stuff up, so the fact that the government had sought to use him anyway wouldn't reflect well on the prosecutors.

On the other hand, Traynor was so hard to believe, and so full of vile claims about Giacalone, that many on the defense team feared that calling him might backfire. The jury could view his testimony as an unfair attack on Giacalone and cost the defense itself some credibility.

Now, amid the deli detritus of half-eaten pickle spears and crumpled butcher paper, the defense lawyers and their clients hashed out the pros and cons of calling Traynor as a witness.

Hoffman could see both sides but didn't think they should call him.

Gotti was opposed to it as well.

Cutler thought they should do it.

Slotnick, after struggling with the question, ultimately came out on the side that they should put Traynor on the stand.

It was a risky but necessary strategy, Slotnick felt.

CHAPTER 60

Sworn in as a witness, Matthew Traynor presented a sorry specimen. A stocky man with brown hair, he was currently awaiting trial on bank robbery charges. He had a sinus problem, which he said was related to the fact that he had only one lung (he had lost the other in his early twenties during a gunfight), and he sounded congested when he spoke. He identified prosecutor Diane Giacalone by pointing a gun finger at her and calling her "the woman with the stringy hair."

As expected, Traynor's testimony supported the defense narrative about the extremes to which the government was willing to go to woo its witnesses. He insisted that Giacalone had tried to get him to give false testimony against Gotti. He said he barely knew Gotti and some of the other defendants and knew of no wrongdoing by them, but "she really wanted to frame Mr. Gotti and the others with him. She told me she didn't like them because years earlier they had ridiculed her for being skinny when she used to walk through the neighborhood where they hung out…She said she needed a pretty strong leadoff witness."

Traynor said that part of his deal with prosecutors was that they'd supply him with Valium and codeine. After the staff at the Metropolitan Correctional Center in Manhattan refused to give him the pills the previous April, the prosecutors had arranged to have him taken to a private doctor, who prescribed the drugs he wanted. Traynor said Giacalone cut off his pill supply later that month, when he went to her office for a briefing and she gave him pizza and beer and he threw up on her desk after taking the drugs. He described, in excitedly graphic detail, the alleged underwear incident and claimed he'd decided not to cooperate with Giacalone after she tried to get him to admit to a murder he hadn't committed.

Slotnick knew that the defense team had to walk a fine line. On the one hand, they wanted the jury to believe Traynor when he described some of the tactics the government had used with him. On the other hand, they wanted the jury to see what an egregious liar he was and to hold *that* against the prosecutors—that they would have considered using someone with so little credibility to make their case.

Under questioning by Cutler, Traynor admitted that he'd lied to FBI agents after a 1978 arrest in order to get a reduced sentence and said that he had offered to cooperate with the government last March only in an effort to get better treatment. Hoffman asked about a document from the FBI from the late 1970s saying that Traynor was unreliable and shouldn't be used again as a witness or informant, and Traynor claimed that Giacalone had told him not to worry—she'd salvage the situation, and it was after this that she put him into WITSEC.

For obvious reasons, John Gleeson, rather than Giacalone, cross-examined Traynor.

Gleeson was aggressive in dismantling Traynor on the stand, eliciting evidence to show that in fact the prosecutors had exercised sound judgment in deciding *not* to call Traynor as a witness. Gleeson asked about Traynor's admissions to a prison psychiatrist that "one of the reasons you wanted to convict John Gotti was because you hated Gene Gotti" and that his anger toward Gotti had later swung toward Giacalone.

Traynor denied having said he wanted to seek revenge. "I don't have any intense hatred for Diane Giacalone," Traynor said, sounding stuffed up, but added, "I may dislike her."

Gleeson entered into evidence a card Traynor had sent to Giacalone from prison: "Sometimes you make me so darn mad, I forget how happy you make me the rest of the time."

"Her panties she gave me to sniff was the closest thing I had to make me happy," Traynor said. "I tried to send her a nice card. You're trying to tell me I hate her."

"Your Honor," Gleeson said. "I would like an instruction about a certain portion of his testimony that he insists on repeating before this jury."

Nickerson spoke sharply to Traynor: "Don't repeat that again."

Traynor was a terrible witness, and Gleeson gave him a thorough beatdown. The prosecutor kept asking Traynor to name a single person, prior to his conversation with Cutler, whom he'd told that the government had tried to get him to lie and falsely implicate the Gottis in murders.

Traynor was evasive, giving nonresponsive answers and

shoehorning in smears against Giacalone. "She said she held him in the palm of her hand," Traynor claimed, echoing what Cardinali had said about Giacalone and Judge Nickerson.

Rather than assume the jury wouldn't give much credence to Traynor's sleaziest claims, Gleeson took Traynor straight on, rigorously questioning him about the alleged underwear gift.

"Did you tell anybody before you met with Bruce Cutler in October of 1986 that you were provided with, as you once put it, a kinky sexual release by Ms. Giacalone?"

"She knows. She gave it to me."

"No, no. Did you tell anybody that before you met with Bruce Cutler?"

"Yes...anyone who would listen. I got busted with—with panties at—"

"Who?...Who listened? Give the jury some names, Mr. Traynor. Give them some names."

"The average person in this jury won't believe the under-handed dealings that these two are about."

"Do you recall saying that the physician who wouldn't pre-scribe Valium for you tried to come on to you in the MCC, tried to make a pass at you?"

"I've been through a lot in my life. I've been shot twenty-three times. I've been through a lot of crap, pal."

"Who was present, Mr. Traynor, when as you claim you were provided with underwear in the United States attorney's office?"

"The lady who belonged to the underwear. She's seated right there. Ms. Diane Giacalone."

"Who else was present?"

"Edward Magnuson." Magnuson was a DEA agent who'd worked with Giacalone on the case.

"Where did it happen?"

"In her office. She was seated at her desk. The right-hand bottom drawer is where she keeps all her used dungarees and underwear that she changes into. I was pressing her to get laid. I wanted a girl. She just cut me off from the alcohol. She said no more alcohol because I threw up all over her desk. So I said fine. I wasn't going to quibble over that. I needed — how about a sexual release. She said you can't have a girl because you're in the witness program. I asked her for a policewoman. She said — she laughed. She said, 'No way.' And then Magnuson or her got a bright idea. They were smiling. Magnuson opened the drawer, pulled out a pair of panties. She smiled. He threw them at me. Told me 'Sniff them and jerk yourself off in the bathroom.' All right. And they smelled like *deep-fried scallops*."

Hearing this description, a courtroom full of faces contorted in disgust.

Gleeson kept pressing Traynor to describe Giacalone's office and exactly where her panties supposedly were. The best Traynor could do was to keep repeating: "It's the bottom right-hand drawer where she kept all her soiled garments."

"Isn't it a fact, sir," Gleeson said, "that you were never in Diane Giacalone's office?"

Slotnick asked for a sidebar, where he said that Traynor had in fact described Giacalone's office and asked "if there is a good-faith basis for that question."

Giacalone fielded that one. "He's never been in my office," she said.

* * *

The snorts and sneers and face making between the opposing sides had continued through the Traynor part of the trial, and finally the jury had had enough. Once again, they sent a note to the judge: "Your Honor, the jury finds it extremely distracting that both the prosecution and defense attorneys display exasperated expressions during the testimony of witnesses. Please don't give any exasperated expressions."

When the jurors were out of the room, it was even more like a kindergarten, with Gleeson saying "I don't care," and Cutler saying, "I care, I care, I care," and Nickerson saying, "Stop, stop now, both of you," and Cutler saying, "And I should care, Your Honor. We should all care," and Nickerson saying, "Please, please."

Nickerson chastised Cutler yet again for shouting, which surprised no one, but Nickerson also had to chastise Hoffman, normally one of the most restrained defense lawyers. Hoffman defended himself by saying of Gleeson, "I was trying to get over *his* shouts."

Slotnick was the one lawyer who managed not to fully regress. During a colloquy on a legal point, he said, "I know I try the Court's patience," and Nickerson said, "No, you don't. You try the Court's patience the least of anyone."

CHAPTER 61

By the time Diane Giacalone gave her summation, on March 2, 1987, everyone—the judge, the lawyers, the jurors, the defendants, the reporters covering the trial—was tired. The trial had gone on far longer and become far uglier than anyone anticipated.

The final month of the trial had focused largely on Traynor—the defense calling other witnesses to corroborate his testimony, then the prosecution calling seventeen witnesses just to rebut him and his smears against Giacalone, Gleeson, and other government agents. By then, Slotnick had become convinced that the jury must be fully perplexed by what the case was even about. The more time the prosecutors spent showing Traynor to be a liar, the more time they were spending calling their own judgment into question.

At one point, the defense had subpoenaed the work records of Gleeson's wife, a nurse who worked at the same hospital that had prescribed Traynor's Valium; Gleeson was enraged, and even Judge Nickerson seemed triggered. "It is just so off the wall," he said, "completely off the wall." He quashed the subpoena. "This case is not going to turn into any more of a circus than the defendants' attorneys have already made it." At another point, after the defense lawyers called Giacalone a liar, she called them pigs.

Now Giacalone's voice was fading. Slotnick listened carefully as she made her closing remarks. She noted that what had happened in the courtroom during this trial—the name-calling, the sleaze of Traynor's testimony, and all the rest—wasn't normal. She spoke scornfully of the over-the-top statement by Cutler that this case was like "the herding of Japanese into internment camps in World War II" and Hoffman's statement that it represented "the rebirth of McCarthyism" and Slotnick's claims that the trial was only taking place "because the government didn't like John Carneglia's friends."

"At some point," Giacalone told the jury, "you are going to have to ask yourselves, is John Gleeson on trial? Is Diane Giacalone on trial? One would have mistaken us for defendants during certain portions of this trial."

She asked for guilty convictions for Gotti and the other defendants "because they kill at their pleasure" and "substituted the rule of law with the rule of force."

Though her summation lasted only an hour and five minutes, to Slotnick it seemed interminable and deadly. Like her opening—and, really, like the whole case—it contained so many disparate elements and names that it was hard to keep track of the whole sprawling thing. All of which made Slotnick indescribably happy. Normally, it was a defense lawyer's job to confuse a jury. Here, the prosecutor seemed to be doing it for him.

The next day, after lunch, Slotnick stood and addressed the jury.

His voice was fading, too.

Slotnick again discredited the government witnesses for all the reasons he'd already done so—their criminality, their financial and legal incentives to cooperate, their endless lies. But his most effective arguments were the most basic and substantive. Slotnick methodically went through the evidence against his client and reminded the jury of its weaknesses. He carefully compared Sal Polisi's taped interview with a Queens detective to his direct examination by Giacalone, convincingly showing that Polisi had tailored his testimony for this trial.

"Strike that one," Slotnick said. "That's not reasonable doubt. That's absolute doubt."

Slotnick highlighted the parts of Polisi's recorded conversation with John Carneglia in which Carneglia, far from coming off as a menacing loan shark, seemed more benevolent than a chartered bank.

Slotnick revealed to the jury that during the period when Gerard Curro had claimed that his brother was chopping up cars with Carneglia, Carneglia had been *in prison*.

And Slotnick homed in on the peculiarity of the RICO law and its flirtation with double jeopardy. "This is a very special case," he said. "Very different. These men are charged with crimes they have gone to jail for, that they have paid their penalties for, and now the government is asking, for certain of those crimes, for that to happen again."

The prosecutors were allowed to give a rebuttal summation,

and John Gleeson's lasted nearly two and a half hours. The gist of it was that the jury should be "outraged" by the conduct of the defense. "These counsel have decided, these defendants have decided, that everybody involved in this case except them is guilty of a crime."

CHAPTER 62

arry Slotnick couldn't sleep again. His insomnia was always worst when a jury was out. He pulled back the sheets, slipped out of bed, and tiptoed toward the bathroom.

"I can see you."

Donna. She was watching him. She knew exactly where he was going.

The first couple of nights the jury was out, Barry had soldiered through a night of tossing and turning and getting up to go to the bathroom and staring at the ceiling, wishing for sleep. But the anonymous jurors were sequestered, and their deliberations went on and on...five days, six days, seven days.

Slotnick couldn't take it anymore. He was exhausted. He knew that a sleeping pill would help. A whole bottle of them was mere feet away, in the bathroom. But Donna hated when he took Valium.

He sheepishly got back in bed and kept staring at the ceiling, struggling to relax.

Waiting for a jury to reach a verdict was always agonizing. It wasn't that he wanted them to come back fast; a quick decision usually meant a conviction. But until he knew the trial's outcome, Slotnick found it impossible to think of anything else.

More than a hundred witnesses had testified in the Gotti trial. The transcript exceeded seventeen thousand pages. Soon would come the moment of truth. If found guilty of the most serious charges, each of the seven defendants could go to prison for forty years. Slotnick ruminated, replaying each moment of the trial and wondering if he'd made the right move here or the wrong move there. He *had* to win. He *had* to get his client off.

During waking hours, at least, Slotnick could pace and smoke cigarettes and chew paper clips and jawbone on the phone with other lawyers, trying to game out what the jury might be up to. At one point, the jurors requested the defense chart showing the criminal histories of the seven most important prosecution witnesses, which included sixty-nine separate criminal acts. It was an interpretive art—trying to glean what such a request might mean about the drift of a jury's conclusions. Slotnick allowed himself to hope that this one meant the jurors were finding fault with the government's witnesses, which meant they were finding reasons to doubt that the government had met its burden of proof.

Slotnick slowly, quietly eased back out of bed again. This time, he made it to the bathroom undetected.

Donna had hidden his bottle of Valium, but he knew where she kept it.

He snuck one and took it.

* * *

Finally, on a Friday the thirteenth in March, shortly after 2:00 p.m. on a chilly day, the jury walked back into the courtroom, which was packed and silent. Juror number 10, the forty-five-year-old ex-Marine who'd served as jury foreman, quietly read the verdict.

First count: "Not guilty."

John Gotti, wearing a tailored double-breasted pin-striped chocolate-brown suit, turned to Cutler and said, "Good job."

"Not guilty."

"Not guilty."

"Not guilty."

When the conspiracy-count verdict was read, Gotti flashed a smile and punched Cutler in the arm.

When the racketeering-count verdict was read, Gotti hugged Cutler.

In the courtroom, there were gasps and looks of surprise. Then the crowd erupted in cheers and clapping and shouts of "Justice has prevailed!"

John Gleeson and Diane Giacalone looked downcast.

Gotti leaped to his feet and pumped his fist. He mouthed "I told you!" at his lawyers. He slapped Slotnick on the back. All the defendants traded hugs and double-cheek kisses with one another and their lawyers. As the jurors were led out of the room by federal marshals, the defense table turned in their direction and clapped.

Moments later, Gotti, flanked by marshals, moved toward a side door. As reporters shouted questions, he pointed to the prosecutors' table and said, "Shame on them! I'd like to see the verdict on them, too."

"How did you beat it?" a reporter asked. Gotti pointed at the now-empty jury box and said, "With these people here." Then he left the room. After getting his personal effects, which had been taken from him when he was returned to jail the previous May, he left the courthouse through a back door.

Outside, more reporters mobbed Gotti. "I told you we would win," he said before adding: "They'll be ready to frame us again in two weeks. In three weeks, we'll be starting again; just watch."

Then he rode away in a gray Cadillac as Slotnick lingered to bask in the journalists' attention.

Gotti and the others were "innocent beyond a doubt," Slotnick told reporters. "I think it was clear throughout that there was nothing to tie them to the evidence except two witnesses who lied through their teeth—and the jury simply didn't buy it."

Over the previous six months, the heads of four other big Mafia families had all been convicted on federal racketeering charges and sentenced to years in prison. This was the first major loss for the government in its onslaught against the Mafia.

"I've had a lot of acquittals in my day," Slotnick said, "but this is the best. This is the very best."

CHAPTER 63

That night, as 7:00 approached, Barry Slotnick prepared to settle into his seat in the spotlight. He had arranged for a press conference at his offices to be carried live on CBS, and he was flanked by all his cocounsels.

The lone microphone was positioned in front of Slotnick. The only earpiece was in Slotnick's ear.

John Gotti was celebrating at the Ravenite, and Jimmy Breslin, of all people, was at the party.

At Slotnick's office, Bruce Cutler was annoyed.

Suddenly, the CBS reporter, after taking a call from headquarters, came over and asked Slotnick to give the earpiece to Cutler and cede his place in front of the microphone to him. Cutler would learn later that one of the other lawyers in the suite had called CBS to alert them that Cutler, not Slotnick, had been Gotti's actual lawyer.

Slotnick did as he was asked but sat on the arm of Cutler's chair, smiling, his arm around his former protégé.

By now, Cutler was just Slotnick's tenant.

They had ended their professional partnership during the trial.

The next day, a heavy box arrived at the office, addressed to Slotnick. It was from Gotti—who in light of his acquittal had received a new tabloid title, the Teflon Don—and contained a case of Perrier-Jouët, Gotti's favorite Champagne.

The US government tried John Gotti three more times. The first two times, he was represented by Cutler and was acquitted, reinforcing his Teflon Don nickname. The third time, however, prosecutors succeeded in disqualifying Cutler as Gotti's lawyer, convincing a judge that Cutler had become "house counsel" to the Gambino family and had a conflict of interest. Without Cutler at his side, Gotti was sentenced to life in prison without the possibility of parole. Cutler was later convicted of contempt of court after he defied the orders of the judge in that case to stop speaking to the press about Gotti, and his law license was suspended for a time.

By then, Slotnick and Cutler had stopped speaking to each other, an estrangement that would last another twenty years.

During the trial, prosecutors Diane Giacalone and John Gleeson had been justifiably concerned about possible jury tampering. After the acquittal of all the defendants, the prosecutors' boss, US attorney Andrew Maloney, asked the FBI to investigate whether the case had been fixed. Later, when Gotti's underboss, Sammy "the Bull" Gravano, turned state's evidence, the truth finally came out.

The jury foreman, George Pape, had taken a sixty-thousand-dollar bribe from Gotti. At the start of jury deliberations, Pape announced, "This man Gotti is innocent. They are all innocent, as far as I am concerned. There is nothing left to discuss." While most of the other jurors disagreed, Pape dug in to a "not guilty" verdict, and eventually the rest of the jury was swayed by him.

Pape was later convicted of obstruction of justice and sentenced to three years in prison.

Would Gotti have been acquitted were it not for the compromised juror? Possibly. Pape was only one out of twelve, after all. It was difficult, in federal trials, for a single juror to sway eleven other jurors.

Barry opened his eyes. He must have fallen asleep on the raft. Donna had insisted that he take a vacation as soon as the Gotti case ended. Seven months on the trial had taken their toll. Slotnick's eyes bagged. He felt exhausted. At moments like this, he even questioned his workload. It was unrelenting. But he didn't see an exit. What else could he possibly do? What else would he *want* to do?

Now, though, Slotnick's exhaustion had caught up with him. The waves were gently rocking the raft, and he turned his head toward the beach. Except there was no beach. Just ocean. He rotated his head and looked in the other direction. He saw the island in the distance, but not the resort where he was staying. He shook off the drowsiness and sat up. Judging by the height of the sun, he figured he must have been drifting for hours. With a mounting sense of alarm, he started to paddle. Hours later, he reached shore.

After a huge case like *Gotti,* Slotnick would usually experience something like postpartum depression, but on the day of the verdict, Justice Crane had announced that jury selection in *Goetz* would start on March 23, with 150 prospects. The next day, the *New York Times* ran an article: "Stage Set for Goetz Trial."

With *Goetz* looming barely a week away, there was too much on Slotnick's mind for him to feel the familiar hollowness.

As far as Donna was concerned, *Goetz* couldn't come too soon.

By coincidence, Jeffrey Hoffman and his wife were also vacationing in Puerto Rico. Hoffman was the one lawyer on the defense team whom Slotnick had clicked with: he felt like Hoffman, unlike many of the other lawyers, had a good sense of humor, a way of carrying even serious matters with a winning lightness.

Hoffman was lounging at his hotel in San Juan when he got a call from Slotnick, suggesting that they get together, maybe drink a couple of piña coladas.

"I just spent the last seven months with you," Hoffman said. "I came here to be away from everyone."

At dinner that night, minus the Hoffmans, Donna and Barry talked about where they were in their lives.

Barry suggested that *United States v. Gotti* represented the end of a chapter.

Donna said she hoped that *The People of the State of New York v. Bernhard Goetz* marked the start of a new one.

PART SIX

CHAPTER 64

Monday, March 23, 1987, dawned sunny and mild, and when Barry Slotnick, his team, and their client arrived at the courthouse in lower Manhattan, pro-Goetz and anti-Goetz protesters were facing off on the courthouse steps, chanting slogans:

"Free Goetz now!"

"Put him back in jail!"

"God bless America!"

A man was selling seven-dollar T-shirts reading THUG BUSTER—ACQUIT BERNHARD GOETZ and HE WHO TAKES, GOETZ IT. Another man was touting a vinyl record of a song titled "Subway Vigilante," by Ronny and the Urban Watchdogs, with lyrics such as: "He had enough and came out fightin' / Drove the rats back into hidin'." Still another entrepreneur was hawking a board game called the Subway Vigilante Game.

The long-delayed trial of Bernie Goetz was finally to begin. More than two years after the shooting and Goetz's arrest and the second grand jury's indictment, attitudes toward the case remained starkly divided between people who saw Goetz as an everyman who'd stood up for them all and those who saw Goetz as a racist lunatic. It seemed like the whole city had been holding its breath, waiting for this moment.

Barry Slotnick was happy he'd no longer have to go to Brooklyn every day, as he had during *Gotti*. The Goetz trial would unfold only a few blocks from where the shooting had occurred, which was much closer to Slotnick's office. But the distance between the courthouses went beyond mere geography.

State court in Manhattan was like the city it served: dirty and run-down and gritty, with small courtrooms, resounding echoes, worn wooden seats, and no climate control. If Slotnick opened the windows, his voice would be drowned out by police sirens. Lawyers openly hawked their services in the corridors, people ran every which way, and the courtrooms functioned as holding pens, bursting with defendants waiting to have their cases heard. Prosecutors and judges in state court tended to be overwhelmed by unmanageable caseloads. Here, Slotnick felt like he had if not the upper hand then at least a level playing field.

Slotnick and his entourage took the elevator to the fifth floor and made their way to room 572. Clad in wood paneling, it was the largest courtroom in the building, with 170 seats, and had been designated for this trial in order to accommodate the hordes of journalists and curiosity seekers who were expected to attend. All the seats quickly filled up, fifty of them with reporters.

The Honorable Stephen G. Crane, now robed, sat in a high-backed swivel chair upholstered in red leather, an American flag at his side and IN GOD WE TRUST carved into the wall behind him, and gaveled the courtroom to order. Three hundred and thirty-three potential jurors had been interviewed in the pre-screening process. Only two of them—one who'd been living for the past several years on a remote island in Asia and another who'd been living in Minnesota—had never heard of Goetz. One hundred and thirty-six prospects remained. It was time to choose the final twelve jurors and four alternates. This, too, would be a process.

CHAPTER 65

Months earlier, on Friday, December 12, 1986, two hundred potential jurors had reported to a courtroom at 111 Centre Street in Manhattan, home to the New York State Supreme Court. Justice Crane's clerk, Robert Hamkalo, summoned candidates one by one to be escorted through an adjacent courtroom to a small jury room, where Crane, Barry Slotnick, Mark Baker, prosecutor Greg Waples, and Bernhard Goetz awaited them.

Goetz had been unhappy about the trial's delay. It wasn't just that his life was on hold and that a sword was dangling over his head. Goetz had also internalized the idea that his case was *important*—that he was personally making a difference for New York, changing the conversation and the culture of the city.

Slotnick didn't really care what Goetz thought, but he did worry about what Justice Crane thought. Crane had already granted several postponements, and he seemed to be losing patience. If the judge were to insist that Goetz find new counsel, it would be a disaster for Slotnick. *Goetz* promised to be the trial of a lifetime. The firm had already donated thousands of man-hours, and Slotnick had an unshakable confidence that he alone could get Goetz off.

There was another reason why Slotnick was loath to lose the case. While his former associate Bruce Cutler had reveled in organized crime work, Slotnick was determined to extricate the firm from that enterprise. Getting fees from wiseguys was always an issue, and the federal government was making it increasingly uncomfortable for defense lawyers to represent them. For Slotnick, Mark Baker would recall later, Goetz was "a knight on a white horse." A victory on his behalf could launch the firm in a new direction.

Finally, Justice Crane had agreed to one more delay of the Goetz trial—"He wasn't a ball buster," Baker says—but on the condition that they move ahead with preliminary jury selection. Unlike Gotti, Bernie Goetz wasn't feared; no one fretted that he might intimidate jurors. But newspaper editorials and talk-radio shows had been full of pro- and anti-Goetz arguments for more than two years, and it was a case so resonant among New Yorkers that it received even more media attention than *Gotti* did. Crane knew that it was going to be difficult to find a dozen impartial jurors, so he planned to assemble five hundred prospects and weed out four hundred of them before real jury selection began. Slotnick would spend one day a week in the supreme court building in Manhattan—on Fridays, the Gotti trial was on hiatus—during the prescreening process for the Goetz trial over the next few months.

In federal court, lawyers didn't get to directly ask prospective jurors any questions, and judges basically picked juries. "How do I pick a jury in state court?" Slotnick said now. He was only half joking. He hadn't tried a state case in years.

The prescreening was designed to eliminate people who said they couldn't interrupt their lives for a six-week trial or who had some other obvious disqualifier. Each prospect would be interviewed for around ten minutes. Crane would question each person first, then the lawyers would get turns. If any one of them wanted a prospective juror out, for any reason, he could get that person out. Prospects who were willing to serve, and were okayed by both sides, would move on to the smaller pool.

The first person they interviewed, a young African American woman who was employed as a social worker, revealed that she believed that all white people were afraid of groups of young Black men. Slotnick thought her attitude could cut either way: it might make her see Goetz's response as typical and therefore "reasonable." Then again, she might just view him as a bigot. Since her overt bias made it unlikely that she'd ultimately be chosen for the jury, both Slotnick and Waples moved to dismiss her.

A white middle-aged man said he'd once been mugged by a Black man, resulting in a yearlong hospital stay, and he thought that Goetz had been in the right. Slotnick was sure that Waples would seek to dismiss the man, but suddenly Goetz piped up: "If the prosecutor could prove to you that I was not the victim of a robbery and I shot four people without justification, would you lose your sympathy for me?"

"Yes," the man said. "Of course."

As a result of Goetz's interjection, which normally Slotnick would have disapproved of, Waples let the man remain in the jury pool for the time being.

Then an African American man came in, and Mark Baker asked, "Do you have any opinions about this case?"

"What case?"

"The judge told you this is about Bernie Goetz."

"Who's that?"

"This guy here. You don't recognize him?"

"No."

"Do you watch TV?"

"Yes."

"Which channels?"

"All of them."

"You've never seen this man?"

"No."

"Do you read newspapers?"

"Yes. Mostly the headlines, though."

"And you don't recognize this man?"

"Nah."

Justice Crane was rolling his eyes. The man was clearly lying, and he was disqualified. "In these high-profile cases," Baker says, "you get people with agendas."

"The Goetz trial was 90 percent jury selection," recalls Gillian Coulter, who as Slotnick's young paralegal was there for much of it, "and 10 percent trial. Jury selection went on forever."

For this new round, groups of eighteen prospects at a time would sit in the jury box to be interviewed and screened for possible bias. Robert Hamkalo, the court clerk, picked names from an octagonal spinning chamber one by one until the first batch of potential jurors had been assembled. When Slotnick addressed the group, he told them that they were "ministers of justice." He emphasized that he wasn't looking for blank slates.

"People who haven't heard about this case have been on Mars," he said. He solemnly declared that his only intention was to find "impartial" and "unbiased" jurors.

Of course, he wanted jurors who *were* partial and biased—toward Goetz. His other unstated goal was to begin to influence their opinions even now. Jury selection was part of the presentation of a defense case, and despite several warnings from the judge, Slotnick made sure, even while he was asking supposedly neutral questions, to repeatedly describe the youths who'd been shot as "thugs and hoodlums." This was a unique opportunity for him to establish a rapport with the jury: once the trial began, the jurors would be just observers, and Slotnick wouldn't have another chance to engage with them directly.

Howard Varinsky, the jury consultant, had written to Slotnick with a proposal: he would provide his services for free, gambling that the publicity would be good for him if Goetz was acquitted.

Slotnick had been picking juries for twenty-five years by relying on his gut, and he found this new breed of scientific "jury consultant" vaguely ridiculous—but he figured he had nothing to lose, so Varinsky joined the team for jury selection. Slotnick theorized that his ideal juror in the Goetz case was a crime victim, and he wanted to keep off the jury the kind of strong-willed person who might dig in and impede a unanimous acquittal. But Varinsky conducted a phone survey of New Yorkers, and it yielded insights that helped Slotnick think more broadly: while liberals tended to oppose Goetz, liberals who were into self-defense viewed him favorably; while Black people tended to disapprove of what Goetz had done, Black women—especially single Black women—who felt victimized living in crime-plagued neighborhoods were open to arguments in his favor.

Each candidate was interviewed in quiet conversation at a long table in the front of the room, where Crane quizzed them alternately on behalf of Slotnick and Waples. Picking a state-court jury was a chess game. Each side received fifteen "peremptory challenges"—meaning fifteen jurors it could veto, with no explanation, even if the other side wanted them. Typically, a bunch of jury prospects would be interviewed, then the judge would say something like, "Okay, numbers 1 through 6. Prosecutor, any peremptories?" Maybe the prosecutor would say, "Number 2." Then the judge would say, "Defense, any peremptories?" If the defense had any, he'd say so. Then the judge would move on: "Okay, 7 through 14. Prosecutor, any peremptories?" Since the prosecutor went first in each round, the defense had a bit of an advantage, but a defense lawyer still had to make nail-biting decisions about how many peremptories to use now and how many to save for later.

Waples was clearly looking for liberals—"Greenwich Village types," as he called them—who hadn't been crime victims and didn't want gun-wielding citizens roaming the subways exacting frontier justice. He used one of his challenges on a Puerto Rican woman who'd been mugged five times and betrayed a bias against people with criminal records, saying that "a person doesn't get arrested for not doing anything" (her son was currently in prison, and she said he deserved to be there).

Slotnick used a challenge to strike an Episcopalian nun. Varinsky thought her life of contemplation would predispose her to passivity, and Baker worried that her nun's habit, symbolizing moral authority, would give her undue sway in a jury room.

Slotnick initially liked an older Jewish lady who'd worked as a psychiatric social worker. She was just the kind of person with whom Slotnick felt he got along well. But Varinsky, who'd been a psychologist in private practice in San Francisco before moving into jury consulting, "knew she'd diagnose Bernie, whether he took the stand or not": she'd see a mental disorder instead of the rationale of a reasonable person in extreme circumstances.

"Barry kept saying, 'No, no, they like me,'" Varinsky recalls of Slotnick's rapport with older Jewish ladies. "I said, 'Not this one, Barry.'"

Eventually Slotnick came around to Varinsky's point of view, arguing to the judge that a social worker who'd worked with combat veterans might be able to lead the jury in a particular direction because of her expertise in trauma reactions; Crane agreed and dismissed her.

One day, an African American prospect gave all the right answers. Baker and Slotnick looked at each other. Something wasn't right. The guy seemed too smooth. A short while later, Roy Innis walked into the courtroom. Innis was the only conservative Black leader in the country, and unlike Reverend Al Sharpton, who saw Goetz and his supporters as racists, Innis was a big fan of Goetz. Baker noticed that the suspiciously smooth guy was staring daggers at Innis. Baker elbowed Slotnick, whispering, "Did you see that?"

Slotnick rose to ask the prospective juror more questions. He asked him directly whether he disliked Innis. "No," the man said unconvincingly. "I like Innis." Finally, Slotnick used one of his fifteen peremptory challenges to have the man dismissed. Later, a court officer told Baker: "Good thing you got rid of that guy. I heard him say, as he was leaving, 'Some other guy will get rid of that motherfucker.'"

Many of the candidates who ended up on the jury fit both sides' criteria. Catherine Brody, a fifty-nine-year-old English professor, had been approached by muggers on the subway, but she resisted, scaring them away. To Slotnick, this meant she could empathize with Goetz's reaction; to Waples, Brody's experience equipped her to distinguish between reasonable, proportionate self-defense and what Goetz had done.

James Mosely had a midwesterner's commonsense attitude toward law and order, which appealed to Waples; in Slotnick's view, Mosely, as a generally law-abiding citizen, would be more sympathetic to Goetz than to the victims, who had serious rap sheets.

Varinsky and Baker had their doubts about a man named Ralph Schriempf, a sixty-three-year-old word processor—he seemed like the kind of independent-minded person who might seek center stage during jury deliberations and block an acquittal—but Slotnick bonded with him over Schriempf's hometown, Sandusky, Ohio, which was where Barry's wife, Donna, was from.

Carolyn Perlmuth and Mark Lesly were both liberal, and neither had been victimized by crime. This made them obvious choices for Waples. But both also studied martial arts, which made them the sort of self-sufficient people Varinsky had pegged as being likely to identify with Goetz.

Varinsky was less successful when he tried to influence Slotnick in a different realm—his attire. Goetz drew his core support from regular people who saw their own grievances reflected in his. "I said, 'Barry, you have to dress down,'"

Varinsky remembers. "He was right out of *GQ*. This is a case about everyman being afraid to walk the streets, afraid of being mugged." The next day, Slotnick showed up in one of his regular three-piece suits—minus the vest. "I don't have dress-down watches. I don't have dress-down clothes," he said. "I can't do it. It's not me." After that, he stuck to his usual finery.

Two and a half weeks after jury selection began, it was over.

"We have a jury," Justice Crane said. "Mazel tov."

It was now possible to get a superficial glimpse of the people who would be deciding Goetz's fate. There were eight men and four women, ten of them white and two of them Black. Six of the jurors had been victims of street crime.

Before opening arguments, there would be a two-week break.

CHAPTER 66

Beside the pool at the Sans Souci hotel in Miami Beach, Barry Slotnick was sprawled on a lounge chair, working on his opening argument and his tan. Nearby, the rest of the Slotnick clan sheltered from the glaring sun in a cabana, which Slotnick had as usual arranged to be equipped with a phone connection. A wire ran out from the cabana to a Trimline touch-tone phone that sat on the ground next to Slotnick, beside a stack of documents.

It was the week of Passover. Slotnick was friends with the hotel's owner, who made it kosher for the Jewish holiday. Slotnick and Mark Baker had brought their families with them for a working vacation. On Friday and Saturday nights, the families shared dinners. The rest of the time, the two lawyers sat by the pool, reading and writing.

Both men felt the usual pretrial anxiety, amplified by the significance of the case and the amount of work still to be done. As the Gotti trial had consumed Slotnick, Baker kept asking:

"When are you going to start reading this stuff?" Now he had an answer. And the stack of documents to go through had just gotten higher. Under New York law, once jury selection was completed, a defendant received a cache of papers from prosecutors called Rosario material. This included the prior testimony of witnesses in police reports and grand jury transcripts. Slotnick had shipped Bankers Boxes full of this material down to Florida.

While Baker and Slotnick sat on their chaise longues by the pool, Baker took a first pass at reading the Rosario documents, while Slotnick immersed himself in prepping for game day, studying witness dossiers and rehearsing his opening.

Most of what Baker was reading was familiar to him at this point. But as he was reading a police statement by Garth Reid, who'd been in Goetz's subway car, a quotation leaped out at him. Reid recalled his wife, Andrea, saying, before the shooting: "Look at those Black kids, what they're doing to the white guy." Baker sat up and turned to Slotnick. He passed him the document. To Baker, the statement was clearly exculpatory—information that the prosecutor should have provided to the defense earlier. Baker immediately began drafting a motion to dismiss based on the withholding of exculpatory material. It was a gray area of the law, and the motion was a Hail Mary.

Meanwhile, Slotnick turned over possible opening phrases and arguments in his mind. Most important, he had settled on a theme. Slotnick believed that themes were vital to defenses, especially during opening arguments. An opening wasn't evidence—it was a road map, a way to prime jurors for ways to interpret what they would soon hear. A theme was what would help it stick in memory.

CHAPTER 67

On Monday, April 27, 1987, despite an overcast sky and a near-constant drizzle, a mob of New Yorkers waited hours to score a seat for opening arguments in the Trial of the Century.

As the start time of 9:30 a.m. approached, 150 spectators and reporters packed the gallery in courtroom 572. Among them were ten Guardian Angels, in their signature red berets, at least as many black activists, a group of college kids with their sociology professor, and prosecutor Greg Waples's father and stepmother, who had flown in from Palo Alto to watch this.

Slotnick's hair was freshly cut, his beard newly trimmed. He wore one of his nicest Fioravanti custom suits. His gold Piaget Polo watch gleamed. Slotnick sat at the far left end of the defense table, closest to the room's center. Next to him was his investigator Frank King, who wore a suit and whispered in Slotnick's ear from time to time. On King's other side was Bernhard Goetz, wearing blue jeans and a white shirt, then paralegal

Gillian Coulter, and finally Mark Baker, who sat on the end so he could quickly step forward to make legal arguments.

A few feet away, at the prosecution table, Waples sat alone, preparing. He would make his opening argument first. Waples was thirty-seven and serious-looking. He was a bachelor who'd grown up in Iowa and gone to Yale and Columbia Law, and there was a solitary intensity about him. He was a runner, and he liked to go camping alone in Canada and Alaska. Today, he wore glasses and his one custom-made suit, which he'd bought only after being ribbed by colleagues. On the table in front of him rested his orange rucksack, a far cry from Slotnick's alligator-skin briefcase. While Slotnick had a tall glass of water on the defense table, Waples drank from the same type of paper cup the jurors did, as if to say: *I am one of you.*

Before calling the jury in, Justice Crane asked whether any of the lawyers had matters to address with the court.

"Defendant is ready for trial, Your Honor," Slotnick said.

"We were ready some time ago, Judge," Waples said, alluding to the delays caused by Slotnick's role in the Gotti trial.

"I think we all were," Crane said.

"At first," Gregory Waples began, "December 22, 1984, seemed a day much like any other day to the twenty or so passengers who were seated in the seventh car, car number 7657, of a ten-car IRT number 2 downtown express train." The prosecutor's words bounced off the marble and hardwood surfaces of the courtroom, colliding in a volley of echoes and overlapping sounds. "The train had begun this particular journey at White Plains Road in the Bronx at 12:36 p.m., and, about 1:40 p.m., this grimy, graffiti-smeared car was lurching and swaying in the noisy and peculiar rhythm that's almost unique to the New York City subway system as the train holed underground from the Fourteenth Street station towards its next stop at Chambers Street."

For the ensuing hour, Waples presented his case. He said that Goetz had acted out of a "twisted self-righteous sense of right and wrong" and was "pathetically obsessed with the idea that he had to carry a gun." He was a *"Death Wish* vigilante."

As he was being described, Goetz stared downward at the defense table. Sometimes he smiled. Sometimes he smirked. Most of the time he had a blank look on his face. When Waples referred to Goetz's "jaundiced mind," Slotnick objected to it as being "inappropriate," and the judge cautioned Waples to avoid such rhetorical flourishes. This happened again when Waples described Goetz as "this human powder keg." For Slotnick, an objection was in part a brushback pitch, a warning to his opponent not to get too comfortable in his aggression. He was also a believer in objection as distraction—a shiny object to derail a foe's momentum.

The rest of the time, Slotnick sat seemingly half listening, as if bored. Waples was telling the seamless story of a day and a moment. To the untutored ear, everything had equal weight. But Slotnick was paying close attention, picking up the important phrases that Waples had artfully woven into the tale, the precise language that would support the specific criminal charges.

Waples spoke of Goetz "firing shots in every direction," including a fifth shot, which missed its target and ricocheted dangerously around the car. Waples talked about two of the youths running away from Goetz at the moment he "gunned them down" and shot them in the back; one of them, whom Goetz shot at twice, was sitting down, "absolutely helpless," when the second bullet hit him, severing his spinal cord. Waples called the shooting of Darrell Cabey "little more than a cold-blooded execution or an attempted execution and is as far from being a legitimate act of self-defense as heaven is from hell." The shots were fired not by "a reasonable person, such as yourselves...but by an emotionally troubled individual." Waples spoke about the fact that Goetz had a quick-draw holster and hollow-point bullets, whereas none of the kids had weapons or had even touched him. Above all, Waples signaled that his main proof would be Goetz's own confessions, recorded on audio and video. Even if the jury didn't find the victims credible, Waples said, the tapes would still be sufficient to convict Goetz.

Then Waples surrendered the floor to Slotnick.

CHAPTER 68

Barry Slotnick had rehearsed furiously, practicing this speech repeatedly, but now, as he paced back and forth before the jurors, he affected a nonchalance, referring only rarely to his notes, as if this were something he was tossing off the top of his head.

He began, as he often did, by stressing that he wasn't required to give an opening statement—or even, for that matter, to cross-examine witnesses or present any case at all. "Remember, I have no burden," he said. "I need do nothing." But the reality was that airy theories about the burden of proof and the presumption of innocence aside, Slotnick would almost never take such a detached approach to a case. This was what he loved doing. Slotnick could be an ensemble player, as he was in the Gotti trial, but it was as a leading man that he was in his element.

Whereas Waples's approach was dry and charmless and concerned with high intellectual principles, Slotnick was out to win—and to appeal to the jury on a deep, emotional level whenever possible. As the star of the Barry Slotnick Show walked around the room, he treated everyone in it as an audience member to be wooed, addressing by turns the jury, the judge, Waples, the spectators, and the press. This was theater in the round.

Slotnick told the jurors that he wished he had recorded Waples's opening so that at the end of the trial he could play it back and they would be "totally insulted, as I was," listening to it. Goetz, far from being the "citizen Rambo" portrayed by Waples, was a man who'd lawfully defended himself against a robbery. "There were times when I sat back there," Slotnick said, "and I believed that I was sitting at a testimonial dinner for these four thugs and hoodlums."

Slotnick did promise the jury that he'd come back to them with transcripts of Waples's opening and his own and ask them which one had been supported by the evidence they'd heard. "I ask you to pull [Waples's] head out of the sand so that you can see what these facts are really all about," Slotnick said. "As a matter of fact, in a strange way, if Rod Serling were alive, he could make a massive serial of this story by calling it *The Twilight Zone*."

And there it was: Slotnick's theme.

"In this courtroom you will find that everything is wrong and displaced. You will find that the victim of a crime, the victim of a December 22, 1984, robbery, sits here as a criminal defendant."

Slotnick wouldn't be defending Goetz, he'd be *prosecuting* the four kids.

"I'm going to try them for robbery. I promise you that. And you're going to convict them and acquit him."

"Quite frankly," Slotnick repeated, in case his point had escaped anyone, "we're proceeding in the Twilight Zone. Everything you see in this courtroom will be contrary to what you know of the law of American justice. Everything's turned upside down."

A trial could be won or lost in the opening. It was Slotnick's first stab at destroying the prosecution's arguments, introducing his defense to the jury, and establishing reasonable doubt. But Slotnick didn't like to give too much detail at this stage. He never knew exactly how the evidence was going to turn out once testimony began, and he wanted to leave himself room to change theories midcase. Slotnick was most interested in painting a suggestive collage of image and feeling and vivid phrases.

First—*admit what you can't deny*—Slotnick hinted at the way he was going to try to overcome his client's confessions. Goetz was "full of stress and fear" and "may have recounted a lot of things that didn't actually happen" but were instead what Goetz wished had happened. In fact, Slotnick said, the evidence would show that Goetz had fired the bullets in a single reflexive burst—with no pausing to premeditate further shots—and that his most damning self-reported statement, "You don't look so bad; here's another," had never been uttered. The jury, Slotnick said, would hear evidence suggesting that seasoned police officers in stressful situations react the same way as Goetz did and are often unable to recall how many shots they fired. "In the imminent moment of stress, the human mind betrays itself."

To undercut the idea that Goetz had been out "hunting," Slotnick openly emasculated his client: "He looks meek; he looks easy; he looks like easy bait...He's not muscular; [he's] unimpressive looking." Slotnick mentioned Goetz's traumatic prior mugging to help explain the extremity of his reaction. "Did he become Rambo, as Mr. Waples would like you to know? No. He just realized that he was not going to be molested and robbed again."

Slotnick repeatedly referred to the kids who'd been shot in disparaging terms: "The four vultures"..."vicious predators of the street"..."lowlifes"..."savages"..."punks." He began the process of discrediting whatever they had to say, sneering at "the good immunity bath given to them by the district attorney of this county," which was "a license to lie." He mentioned the multimillion-dollar civil suits that two of the youths had filed against Goetz. Slotnick repeatedly referred to the kids as a "gang of four"—he needed jurors to view Cabey as part of the whole rather than someone who should be accorded special sympathy or used as the basis to find Goetz guilty of the most serious charges.

Most powerfully, Slotnick anticipated the testimony of James Ramseur.

"'James Ramseur, where do you live?'... He'll tell you, 'State's prison.'

"'Mr. Ramseur, what were you convicted of? Was it rape, robbery, and sodomy of a pregnant woman?' And the answer will be 'Yes.'"

Slotnick faced the jury, a look of utter disbelief and disgust on his face. "'And was it this same woman, when you got done with her, who needed eighteen stitches in her anus, was taken off a rooftop, and spent time in a hospital?' And the answer will be 'Yes.'"

What happened to the woman, he suggested, was vivid,

horrifying evidence of what happened when Ramseur carried a crime to completion: had Goetz not defended himself, Slotnick implied, he, too, would have been brutally victimized in some way.

"And that's your decent, law-abiding young lad who has been dealt a sad hand by society," Slotnick said. "Yes, James Ramseur, that same dear, sweet individual that this man will put on the witness stand."

As Slotnick spoke, he kept his eyes fixed on the jurors, looking at them one by one and gauging their reactions.

"Bernhard Goetz was surrounded by four mean, vicious-looking men with no pity in their eyes. Let no one kid you—he's the victim. And now he's a double victim by being here in the courtroom." Slotnick was pointing his finger at Goetz.

The lawyer's voice had been slowly rising, and by now he was brimming with indignation. Waples's remarks, Slotnick boomed, were "*insulting*…We have no obligation to submit to street violence. No one can walk up to me and say, 'Give me that watch, or that ring, or five dollars.' If they do, heaven help them if I'm armed, because I know what the law allows. . . . [Goetz] did what the law allowed."

Slotnick had to pause his opening while the trial broke for lunch, but for him, this was just another chance to show flashes of the folksy humor that tended to bond him with juries. "I wish you all a hearty appetite, good lunch, drink lots of coffee."

Outside the courthouse, the picketers had multiplied. There were now people marching with signs that said things like WILL GOETZ BE ANOTHER RACIST WHO GOES FREE? and SOUTH AFRICA TO THE U.S.A., RACIST RAMBOS ARE GOING TO PAY.

At 2:15 p.m., Slotnick resumed his opening. "I'm coming to the end," Slotnick said. "Everybody is smiling...

"I told you at the beginning we had entered the Twilight Zone and everything was upside down. That's correct. We might as well switch tables, because I'm going to prosecute those four, and you're going to see that those four were committing a robbery...you're going to convict them and acquit him."

Two hours after he had begun, Slotnick sat down. He felt good. He thought that his opening had been dramatic and effective.

CHAPTER 69

As Greg Waples began to present evidence, Slotnick's triumphal feeling turned to vapor. The first few prosecution witnesses were outsiders who'd reached the subway car right after the shooting. John Filangeri, the paramedic who had arrived first, recalled the scene. These were powerful images that would be hard for Slotnick to overcome, but in cross-examining Filangeri he scored an important point when Filangeri agreed that Cabey's wound and the bullet trajectory that it implied were inconsistent with a scenario in which Goetz had moved directly in front of Cabey and said, "You don't look so bad; here's another," and fired directly at him.

Waples's next witness was a crime-scene investigator, Detective Charles Haase. Haase described the disarray of the subway car after the four kids had been taken away to hospitals. As Waples questioned him, jurors were shown black-and-white photos of the shooting's aftermath: clothes strewn about, scattered pools of blood, the dent in the metal wall of the conductor's cab from a bullet, and some bullet fragments on the bench beside it. Haase had also recovered from the scene the kids' jackets and three screwdrivers they'd been carrying. Waples used the jackets, and the placement of the bullet holes in them, to reinforce his scenario of where Goetz was standing relative to each youth when he fired. When Slotnick cross-examined Haase, though, he focused on the fact that they were reversible jackets; as Slotnick walked back and forth in front of the jury, he turned a red-and-blue jacket inside and out, suggesting through his questions that such a jacket was "the uniform of a mugger."

The courtroom itself was proving problematic. The jurors could hardly see what was going on because the front of the jury box was eight inches too high. Justice Crane kept complaining about the acoustics, saying he was hearing himself speak in stereo. Jurors repeatedly had to ask to have witness testimony read back to them. Court officers rearranged the sound system's speakers, trying to find a configuration that would eliminate the echo. The trial was off to an awkward start.

On Wednesday the twenty-ninth, the third day of the trial, Slotnick opened the *Daily News* with more than his usual amount of anticipation. He knew there'd be coverage of the Goetz trial, but he was interested in one article in particular.

The previous morning, when Slotnick was scanning the gallery, he'd spotted Jimmy Breslin. Trawling, Slotnick had no doubt, for column fodder.

Sure enough, there it was on page 3, above Breslin's familiar mug and block-caps name: UP HIS SLEEVE: THE TURN OF THE SCREWDRIVERS. Slotnick skimmed the text. Breslin described

Haase's testimony about the bullet fragments. Then the article jumped a few pages.

Recounting Slotnick's cross-examination of Haase, Breslin described the lawyer pacing with the reversible jacket, turning it inside and out, and showing the three screwdrivers—which the *Daily News* alone, Breslin noted, hadn't erroneously described as sharpened.

"Start confusing them right off," Breslin wrote, sliding into his characteristic sarcasm. "A criminal defense lawyer in this country, under our Constitution, has two duties. First, he must get paid. The lawyer's next duty is to approach twelve citizens, who sit in a jury box and do not get paid, and try to confuse them so much that at the end they will have no idea of what they have heard and what it all means. They will go home broke and disgusted and the lawyer will go home with his money."

Slotnick rolled his eyes, but a trace of a smile played on his lips. Breslin wasn't so far off the mark.

CHAPTER 70

Prosecutor Greg Waples announced that the jury would hear an audiotape of Goetz's first spoken confession to New Hampshire police. A few improvements to the courtroom had been made. Another audio speaker had been added, along with two more microphones—one for the judge and one for the attorneys. Overnight, the jury-box railing that had obstructed the jury's view of the courtroom had been removed. Each juror was now provided with a set of wireless headphones and a copy of the forty-seven-page transcript of Goetz's confession. An amplifier would broadcast the recording for everyone else in the room.

Waples pressed Play, and suddenly the jurors were hearing Goetz's voice for the first time. "The mood of the courtroom," as one observer later described it, "shifted from excited observation to the meditative silence of parishioners absorbing an awesome moment."

For more than two hours, there was hardly any other sound

as a rapt, packed courtroom listened intently to the scratchy recording. Jurors glanced periodically at Goetz, as if they were trying to reconcile the slight, awkward, seemingly mild-mannered man in the room with the anxious, angry, intense man on the tape. They heard him say he'd been "cold-blooded" but also that he'd been "out of control." They heard him say, about shooting Cabey: "I know this is gonna sound vicious. And it is. I mean, how else can you describe it? I said, 'You seem to be doing all right; here's another.'" They heard him talk about his quick-draw holster and hollow-point bullets. Every now and then, Slotnick was dismayed to hear disbelieving gasps in the room, stark expressions of skepticism that Goetz had acted in self-defense.

But Goetz's confession was also self-lacerating to the point of being legally suicidal, which Slotnick told himself reflected well on Goetz, in an odd way. "What a lawyer would do," Goetz said on the tape, "is tell me what not to say. He would say, 'Well, don't say this, and don't say that,' and—and you get off on the technicalities. And that just makes me sick. Because if you did it, and it's true, you should be judged, you know, on the truth, and what is right and what is wrong."

By 12:45 p.m., when Waples pressed Stop on the audio player, the jury had heard the whole stew that Slotnick needed to over-come: Goetz's incriminating statements, his palpable fear, his guilt and anguish and anger, and his sincerity, which gave the incriminating statements even more weight. At the same time, Slotnick hoped that Goetz's humanity came through on the tape in a way that might let the jury understand him better.

At this point, Slotnick was limited in his options to try to undercut Goetz's own words, but in cross-examining the New

Hampshire detective who had introduced the audio, he was able to draw out a few points: Goetz had "appeared to be a meek, quiet individual"; Goetz had spoken voluntarily and without exercising his right to have a lawyer present; Goetz had talked about how fast everything had moved; Goetz had told the detective that the gun was for self-defense; Goetz had explained that "the mind sometimes takes over the body."

Slotnick cringed but wasn't surprised the next day when newspapers focused on the lines most harmful to his client, including "my intention was to murder them." The *New York Post* splashed another on its cover: I WANTED TO MAKE THEM SUFFER.

Next, Waples called his first eyewitness—Sally Smithern, a student at something called the Ohashi Institute. Smithern was young and blond and pretty, and she had come forward to say she'd been on the train during the shooting.

When Smithern took the stand, she was clearly nervous.

"I was reading," she recalled. "I heard a loud bang that I perceived as a shot. I looked up; my eyes went directly to a very—a person standing, a very light image, puffy light coat, some kind of hat, light hat, his arm—this person's arm was pointed outwards, and I heard the shots, then I saw the hand go like this in a sweeping motion, and, like, stop, and each time it stopped, three times, I heard another shot, and that's what I saw."

As Waples questioned her, Slotnick shared a look with Frank King. Smithern's description of what she'd seen was weirdly vague.

Had what she'd seen occurred in her car, Waples asked, or somewhere else on the train?

"Oh, I'm sorry, it was through the, through the windows of the next car, the south car, right in front of me that I saw this. It was very clear."

"Okay," Waples said. "Now, tell the jury—I—" He broke off.

Slotnick couldn't believe it. It seemed like Waples was only now learning that Smithern had been in a different car from the one where the shooting occurred.

"I got the impression it was a man just by the stance," Smithern continued, "but I couldn't say for sure."

Slotnick felt a familiar, rising excitement—the tingle a hunting dog gets when it smells prey.

Waples asked Smithern to describe the spacing of the shots.

"Bam, bam, bam, bam."

Maybe a second apart, Waples said for the benefit of the stenographer, whose transcript wouldn't capture the pauses.

Before Waples ended his direct examination of Smithern, he put up a diagram of the subway car on an easel and asked her to initial the spot where she'd been sitting and draw an arrow showing the direction in which she saw the arm moving.

Slotnick began his cross-examination by asking Smithern to detail her educational background. She said she had studied "holisticology," among other things. He asked for her home address at the time of the shooting. She described a transient-sounding life. "What you are telling us," Slotnick said, "is you don't remember right now where you lived during that Christmas season, 1984, is that correct?"

"No. Like I said, I live a lot of places for two months and move. I'd have to go to my list."

Slotnick asked when she'd first told the police about "what you had allegedly witnessed on the train."

Allegedly. Slotnick was now doubting whether Smithern had even been on the train.

Smithern replied that she'd heard on the radio that the police were looking for witnesses, so she'd called them and anonymously told her story. Slotnick tried to pin her down on the timing. She said it had been "a few weeks" after the shooting. She acknowledged that in the intervening period she'd absorbed a lot of news about the case.

"As a matter of fact," Slotnick said, "you called the police in March of '85, isn't that correct?"

He showed Smithern a statement to police dated March 7, which she acknowledged was in her handwriting.

Slotnick's tone remained matter-of-fact, but his questions took on a sharper edge.

Hadn't she initially told Waples that she got off the express train at Canal Street, where there was no express stop? Yes.

Though she'd claimed to have drawn a diagram for Waples, she hadn't actually drawn one, had she? "On paper, no. Then I guess I didn't."

"Well, is there anything else that you draw a diagram on? How about on wax, or on the floor, or on a rug, or anyplace else?"

Slotnick's disdain was both sincere and calculated. It was a nudge to the jury, a whisper about how much weight they should give to what they were hearing.

"No," Smithern said in a barely audible voice.

Was there anyone who could corroborate that she'd been on the train? No.

"Now, Miss Smithern, did Mr. Waples tell you that a lot of

people have come forward in this case that weren't on the train, that were just here to give testimony, or to take the witness stand in a highly publicized case?"

"No."

"And do you have any thought that if they ever make a movie of this trial, that you might be one of the people that would be depicted in the movie?"

"No, I doubt it."

Slotnick locked Smithern into her testimony that she had been able to see from her position through the door at the end of the car to "the arm" she'd seen shooting.

Was she seated or standing? Standing.

How tall was she? Five feet five.

And she was standing? She corrected herself. No; she was seated.

Slotnick entered into evidence another diagram of the car, which was shown to the jury.

"Now, do you remember anything unusual about the hand?"

"No."

"How about the fact that for you to have seen what you say you saw, you would have had to have been seven feet in the air?" Slotnick asked. "Did you notice that?"

Smithern, clearly rattled, took Slotnick's purple pen and started drawing on the defense exhibit.

"Please don't draw a bigger window," Slotnick said.

Waples objected, and the judge sustained the objection.

"I'm almost finished," Slotnick said. "I think it's time Miss Smithern went home, Judge."

Slotnick turned back toward the witness.

"Miss Smithern, have you ever been under psychiatric care?"

CHAPTER 71

At the back entrance of the courthouse, as the day's proceedings drew to a close, a throng of media and curiosity seekers had gathered.

As Greg Waples hurried mutely past them, reporters played at composing a song called "Lighten Up, Greg." Three days into the trial, they had begun to grasp the distinct rituals of the opposing legal teams.

While Slotnick stood up every time the jury was ushered into the courtroom, Waples remained seated. Waples was always alone at the prosecution table. At lunchtime, the defense team stayed in the locked courtroom to eat kosher New York deli food brought in by Frank King.

Waples entered the court building each morning without engaging with reporters. When Slotnick arrived, trailed by his entourage, he'd single out reporters by name. Now Slotnick emerged from the building, eager to field questions and dispense quips and insights about what had happened in the courtroom that day. He still had traces of a bridge-and-tunnel accent and salted his conversation with name-dropping anecdotes about Sammy Davis and "Frank." The reporters were already calling Slotnick's daily Q&A sessions the "five o'clock follies."

Finally, Goetz appeared. Since the defense team didn't trust him not to say the wrong thing, he'd been waiting inside, with Frank King at his elbow, until Slotnick was done with the press. Then King reminded him just to smile, saying, "This is all show, and this game is a game of hardball."

"Fuck you, Frank," Goetz said, but then he mostly complied with his lawyer's wishes, looking down at the ground and silently making his way to Slotnick's Cadillac amid the clamoring mob.

"It was scary sometimes," Gillian Coulter says. "Very often we had to be escorted to the car by court officers."

Normally, the moment when a crime victim testified was Slotnick's least favorite part of a trial. During direct examination, Slotnick would have to sit quietly, respectfully, concealing his dismay, even showing a modicum of sympathy for the victim's plight.

And when Troy Canty appeared in court on Friday, May 1, he looked good. He wore a beige plaid suit and a brown-and-gold-striped tie. As Waples began to examine him, Canty described himself as a young man trying to better himself. He had been living at Phoenix House Academy, a drug rehab center in Westchester County, for the previous two years, and he had plans to attend culinary school. In case jurors were inclined to compare Canty's imposing size with that of the bantamweight Goetz, Waples had his witness confirm that he had been shorter and thinner three years earlier.

Then Waples walked Canty through the moments surrounding the shooting.

Canty said he'd asked Goetz: "Mister, can I have five dollars?"

"He got up and turned his back towards me. He walked and he was zipping down his jacket. Then he turned around and pulled out his pistol."

"What were you doing when you saw the gun?"

"Standing."

"What happened?"

"He fired. I grabbed my chest. Then I went to the floor."

Goetz was seeing Canty for the first time since the shooting and stole occasional glances at him.

Waples kept Canty on the stand for an hour. Canty told a tidy, streamlined version of events that portrayed him as a reformed drug addict and petty criminal who'd done nothing to warrant Goetz's violent assault and Goetz as a madman with a gun. Then Waples turned his witness over to Slotnick for cross-examination.

A victim was often a defense lawyer's minefield, and in cross-examining one, Slotnick had to tread carefully. Act too aggressively, and Slotnick would lose the jury. Be too gentle, and the jury would simply accept everything the victim said as the gospel truth.

But Slotnick saw Canty as a precious opportunity to flip the script of this whole proceeding, turning him into the living embodiment of the case's down-is-up reality. "Troy Canty is the most unbelievable person to pass across this planet," Mark Baker had said earlier. "He is wholly unworthy of belief. There is not one iota of trust in what he will say other than the fact that he was on the subway train. We have always relished the thought of confronting Troy Canty."

When the jury returned from lunch at 2:15 p.m., the well of the courtroom had been made over as a photography exhibit. An easel in front of the jury box held a three-foot-by-three-foot blown-up image of Canty from around the time of the shooting. Beside it were three other easels, each containing a similar enlarged photo of the other kids. Waples's question about Canty's physical growth had opened the door for Slotnick to enter these pictures into evidence.

Mark Baker had told Frank King to get the meanest-looking pictures of the kids he could find. In these photos, the foursome looked confident and streetwise. Slotnick's overarching goal was to try to make the jury feel the way Goetz must have felt so that they would judge his actions as reasonable, and part of that meant conveying the perception Goetz would have had of the youths as he encountered them. The jury was now looking at the four teens as they might have appeared to Goetz: young and cocky and hard.

The one of Canty showed him with arms crossed, his eyes narrowed, his jaw set, his face a mask of bitterness and contempt.

"Mr. Canty," Slotnick began, "in December of 1984, when you were aboard the railroad train, you weren't wearing that nice suit and the tie and the shirt, were you?"

"No, I wasn't."

Slotnick made a sport of discrediting Canty, keeping him on the stand for two days. He brought out that Canty stood to gain from a civil suit against Goetz. After Canty said he'd changed and "learned that life is not peaches and cream," Slotnick suggested that was a line he'd been coached to say by a district attorney on a mission to get a win: Canty revealed for the first time that he'd testified before the second grand jury only after receiving immunity (meaning that he wouldn't be charged with robbing Goetz) directly from DA Robert Morgenthau in a face-to-face meeting he attended with his mother.

Slotnick confronted Canty with past statements that contradicted what he was saying on the stand. There was a *National Enquirer* interview Canty had given, for which he acknowledged receiving three hundred dollars. He said he split the money with Barry Allen but denied all his quotations and said he didn't remember anything Allen had said. There were statements Canty had made to police about Goetz having looked "soft" and that "we were robbing the white guy and he shot us." Canty denied those, too. There were a bunch of statements he'd made to the grand jury, which he also denied. Canty denied so many things that his denials began to seem implausible. And when he didn't deny something, he said he'd forgotten it. More than sixty times, Canty said he didn't remember. When Canty said he hadn't behaved in a threatening way toward Goetz, a man in the courtroom laughed loudly and was ejected.

Canty repeatedly denied knowing the names or recognizing the faces of people who'd made other criminal complaints against him. Even when Slotnick showed Canty a police complaint documenting his arrest, Canty said he didn't remember any such incident.

At this point, as Slotnick had choreographed it, the complainants themselves entered the courtroom. Still, Canty denied having any idea who they were.

While Slotnick's theatrics were effective, Canty wasn't a pushover. He was adroit at boxing off whole areas of inquiry by saying he didn't remember anything. As Slotnick counter-punched, embedding information he wanted the jury to hear into his questions, Waples objected several times, and the judge repeatedly reminded the jury that questions aren't evidence, and that since Canty kept saying he didn't remember things, the jury was to disregard them. But the reality was that Slotnick was methodically, relentlessly injecting facts and images and innuendo into the jurors' minds. They might sincerely claim to disregard it, but they would nevertheless be affected by it.

Things finally boiled over when Slotnick grilled Canty about spending a year at the Bronx-Lebanon Hospital Center's department of psychiatric care.

"And could you tell the jury why you went to the Bronx-Lebanon psychiatric center?"

"I don't really recall going there."

"And that's your answer, is that correct?"

"Yes."

"So if I ask why you went there, and things of that sort, you just wouldn't answer me?"

"I wouldn't know."

"Remember you testified you had beaten up a teacher and were suspended from school, on Friday, remember testifying about that?"

"Yes."

Under the rules of cross-examination, Slotnick was barred from asking specific questions about events not remembered, but he plowed ahead with his line of questioning.

"You remember going to the Bronx-Lebanon psychiatric

center afterwards in which they discussed the issue of why you beat up the teacher and they told you you had been arrested for it, remember that?"

"No, I don't."

"Is there anything you remember about the Bronx-Lebanon psychiatric center?"

"No."

"Does it refresh your recollection that a doctor said or several doctors said that you, Troy Canty, were hostile and assaultive?"

Canty continued to not recall anything Slotnick asked.

Waples kept objecting, and finally Justice Crane said Slotnick could ask just one more question on the subject, "so choose wisely."

"Were you told at Bronx-Lebanon Hospital Center that there's a possibility you could go [to a junior high school] if you toned down your behavior and were not so vicious?"

"I don't recall ever going there."

Despite Justice Crane's instruction, Slotnick kept finding new ways to ask. "Is it that you don't remember because at the time you went to Bronx-Lebanon psychiatric center, not only did you have a marijuana problem but you also were using PCP, or angel dust, on a constant basis?"

Waples objected, and Crane sustained the objection.

Slotnick spent a few minutes on other topics, then once again said: "Bronx-Lebanon psychiatric center. Does it refresh your recollection—"

"Your Honor," Waples interrupted, "this is in flagrant violation of your last ruling."

"That's correct," Crane said.

Slotnick asked again, and Waples exploded: "This is *misconduct.*"

Crane admonished Slotnick once more, but by now, after keeping Canty on the stand for two days, Slotnick had completely destroyed his credibility.

And Slotnick was almost salivating at the prospect of toying with the next witness—if the next witness appeared.

CHAPTER 72

The men and women in the jury box were experiencing only the most visible part of the trial. There were dozens of smaller skirmishes outside the jury's hearing in which Slotnick and Baker and Waples fought about which evidence would make it into the courtroom. Inevitably these arguments culminated in hearings before Justice Crane, who would hold them in the morning before the jury arrived or at the end of the day, after the jury was gone.

On the first day of the trial, Baker moved to dismiss the case altogether on the basis that "highly exculpatory" evidence had been concealed by the prosecution, presented to neither the first nor the second grand jury. This was in reference to the police report Baker had discovered poolside in Miami only days before the trial began, which revealed that Garth Reid, a passenger on the train, said he'd heard another passenger say, "Look at those four punks; they're bothering that guy," and that Reid himself "saw the kids hassling the white guy, who was doing nothing."

Waples had countered that Reid had been an "evasive" witness whom his office hadn't been able to find when the second grand jury was convening. Crane ruled in favor of the prosecution, in part because he didn't think Reid's testimony would actually be exculpatory.

In a smaller but still consequential setback for the defense, Justice Crane disallowed hearsay testimony by paramedic John Filangeri, who stated that Darrell Cabey, as Filangeri was driving him to St. Vincent's Hospital, said, "The guys I was with were hassling this guy for some money."

"I need this statement for my case, Your Honor," Slotnick told Crane.

"I know, Mr. Slotnick," the judge said, before ruling against him.

Another of the teenagers, Barry Allen, had not been granted immunity, so when he was called as a witness by Waples, he was able to avoid answering Slotnick's dozens of questions simply by pleading the Fifth, and he was allowed to do it outside the presence of the jury. Slotnick kept asking his questions anyway, and Waples accused him of "grandstanding... We could be here until Mr. Slotnick gets laryngitis."

"That won't happen," Slotnick said, in a statement that in hindsight would come to seem highly ironic.

The fourth teen, James Ramseur, posed a different problem. He had been given immunity, which meant that he was required to testify, but now he was refusing to do so. Slotnick at least wanted the jury to witness Ramseur's refusal in open court, but initially Justice Crane sided with Waples, agreeing that it could happen outside of the jury's presence.

"Unless this man is called," Slotnick said, "I have a right to a mistrial."

Waples erupted. "I think this pious talk most—I find it *disgusting*, especially in view of some of the things I've seen in this courtroom the last couple days."

Crane said he wanted everyone to calm down. Then he ruled in Slotnick's favor. Waples had to call Ramseur as a witness in front of the jury.

Unlike Canty, who'd worn a jacket and tie during his testimony, Ramseur came into the courtroom wearing prison pants and a Windbreaker and escorted by a court officer, as if he were there against his will, which he was.

Ramseur was temporarily living on Rikers Island, in cell block 74, while in the city to testify. For the long term, he was living at the Green Haven Correctional Facility, sixty miles north of Manhattan, and serving an eight-to-twenty-five-year prison sentence for the brutal rape of Gladys Richardson.

Slotnick had been looking forward to cross-examining Ramseur. He was the worst of the four, the living embodiment of the reason Goetz had been justified in his actions.

Ramseur got in the witness box. He wore a bitter smirk on his face, alternating with a surly grimace.

"Place your left hand on the Bible," a court officer said.

Ramseur pushed the Bible away and said, "I'm not taking the stand. I refuse to."

"Sorry, Your Honor," Slotnick said, in an apologetic tone that did little to mask how much he was enjoying this. "I can't hear the witness."

"I refuse to take the stand!" Ramseur repeated.

The judge directed him to stand up and take the oath, and

Ramseur again refused. The judge then cited him for contempt, and Ramseur was taken out of the courtroom.

Slotnick was glad that the jury had experienced Ramseur and his demeanor, but he wasn't happy about Ramseur's contempt. As far as Slotnick was concerned, the more time the "victims" spent in front of the jury, the better it was for Goetz. Slotnick couldn't prosecute them, as he'd told the jurors he'd do, if they refused to be in the courtroom.

CHAPTER 73

Prosecutor Waples next called a series of eyewitnesses to the shooting. These were people who'd been in the subway car, regular folks the jury might identify with. Unlike Troy Canty, they had nothing obvious to gain by lying. If they confirmed the details of the story Goetz told, Waples stood a good chance of winning.

Victor Flores was a fifty-year-old native of Puerto Rico who'd worked as a cleaner for the city's transit authority for more than twenty years. On the afternoon of December 22, 1984, he had been on his way to Brooklyn to help his brother, a building superintendent. He testified that Goetz, as he shot the kids, "looked like he was very mad, like he was angry," but Flores didn't provide any details confirming the key points of Goetz's confession.

When Slotnick cross-examined Flores, he elicited a description of the youths as having been "bunched together" near Goetz before the shooting.

"After the rapid succession of shots, you never heard another shot?"

"Right."

If anything like Goetz's alleged Cabey moment—when he'd gone back over to him, said, "You don't look so bad; here's another," and fired again—had happened, Flores said, "I was not there" to see it.

"What are the duties of a conductor on our subway system?" Waples asked his next witness, Armando Soler, who'd been the train's conductor.

"Basically to operate the doors and make sure everybody arrives to their destination safely," Soler said.

The whole courtroom burst out laughing at the unintended irony.

Soler reddened.

He described entering the car after the shooting. He said Goetz was sitting calmly and told him, "I don't know why I did it. They tried to rob me."

Slotnick wasn't hearing anything he thought was harmful to his client, and on cross-examination, Soler, like Flores, recalled the shots happening "in rapid succession," in a single burst lasting only "about a second."

Slotnick's angles of attack began to gel. With each of the next several witnesses, he repeated the phrase "rapid succession." He'd begin a question with "After hearing those four or five shots in rapid succession..."

None of the witnesses recalled the extra, gratuitous *Death Wish* shot at Cabey.

Slotnick and Baker couldn't understand why Waples had called these witnesses, given their unanimous agreement that the shots had been fired without a pause. "He's a bright guy," Baker says. "I couldn't figure out how he thought that would be helpful to his case."

Waples had made another misstep, Slotnick thought. The prosecutor had asked each of his witnesses if they'd been afraid of the four youths. The first time he did this, Slotnick objected. Waples was obviously trying to distinguish the other passengers from Goetz, to make the case that Goetz hadn't simply behaved as a reasonable person would. But in doing so, Waples was opening the door for Slotnick to cross-examine them on the same point, which could be useful to the defense. Justice Crane even cautioned Waples, asking whether he was sure he wanted to open that door. But Waples strode blithely through it.

With subsequent witnesses, this became a focus of Slotnick's cross-examinations.

Loren Michals, a thirty-three-year-old credit manager, said he'd been sitting with his friend Christopher Boucher around forty feet away from the kids. Slotnick asked: "But even at that distance you found them noisy and rude?"

"I didn't say rude particularly," Michals said.

Slotnick then showed Michals a transcript of his grand jury testimony, in which he had recalled the youths being "a bit noisy and rude."

Slotnick routinely smuggled into his leading questions the facts he wanted the jury to be aware of, or the interpretations he wanted to suggest were the correct ones, but it looked like he had gone too far with this tactic when he was cross-examining Garth Reid, the twenty-six-year-old computer programmer and student from Jamaica. Reid had been traveling with his wife and baby from their apartment in the Bronx to the Borough of Manhattan Community College, at the lower tip of Manhattan, when the shooting occurred.

"And, as a matter of fact," Slotnick said, "isn't it true that the reason you took notice of these four individuals is because someone said, 'Look at those four punks bothering that man'?"

"Objection," Waples said.

This was a matter that had already been discussed in a sidebar, and Crane had expressly said he wouldn't allow it.

Crane agreed and looked at Slotnick sharply. "Please don't include something that's not in evidence in your question," he said.

When Slotnick protested, Crane ordered another sidebar. He was angry, and his usual sidebar voice, louder than a whisper but below normal speech, shot up a couple of notches.

"I thought we had an understanding this would not happen again, Mr. Slotnick," Crane said.

"Judge," Slotnick said, "you can speak a little louder and the jury can hear you."

"I'm upset with your conduct," Justice Crane said.

"I'm upset with *your* conduct," Slotnick said.

"You know where you can go with that," Crane said.

Slotnick was treading awfully close to insulting the most powerful man in the room, but he continued to defend his questioning, and Justice Crane eventually came around to Slotnick's argument that Waples had opened the door to this type of question. While hearsay wasn't allowed, statements relevant to a witness's state of mind were. Crane's about-face ratified Slotnick's sense, earlier, that Waples had miscalculated when he started asking the eyewitnesses about their feelings on the subway that day.

Slotnick felt that these witnesses, far from strengthening the prosecution's case, had been more helpful than not to the defense, and Slotnick had done real damage to the credibility of several of them.

There was little doubt that the Goetz jury was confused. The accounts they'd heard conflicted with one another on nearly every point. Juror Mark Lesly wrote in his diary that night: "We still haven't seen anybody who can definitively corroborate one way or another what happened on that train."

CHAPTER 74

Greg Waples had saved his most important eyewitness for last. The earlier ones had all testified that they'd seen only a fraction of what happened, and none had confirmed the most damning part of Goetz's confession. Christopher Boucher, a thirty-three-year-old department-store display artist who'd been riding the subway with his friend Loren Michals, who'd already testified, was the lone exception. He said he had witnessed the whole thing, including Goetz's point-blank shot at Darrell Cabey.

"My eyes went directly to the action," Boucher recalled as Waples examined him. Goetz had been "standing, looking down" at Cabey, who'd been "sitting back with his hands, like, grasping the bench and a frightened look on his face. When it caught my vision, his hand was already up with the gun...He was standing holding the gun pointed at this individual and in just a matter of seconds he fired."

"Is there any doubt in your own mind that you saw a person sitting in that seat when that shot was fired?"

"No, no doubt."

As Boucher gave his unswervingly confident answers, Slotnick cast sidelong glances at the jury. It seemed like they were buying what the witness was saying.

When Slotnick stood to cross-examine Boucher, he tried to point out inconsistencies between the witness's testimony and statements he'd made to police right after the shootings. He also questioned Boucher on his peculiar insistence that he hadn't been particularly upset by the incident. While Michals had testified that Boucher was "shaken up" by what happened, Boucher denied that he'd been traumatized or that his memory of the events might be distorted in any way.

"Your adrenaline was flowing?"

"No."

Boucher specifically rejected the "rapid succession" idea, saying there was a distinct gap between each shot. And he ended on a resolute note that reinforced the impact of his testimony.

"Is there any doubt in your mind that on December 22, 1984, you saw this tall blond man firing a gun at a person who was sitting in that seat?"

"I have no doubt about it, no."

During lunch, a twenty-seven-inch Sony TV was wheeled into the room on a trolley and positioned in front of the jury box. Four other monitors were brought into the room: one for the judge, one for Goetz and both sides' lawyers, and two for the spectators. The jurors were given wireless headphones, and the prosecutor called New York City detective Mike Clark to the stand. Clark had been present in New Hampshire when

Goetz was interviewed by police, and he was there to introduce Goetz's videotaped confession. Slotnick was dreading this
moment. It was a smart move by Waples, waiting until the confusing testimony was over before dropping his most powerful
piece of evidence. The lights in the courtroom dimmed.

When Slotnick was defending a case in which there was
videotape, he typically focused on either getting the tape
suppressed, if it had been improperly obtained, or justifying
the recorded crime as an act of insanity or self-defense. Years
earlier, Slotnick had represented a man who'd been captured
on video jumping a turnstile and, later, robbing a bank. The
man was arrested a block and a half away with the money in
his hands. There was no getting out of what he'd done—the
prosecutors had the videotape—and it went to trial. In court,
his accomplice testified against him. But Slotnick appealed to
the jury's sympathy. His client had believed he was terminally ill
and robbed the bank to provide a nest egg for his family. When
he got home, his wife told him he'd lost his moral compass, and
she made him return the money. Before he reached the bank,
he was arrested. The jury returned a not guilty verdict.

Slotnick and Baker had initially been confident that they
could get the Goetz videotape suppressed. On the tape, Goetz
waived his Miranda rights. But a few seconds before he did that,
at the very start of the tape, Goetz asked for a lawyer. Once
that happened, under New York law, the subsequent waiver of
rights without a lawyer present was invalid.

Getting the video tossed might have been helpful to the
defense, but even though Goetz came off as a vengeful kook,
his lawyers also thought that the tape made him sympathetic in
certain ways. And Slotnick knew he could never put Goetz on

the stand, so if he wanted the jury to see and hear Goetz speak, his only option was the video confession. If Waples hadn't introduced it as evidence, Slotnick might have done so himself. Still, having the jury see the video was a big risk.

As it played, the room was somber and completely silent except for the voice of Goetz. At the defense table, Goetz squirmed in his seat. Slotnick had watched the video a few times, but he still winced inwardly at the worst of Goetz's moments, his greatest socially unacceptable revelations, which did nothing to support a claim of self-defense: "I turned into a vicious animal," "sadistic," "a monster."

Slotnick kept glancing at the jury to see their reactions. He was at his core a pessimist. It was part of what made Slotnick so good at what he did. By always contemplating the worst outcomes, he approached difficult situations with multiple strategies in his pocket based on every possible contingency. That way he could quickly pivot when necessary. But his feeling about the playing of the videotape went beyond his usual expectation of doom.

"We just lost," he told Baker afterward.

Baker shook his head. "Are you crazy?"

"You could hear a pin drop," Slotnick said. "They focused on what he was inculpatorily saying." Slotnick had a rare look of despondence in his eyes.

"This isn't bad," Baker insisted. "This is good. I disagree with you."

"I'll bet you," Slotnick said. "If they acquit, I'll buy you a car."

CHAPTER 75

Greg Waples had planned to rest his case at this point. The videotape was the capstone of the people's argument. It was emotional, damning, memorable, and seemingly irrefutable.

But a witness who'd had a scheduling conflict earlier in the trial was now available, and on May 19, after a five-day break, Waples called Andrea Reid, another eyewitness from the train. A statuesque part-time model who was studying criminal justice in the hope of becoming a police officer, she was married to Garth Reid, who'd testified earlier. They'd been on the train together, along with their baby, on the day of the shooting.

It was unseasonably warm, and jurors were yawning as Reid took the stand, wringing her hands and radiating nervousness and tension. Many of the prior eyewitnesses had testified that before the shooting they hadn't paid particular attention to the kids at the end of the subway car. But Reid spoke of her constant state of fearful alertness on subways, which had caused her to closely monitor the rambunctious foursome.

At first, her testimony sounded almost helpful to Goetz. She described the youths as "moving about, swinging on the bars, banging on the seats." She described one of them asking a white man, "What's happening?"

"When you noticed that, or heard that individual address the white man," Waples said, "did you say anything to your husband?"

"I said, 'Look at those four punks messing with that white man.'"

Describing the shooting, Reid recalled hearing a shot, then turning and seeing "a white man standing, and he was continuing shooting." Then she turned to grab her baby, walked toward the door, turned back, and "saw the last shot."

But when Waples asked whether Goetz was the same man she'd made the "four punks" comment about, she said, "No. It could have been—I don't know. But I don't think so. I thought that particular man walked off the train."

Other elements of her testimony were potentially damaging to the defense. She said that prior to the first shot, she didn't see any of the youths approach Goetz, and she never saw any of them standing over or surrounding him. Waples asked her to describe the spacing of the shots. Like Boucher, she recalled pauses between some of them, suggesting that Goetz might indeed have made his *Death Wish*–style statement and premeditated some of the shots. She'd heard "probably five" shots. She said there was a slight pause between the first and second and between the fourth and fifth. The middle three were "very rapid."

Despite all this, as Barry Slotnick rose to cross-examine her, he felt good about his prospects. Even under friendly questioning by Waples, she had contradicted herself several times. And Slotnick had a surprise up his sleeve.

A couple of weeks earlier, two investigators working for Slotnick had gone to see Reid in the Bronx. John McNally had sent the investigators to see her, and she told them that the youths "were standing over" Goetz. She said, "I know the guy's mother," referring to Darrell Cabey's mother, Shirley. "That's why I didn't want to get involved, because I didn't want them to know where I live at."

When the investigators told Slotnick what they'd learned, he was very pleased. Then he asked them for the tape.

"What tape?"

Slotnick needed a tape. He always had his investigators surreptitiously record interviews in case he needed to confront a witness with contradictory testimony. But in this case, the investigators had failed to do so. Slotnick told them to go back and redo the interview, this time on tape. The investigators pushed back. They'd already gotten a good interview, they said, and didn't want to bother Reid again. Slotnick had McNally send a different pair of investigators back to see Reid.

Six days before Andrea Reid took the stand, on the evening of Wednesday, May 13, the new investigators arrived at the tan-brick building where the Reids lived.

They identified themselves as investigators for Slotnick and were buzzed in.

One of the investigators had a Sony microcassette recorder rolling in his vest pocket.

An hour later, they left Reid's apartment, tape in hand.

* * *

On the stand, Andrea Reid was still nervous.

"Mrs. Reid," Slotnick said. "Please take some water. Calm down."

Slotnick started gently. He didn't ask anything directly confrontational.

Reid acknowledged that she hoped to become a police officer and that she had spoken about her ambition with the prosecutor. She agreed that Waples had power over whether she became a cop. She agreed that because of her training she understood that criminal prosecutions were very serious, that she should tell the truth to whichever side spoke with her, and that she should do the same on the witness stand. Slotnick locked her into testifying that anything she had told anyone about the case was the truth.

Reid also agreed that Waples had told her that if her husband testified, she wouldn't need to do so herself. Slotnick asked Reid whether she'd told his investigators that she was angry that Waples was now forcing her to testify anyway.

Reid hesitated.

"Now remember, Mrs. Reid, you're under oath."

"I'm trying to recall. I don't remember."

"By the way"—time for Slotnick's big reveal—"do you know that when my investigators came to speak to you, they wore a tape recorder and tape-recorded everything you said?"

Reid appeared stricken. "No."

Slotnick again asked whether she'd complained to his investigators about Waples forcing her to testify.

"Maybe, maybe not. I don't remember saying it like that."

"Do you think you might have said it?"

"Yes, because I never did want to get involved with this whole situation."

Slotnick now made a subtle pivot, asking a series of questions couched as statements she might have made to his investigators. That three or four guys had surrounded Goetz. That her "four punks" remark might have been about Goetz. That she made the remark after the train stopped at 14th Street.

Reid said she didn't remember whether she'd talked about wanting to be a police officer with Waples during their most recent conversation, on Sunday, but then Slotnick said: "Well, did you tell my investigators last night that you had that conversation with Mr. Waples?"

"Yes."

"Did you also tell my investigators, 'Well, you know, that's not a bribe?'"

"Yes."

"And did you also tell my investigators, when they spoke to you, that you heard four or five shots in rapid succession, wasn't that your term?"

"Yes."

Slotnick made another pivot. Now that Reid was on notice that there was a tape recording, he could begin every question with "And isn't it true you told my investigators..." Whether the statement that followed was actually on the tape—whether it had even *been said*—Reid, and the jury, would assume that it was and had been.

"And it's also true, is it not, that when you saw those four men, you were afraid, and you were afraid they would come and mess with you, your husband, and your baby, is that correct?"

"Yes."

"Isn't it true that you told my investigators that the shots—you thought it was firecrackers, one after another?"

"Yes."

"Isn't it also true that you told my investigators that after the shots, one after another, you never heard any other shot?"

"Yes."

Slotnick knew that performing a good cross-examination is like boiling the proverbial frog in water, making imperceptible increases in the temperature so that the witness barely notices what's happening. He asked for a break because of "a mechanical situation." He went over to investigator Frank King, who handed him a microcassette recorder with an earpiece attached.

Now Slotnick took Reid back to the night his investigators had come to see her. He had her put the earpiece in her ear while he played a moment from the tape for her.

"Did you hear your voice saying, 'At least two guys stood over the white guy?'"

She did. Then, without playing any more of the tape, Slotnick quoted her as saying, "They were standing right over him."

It wasn't clear whether that was actually backed up on the tape, but once again, there was an assumption that it was.

"No," Reid said. "I never seen anyone stand over him."

Slotnick suggested that on December 22, she'd told her husband, "Those four, they got what they deserved."

Reid denied saying "they got what they deserved" to anyone, including Slotnick's investigators.

Slotnick played the tape for her and asked again. "Does that refresh your recollection that you told one of my investigators upon his questioning, 'What was your immediate reaction?'...you said, 'They got what they deserved'?"

"Yes."

After Reid left the witness box, Justice Crane ordered a lunch break.

Reid's courtroom testimony, much more damaging than it would have been had Slotnick not persisted in making his investigators capture her unguarded disclosures on tape, had not helped the prosecution. Slotnick figured that Waples had been overly confident in Reid's strength as a witness. Instead, her own visceral fear, demonstrated in the witness box, had conjured in the courtroom the same terror Goetz must have felt on the train.

CHAPTER 76

arry Slotnick had expected the prosecution to rest, but after lunch another witness appeared. James Ramseur, wearing a black shirt, a black sport jacket, and gray pants, entered the courtroom through a side door. Offered the chance by Justice Crane to "purge his contempt"—undo the punishment he had coming his way for refusing to testify earlier—he had decided to take the witness stand after all.

Slotnick brightened. This was an unexpected gift. Even after Andrea Reid's testimony, Bernhard Goetz's videotaped confession was still fresh in jurors' memories. But it would surely fade once the jury spent some quality time with Ramseur.

Slotnick almost felt sorry for Greg Waples, who'd had no choice but to call Ramseur: if he hadn't, Slotnick could ask the judge to tell the jurors that Ramseur was a "missing witness," meaning they could infer that his testimony would have been harmful to the prosecution's case.

Waples did his best to salvage the situation, dutifully walking

Ramseur through his memory of the shooting and asking many of the same questions he'd put to Troy Canty—confirming, for example, that Ramseur had been physically smaller three years ago—but Ramseur contradicted other witnesses' accounts on several points. Slotnick listened quietly, except when he objected from time to time that he couldn't hear what Ramseur was saying and asked Justice Crane to instruct the witness to speak louder.

When Slotnick stood to cross-examine Ramseur, the giant menacing photos were back up on their easels, and Slotnick didn't even bother asking Ramseur about the shooting. He felt confident that when it came time for the jury to puzzle out the truth of what had happened that day, they wouldn't give much weight to Ramseur's account.

Instead, Slotnick had a single aim with Ramseur—to make the jury *feel* what Goetz had been up against. Right away, Slotnick began aggressively undermining Ramseur's credibility. One of Slotnick's first questions was, "And you're the same James Ramseur who was convicted for sodomy of a pregnant woman by the name of Gladys Richardson and caused her [to have] eighteen stitches in her anus, is that correct?"

Slotnick had Ramseur acknowledge that he had a potentially lucrative civil suit pending against Goetz. He asked him about various discrepancies in his past testimony. He asked him about his criminal record and current residence. Ramseur acknowledged that he was serving a prison sentence but denied committing any of the crimes for which he'd been convicted.

As Slotnick kept needling him, Ramseur began talking back.

"He's going to be found not guilty anyway," Ramseur said of Goetz. "I know what time it is."

The following morning, Crane announced to the lawyers that alternate juror Augie Ayala had chest pains and was being checked out at Bellevue hospital. Crane offered to proceed without Ayala, but Slotnick said, "I would rather lose half a day than an alternate." It was a curious preference, but Frank King suggested to Goetz a motive for Slotnick's flexibility: Ramseur's morning meds, given at dawn at Rikers, would be wearing off by the afternoon, making Ramseur more easily provoked. This was where Frank King shined, as a brilliant, down-and-dirty strategist, and why Slotnick never went to trial without him.

At 2:30 p.m., with Ayala cleared for duty by his doctor, Slotnick continued his cross-examination of Ramseur. Overnight, several additional court officers had been assigned to the trial. They now ringed the courtroom, all wearing guns. The jury was afraid of Ramseur. Among themselves, they had come up with a plan, which they'd informed court officers about: if Ramseur got violent, Ayala (who sat closest to the exit) would get up and open the door, and they'd all run out.

Whether for pharmaceutical reasons, or because of Slotnick's deft baiting, the witness quickly melted down.

Slotnick asked about Ramseur's history of stealing and robbing with Canty, Allen, and Cabey.

"We never stole and robbed nobody. We broke into machines. Why you putting robbing in? We never robbed anybody together...Don't try to convince the jurors that I'm a robber."

"Well, let me ask you a question, Mr. Ramseur. Weren't you

convicted of robbing from Gladys Richardson on the day that she was raped and sodomized? Yes or no?"

"Yes, I was. I never committed that crime."

"I guess the jury believed that when you were on trial, didn't they? Yes or no?"

"I guess they did. They was paid to. I was set up."

"How many jurors were paid?"

"All of them. You probably paying the jurors now."

Slotnick looked at the jurors and smiled. "I pay the jurors?"

"This could be a setup. I don't fuckin' know."

This was the first profanity Ramseur had uttered in the jury's presence, and juror Diana Serpe, a thirty-three-year-old airline sales rep, turned, mouth agape, to share a look with another juror.

"Mr. Ramseur," Slotnick continued, "have we ever met?"

"No, we never ever met, but I heard about you."

"I hope it was nothing unpleasant."

"It *was* unpleasant. I know about you, baby."

Slotnick began pressing Ramseur about his actions on the day before the shooting.

"It's none of your business," Ramseur said.

"Your Honor," Slotnick said. "I don't have to take this abuse, and I ask the Court to intercede."

The judge suggested a five-minute break for Ramseur to calm down, and the jury was ushered out of the room.

Justice Crane then explained to Ramseur that his time on the stand was almost over: if he just answered a few more questions, he'd no longer face a contempt charge.

"Let me tell you something, Judge," Ramseur said. "I think this is all bullshit. They all fuckin' together. Just take me out of here."

Crane patiently asked if Ramseur would cooperate.

"I'm ready to cooperate, but he playing fuckin' games."

At this point, Waples could no longer remain silent: "James, why don't you shut up?"

It was a stunning thing to hear a prosecutor say to his own witness, but Ramseur was becoming an existential threat who might single-handedly sink Waples's case. He was exhibit A for a cynical adage popular among DAs: *A murder case is an assault case without the victim to screw it up.*

Crane addressed the witness again. "Just answer the questions, Mr. Ramseur. Don't volunteer anything, and don't put on a show."

The jury was ushered back in, and Slotnick tried once more, but Ramseur again accused Slotnick of "playing fuckin' games."

"Your testimony is important," Crane told Ramseur, with almost saintly tolerance. "I don't want to give you contempt because I want you to answer the last questions. Can't you do that last little bit?"

"No."

"Do you think tomorrow morning, after you talk to whoever you are with at Rikers Island, you might feel better if you came back tomorrow?"

"No."

Slotnick chimed in. He didn't like to see "the Court humbling itself to the point it has" with Ramseur. "How dare he use the language that he has used in this courtroom, and—I'm sure the district attorney joins with me—how dare he use and abuse the majesty of this Court?"

Crane drily suggested that the majesty of the Court wasn't really relevant to the discussion.

Slotnick again addressed Ramseur: "Prior to December 22, when was the last time you were with Darrell Cabey, Troy Canty, and Barry Allen?"

"When was the last time you got a drug dealer off?" Ramseur snapped.

Slotnick started to ask another question, but Ramseur wasn't even listening. He "leaned forward in his chair, his left fist planted firmly on his lower jaw, a bemused smile flickering across his face," as an observer later described him. As Ramseur had become more agitated, several court officers had moved closer to the witness box, until there were four behind it and two on each side, almost at Ramseur's shoulders. Ramseur started shaking his head. Then he crossed his right leg over his left and reached down.

What he did next would be the subject of debate and grow into a legend. But what Slotnick did at that moment was specific and intentional. He visibly flinched, recoiling as if Ramseur was about to attack him. As a result of Slotnick's reaction, the court officers reacted, too, several of them crowding in on Ramseur, which produced a stir in the courtroom.

Ramseur mutely refused to answer any more questions, other than to tell Slotnick, "You paid Gladys Richardson" and tell Crane, "Take me back, Judge. I'm tired of this bullshit." Crane gave him five contempt citations and had him removed from the courtroom. The prosecution finally rested, and Ramseur would later have six months added to his prison sentence.

After court adjourned for the day, Slotnick swung into action. Making his regular appearance before the press outside, he insisted that Ramseur "took off his shoe and was about to throw it at me. If he had a gun he would have shot me... The James

Ramseur of December 22, 1984...is the same James Ramseur the jury saw today."

The next day, the *New York Post* ran a cover story: GOETZ TRIAL EXPLODES; RAGING RAMSEUR; GUARDS SWOOP ON BERSERK WITNESS. According to the *Post,* Ramseur had removed his black loafer with both hands. "Then he glowered directly at Slotnick as some jurors among the eight men and four women appeared frightened and nervously shifted their weight and seemed to move slightly backwards in their chairs. In an instant, Ramseur started to pivot in the witness box and his shoe was waist high as he prepared to hurl it towards the well of the court. At that moment, three of the seven armed and uniformed court officers who had been hovering near Ramseur during his testimony—and during his sullen silences—pounced from behind and alongside him. He was forced to put his shoe back on."

Even the *New York Times* reported that Ramseur "almost hurled his shoe across the courtroom at the defense attorney," having reached down "in a jerky, nervous movement," scratched his right foot, and put his shoe back on. A few days later, Slotnick was still talking about it: "I'm happy he didn't throw the shoe at me," Slotnick said. "He's an angry, frustrated individual. He's a street urchin. He's a liar, and he broke under cross-examination."

When juror Mark Lesly asked a court officer what happened, the officer told him that Ramseur had merely reached down to scratch his foot. Justice Crane, too, would later say that the incident was much ado about nothing. Crane was sitting right next to Ramseur, and Ramseur simply "had his legs crossed and was adjusting his loafer." But facts were secondary; Slotnick had effectively defined for the jury and the public how to interpret what Ramseur had done.

Because Slotnick had been denied the opportunity to finish his cross-examination of the witness, Justice Crane instructed the jury that all Ramseur's testimony was to be stricken from the record and disregarded. But the damage had been done. As far as Slotnick was concerned, it was the perfect ending to the prosecution's case, with the images fresh in the jury's mind of Ramseur as thug. The jury feared Ramseur, which was exactly what Slotnick wanted.

Well after the trial was over, in the spring of 1989, Slotnick received an envelope in the mail from the Attica Correctional Facility, postmarked March 28, and addressed to "B. Slotnick."

Inside, written in red block-capital letters, was a letter from "J. Ramseur."

It read: "From Mr. Rambunctious. I'd like to let you know that it was very dirty, for a so called good lawyer as yourself to use those charges that you know I didn't do to win that case. Your not a real winner and your paranoid, schizophrenic, hypochondriac client's uncle Tom puppet acted as a real agent provocateur! Got that girl thinking she's going to win money from the city in twist my freedom. If you don't know about them framing me you don't use what you don't know about. Or is it anything to win. Ramseur."

Slotnick's assistant filed the letter away in a folder titled "Not Nice Mail."

On December 22, 2011, the twenty-seventh anniversary of the Goetz shooting, James Ramseur would kill himself in a motel room in the Bronx.

CHAPTER 77

Starting at 8:30 a.m. on Thursday, May 22, 1987, the second day of the defense's presentation of its case, Slotnick and Frank King spent an hour marking off the floor in the well of the courtroom with white masking tape, replicating the dimensions of the rear portion of an R22 subway car. The defense and prosecution tables were both moved slightly to accommodate the diagram, which Justice Crane entered into evidence, saying it should remain in place until the trial was over.

Slotnick was feeling uplifted. As soon as the prosecution rested, Mark Baker had filed a motion to dismiss the case, focusing on the "rapid succession" of Goetz's gunshots. Crane had denied the motion, but based on its arguments, Slotnick now saw a skeleton for his summation.

Slotnick's first witnesses, as he'd begun presenting the defense's case, included a police officer who'd assisted Goetz when he was mugged years earlier and the orthopedist who'd treated Goetz for the knee injury sustained in the mugging. Slotnick also called a stenographer who'd documented Troy Canty's grand jury testimony (to try to show inconsistencies in Canty's various accounts of what happened) and the investigator who'd secretly recorded Andrea Reid—and who could buttress Slotnick's contention that Reid had said things to him that she denied in her courtroom testimony.

Now Slotnick asked Crane to let him bring four "props"—young men—into the courtroom to enact his next witness's testimony. Normally, court officers would be used in such a demonstration, but Slotnick, over Waples's angry objections, argued that these kids were the exact heights of the kids who'd surrounded Goetz and were here and ready and would save time. Crane allowed it.

Slotnick then pointed to the young men, who were standing at the back of the courtroom. In casting his reenactment, Slotnick had left nothing to chance. The four youths were African American Guardian Angels provided by Curtis Sliwa, the organization's founder and a vocal Goetz proponent. Slotnick had asked Sliwa to send him kids who looked intimidating, specifying that they should dress in teenage street garb.

The stated point of the exercise was to illustrate testimony by Joseph Quirk, a ballistics expert. As Quirk testified, Frank King stood in front of the jury box. With a giant gut, the ruddy face of a drinker, and the seen-it-all eyes of a disgraced big-city detective, King bore only one physical similarity to Bernhard Goetz—both men were white. Right now, though, in Justice Crane's courtroom, King was playing Goetz. He was surrounded by the four large young Black men in the small taped-off rectangle, which was designed to show just how cramped a space the shooting had occurred in. As Quirk spoke, the youths arranged themselves around King in the precise formation that was being testified to.

Of course, Slotnick's real game, as it had been with Ramseur, was to re-create in the courtroom what it had been like to be Goetz on that day. Slotnick wanted to imprint upon the jurors—vividly and scarily—a sense memory of what Goetz had experienced. The scenario laid out by Quirk matched the ballistics: the four young men were surrounding Goetz, facing him, when he began to shoot. He fired the bullets in quick succession, leaving the young men time only to flinch their bodies away. Quirk's testimony about Allen and Cabey directly refuted the prosecution theory. In the Waples version, Allen had been running away when Goetz shot him in the back, and Cabey had been sitting when Goetz, after missing him with the fourth bullet, moved directly in front of him and fired the fifth bullet into him, severing his spine.

The most serious charges against Goetz hinged on these details. Waples had argued that there was a pause between the fourth and fifth bullets, indicating premeditation before the most damaging shot, and that fleeing or sitting victims under-mined Goetz's claim to have felt threatened. But Quirk testified that Allen had been standing near Goetz and reflexively ducked, accounting for the bullet wound in his back. Quirk insisted that Cabey had also been standing in front of Goetz and that he'd been hit by the fourth bullet, which had pushed him back into the seat. The fifth bullet had missed altogether.

When Waples rose to cross-examine Quirk, the prosecutor was openly hostile, his hands trembling. Quirk had been so defini-tive about what transpired—there was *no way* the kids were shot in the back or while running away, and *no way* that Cabey was sitting when shot—that Waples explicitly suggested, in questioning Quirk, that the witness was beholden to Slotnick for work and willing to say whatever the lawyer needed him to say.

Then Waples said, "You've heard the phrase, 'Garbage in, garbage out'?" Quirk acknowledged that he had. Waples elaborated, for the benefit of the jury, that he meant that a conclusion based on faulty data would inevitably itself be faulty, and Quirk again agreed with him. Slotnick wasn't entirely sure where this was going, but he didn't like it. He started interrupting with objections, trying to knock Waples off his stride.

Waples showed Quirk some photographs of Barry Allen's torso. The bullet wound to Allen's back, far from being in the location Quirk had based his testimony on, was in the center of the back, and the scar on Allen's front left shoulder was from surgery to remove a bullet fragment. Contrary to what Quirk had so confidently asserted on direct examination, the wounds suggested a trajectory from back to front rather than front to back. Quirk acknowledged that, based on these photographs, the scenario he'd presented was physically impossible.

It seemed like Waples had just obliterated any gains Slotnick had made with his witness, but Slotnick leaped to his feet and demanded a sidebar. Quirk had based his testimony on information provided by the prosecution's own medical experts; Waples couldn't now introduce new evidence undermining that. Slotnick called for a mistrial.

"I will not be sandbagged at this point," he said.

"This is outrageous," Waples said.

"There is no such [thing as] trial by ambush in this state," Slotnick said.

"This is ridiculous," Waples said. "*This* is the ambush."

They were getting loud now, and Crane said, "Gentlemen, take it easy."

The air in the courtroom was warm, and Crane suggested that everyone was becoming "hot under the collar." He decided to adjourn for the day.

CHAPTER 78

When the trial resumed, another decision by Justice Crane broke Barry Slotnick's way. The judge struck from the record the questions Greg Waples had asked ballistics expert Joseph Quirk using his new medical facts. What remained of Quirk's testimony about Barry Allen was helpful to Goetz.

The courtroom reenactment had been vivid. It was one thing for the jury to hear a description of what happened. But to see it in the flesh, even if it was hypothetical and based on facts that were in dispute, lingered in the mind and made an impression. The jurors, a newspaper said, were "mesmerized" by the show Slotnick had put on, and the headline NIGHTMARE REPLAYED was splashed across the front page of the *Daily News*.

When Slotnick's next witness testified, it became clear that Waples was catching on to the power of Slotnick's theatrics. Dr. Dominick DiMaio, a former chief medical examiner of New York City who'd performed more than twenty thousand autopsies over the course of his career, testified that based on the medical records, none of the youths could have been shot in the back and that Darrell Cabey must have been standing when he was shot. But this time around, Slotnick was forced to use court officers as his props, because Waples had successfully protested the use of the Guardian Angels as unnecessary and prejudicial.

And when it was time for Waples to cross-examine DiMaio, the prosecutor had an X-ray viewing device wheeled into the courtroom to provide visuals as he tried to get DiMaio to admit that his testimony, which he'd expressed in absolutes, wasn't quite so black and white.

"Doctor, you are making certain assumptions about the way people run, right?"

"It's not an assumption, it's a practicality," DiMaio said. "It's an obvious fact. Nobody runs sideways."

No matter what Waples asked DiMaio, the former medical examiner stuck to his story. Finally, with nowhere else to go in his questioning, Waples tried to suggest that DiMaio had resigned under a cloud after a 1976 autopsy screwup.

"Is it not a fact, sir, that you were forced into retirement because—"

"Go ahead; say what you want to say."

"Because a mayoral committee...appointed to oversee the office that you were running determined that your administration was not satisfactory?"

"You are wrong. What the committee insisted was that at sixty-five I retire, and I did."

On May 26, after a four-day break for Memorial Day weekend, Slotnick called police officer Peter Smith to the stand. Smith had been one of the first cops on the scene of the shooting. Smith testified that Troy Canty, lying on the floor of the subway car, told him, "We were going to rob him, but he shot us first." After just three minutes of direct testimony, Slotnick was done.

Waples, cross-examining Smith, tried to discredit him as an inexperienced cop who'd been under stress and repeatedly asked whether Smith might have misheard, misunderstood, or misremembered Canty's exact words. Smith stuck to his story, but Waples noted that Smith hadn't recorded Canty's remark in his logbook or mentioned it to detectives at the scene or told any detectives at all about it for another year. Smith responded that he'd told Detective Mike Clark on the afternoon of the shooting that he had a statement and that Clark had said, "Don't worry about it. I will get back to you." Clark got back to him eight months later. After half a day of cross-examination, Waples wasn't yet finished with Smith when the trial adjourned that evening.

Stuart Slotnick, still in high school, had become an obsessive recorder of TV news items that concerned his dad's cases. That night, channel 4 aired an interview tape it had unearthed in which Smith, right after the shooting, spoke briefly to one of the station's reporters.

When his dad got home that night, Stuart told him about it, and they sat and watched the recording together. The news item showed Smith sitting in his squad car outside the entrance to the Chambers Street subway station, being interviewed by the reporter. "They said they were involved in—they said they were just fooling around with the guy," Smith said, "so I would assume that that would be possibly harassment; I'm not sure; it's hard to say; it all happened so quickly."

"Play that back," Barry Slotnick said to his son.

Stuart rewound the tape, and they watched it again.

"You see that?" Barry said.

He had a knowing look. Smith's TV sound bite seemed to contradict what he'd just testified to, and Slotnick knew that Waples would try to exploit it the next day. But watching the tape, Slotnick and his son could see and hear a slight pause—a stutter step—at the point where Smith had changed course. He had started to say one thing ("They said they were involved in"), then pivoted and said another ("they said they were just fooling around with the guy").

"He decided, right there," Barry told Stuart, "he wasn't going to talk to the press about what Canty had said."

Sure enough, the next day, Waples asked the judge for permission to reopen cross-examination. Slotnick objected, and the judge overruled him. Slotnick then asked the judge to let him introduce a polygraph exam Smith had taken and passed, and Justice Crane denied the motion.

When Waples resumed his cross-examination, Smith said that his testimony was the truth but that what he'd said to the reporter had been "somewhat" of a lie. He had felt that he shouldn't reveal an "important statement" to the media before he'd told a superior about it. Slotnick knew that damage had been done to Smith's credibility, but he had high hopes for his next witness.

That afternoon, Slotnick called to the stand Dr. Bernard Yudowitz, a neuropsychiatrist who'd worked with cops who discharged firearms under stressful circumstances. Yudowitz testified about the autonomic nervous system, the fight-or-flight mechanism that could switch a person into "automatic pilot" mode. Goetz, in his confessions, had spoken of being overwhelmed by adrenaline, so Yudowitz's testimony supported the defense theory that Goetz continued shooting even after the kids were no longer a threat because he was in a trauma-induced state. It explained why Goetz might have fantasized what happened, morphing a legitimate act of self-defense into a Charles Bronson vigilante scenario by inventing in his memory a pause between bullets and the operatic, premeditated "You don't look so bad; here's another." Yudowitz provided a scientific underpinning for Slotnick's big argument—that the jurors should distrust Goetz's confession.

CHAPTER 79

Rush hour was over, but a New Yorker who happened to find himself in an unused portion of the Chambers Street subway station on the morning of Friday, May 29, 1987, would have seen an odd sight. There, eight cars were attached to an engine idling on a platform that was normally empty. Inside the cars, men and women in regular attire moved around, taking turns sitting and standing and changing positions, seeming to playact, while a small group of men in suits silently observed and a woman sitting on one of the benches pecked at what looked like a small typewriter on her lap. Reporters and photographers stood on the platform, pressing their faces against the car's glass, taking pictures and jotting notes. It was like stumbling upon a bizarre museum exhibit, a live diorama titled *The Subway People*.

In Slotnick's continuing campaign to make the jury see, hear, feel, and smell what Goetz had seen, heard, felt, and smelled, the lawyer had been pushing, in motions outside the jury's presence, for Justice Crane to let the jury visit an actual subway car like the one in which the shooting had occurred. Slotnick wanted the jury to experience how small an area it was and to feel Goetz's cramped sense of "confinement." Waples had consistently argued that such a trip was simply unnecessary: the jurors had already seen sketches and photos, and anyway, a jury of New Yorkers surely had experience with the inside of a subway car.

"Quite a bit more experience than Mr. Slotnick has," Waples added in a jab.

Slotnick, however, had argued that the Goetz car, the R22, was an older, more cramped model that was being phased out—one that 1987 straphangers might be less familiar with. Goetz's feeling of being confined and surrounded was essential to his defense, and the subway car was "the most important piece of evidence in this case."

Car 7657 itself had since been gutted and repurposed as a work train, but an identical model was available to look at, and Crane visited it with the lawyers in advance. He was surprised by some of the distances and angles, and not necessarily in Goetz's favor. Seeing the car from the inside, Crane realized that the dent in the conductor's cab's steel panel that had been made by the errant bullet was much lower than he'd envisioned, supporting the prosecution's contention that Goetz had fired at someone who was sitting down. Crane agreed to a visit by jurors under the condition that no one would speak to them while they were in the subway car. They would inspect it silently.

While the stenographer sat on a gray bench typing, the jurors started to move around, trying out various positions. With the media mobbing the car on the outside, one juror would later write, "We . . . felt like fish in an aquarium."

After five minutes, Crane directed that the conductor move the train away from the media, and the train pulled south out of the station so that the jurors could continue their inspections without distraction. Slotnick, Waples, Crane, Baker, the court officers, and the transit cops walked into the next car, but Slotnick kept an eye on what was going on in the other car. He saw the jurors taking turns in the different roles, with whoever was playing Goetz pointing his finger at jurors who were playing the roles of the youths.

At 11:30 a.m., the train returned to the station, and the jurors were bused back to the courthouse, where Crane adjourned the trial until Monday. Slotnick felt confident that the jurors had seen how trapped Goetz would have felt. How he really had nowhere to go. And why he'd have kept firing out of fear that one or two of the kids would have time to counterattack.

On June 2, Slotnick called his tenth and final witness, former transit detective Charles Penelton, who testified that he'd interviewed Troy Canty in the hospital and that Canty had told him, "We went over and stood around the white guy," targeting him because he "looked soft."

Penelton's testimony was being admitted only to counter Canty's testimony rather than as evidence itself. And Waples, cross-examining the detective, suggested that Canty had been heavily sedated, so anything he'd said couldn't be trusted. But of course, a jury couldn't unhear things, and Slotnick thought that Penelton's testimony put a nice finishing touch on the defense case. It came at an opportune moment, too, since Slotnick's voice was beginning to go. As Penelton exited the witness box, Slotnick said, in a reedy voice: "The defense rests."

Waples was allowed to put on rebuttal witnesses at this point, and he called two medical experts in an attempt to take back the ground Slotnick had won through his expert witnesses. Dr. Charles Hirsch, chief medical examiner of Suffolk County on Long Island, testified that DiMaio's statement that it was "impossible" that Cabey had been seated when shot was "completely false." Waples presented a bosomy cloth-covered mannequin torso as a stand-in for Cabey ("Your Honor, this is not anatomically correct," Waples acknowledged as spectators laughed), and Hirsch stuck a wooden spear through it to show the path of the bullet.

When Slotnick cross-examined the witness, Hirsch's body language was odd. He did not make eye contact with Slotnick but stared at the jury during questioning, which had an effect that was both haughty and timid.

"Could you speak to me, if you could?" Slotnick asked.

"I prefer to speak to the jury, sir."

Slotnick made much of the fact that Hirsch was from Suffolk County, as if Waples had had to expand his search area to find a medical examiner who'd testify in a way that suited the prosecution case, but ultimately, Slotnick was counting on the burden of proof to save Goetz. It wasn't enough for Waples to undercut the authority of the defense witnesses. They had still muddied Waples's evidence, and mud—i.e., doubt—would always work in Slotnick's favor.

CHAPTER 80

Slotnick was preparing his summation for *Goetz* at the worktable in his basement, obsessively tabbing transcript pages, scrawling ideas with a Sharpie on a legal pad, and highlighting passages from his cross-examinations.

In a closing argument, Slotnick had to do several things. He had to recap six weeks of testimony. There had been forty-five witnesses and more than 150 exhibits. He had to cover each of the thirteen counts in the indictment. He had to try to frame or reframe the testimony of every witness who'd been helpful or harmful to Goetz. He had to hammer home his theme and certain crucial points and arguments.

Above all, Slotnick needed to connect with the jury and hold their attention. (In Frank King's trial, Slotnick had noticed that a woman juror was wearing a piece of jewelry with a foreign-language inscription on it, and he'd had it translated. It was an expression of affection, and Slotnick had incorporated it in his closing argument.) Slotnick was always making eye contact during his summations with one or another of the jurors. He thought it better to say too much than too little, but if the jurors looked tired, he believed in stopping right there.

Often, Slotnick would include an element of surprise in his summation. Years earlier, he had represented a man named Larry Stillwell in a drug case. The prosecution was relying heavily on a taped call police had set up in which one of their informants called Stillwell. On the tape, Stillwell was heard saying, "Who is this? I don't know who you are," which the police believed proved consciousness of guilt. When Slotnick had asked Stillwell about it, though, and shown him the phone number connected with the taped call, Stillwell had said, "I don't know whose number that is, but it isn't mine." When Slotnick was cross-examining the informant, he had him confirm that the number was the number he had called. Slotnick was laying a trap, which he wouldn't spring until later. Then, during his summation, Slotnick produced telephone records showing that the police had had the informant call a wrong number, belonging to a different Larry Stillwell. "Look," he told the jury, "their whole case is resting on this call with someone who wasn't even my client." Stillwell was acquitted.

Slotnick also liked to cite page numbers in his summations, which was a bit of a trick. Lawyers often tried to create an aura of doubt around an opponent's closing argument by objecting and claiming that the other side was mischaracterizing what a witness had said. Slotnick, who had binders full of relevant pages tabbed, was always prepared to shut down these maneuvers. He'd say, "But don't take my word for it or theirs. You can have it read back to you." Then he'd furrow his brow and thumb through one of his binders and say, "From the transcript, page..." After reading the text, confirming the accuracy of what he'd said, Slotnick, like a parent disappointed by his child, would look first at his opponent and then at the jury, as if to share with them a moment of mutual moral disapproval of the opponent's tactics.

And only in his summation would Slotnick make obvious what he had been up to in his cross-examinations, which he often conducted in such a way as to obscure which of the nuggets he was gleaning were most precious. Only in the closing did the precise argument by which he hoped to convince the jury resolve into focus. "Barry's not a linear thinker at all," his ex-clerk Jay Breakstone says. "He'd get these pearls, drop them in his bag, then on summation—my God, he'd have three strands of beautiful Mikimotos. It was diabolical."

CHAPTER 81

On the morning of Wednesday, June 10, 1987, Slotnick arrived to court early, wearing a black three-piece suit, a white shirt, and a tie. He checked the microphone, which he planned to detach from its stand so that as he moved around he wouldn't have to speak any louder than necessary. He arrayed several boxes of Luden's cough drops, in various flavors, on the defense table, within easy reach.

It was the most important day of the most important case of his life. All his decisions in the trial had been geared to this moment. In the past several weeks, Slotnick had been buttonholing people to help him road test his *Goetz* summation, trying out various arguments. Donna, as usual, had weighed in with tweaks and word changes. Raoul Felder, New York's most famous divorce lawyer, had sent a letter offering unsolicited suggestions for Slotnick's big speech.

The summation was Slotnick's opportunity to weave everything the jurors had heard—the conflicting and confusing and complex testimony—into a coherent story that could win hearts and minds. Slotnick believed the summation was the key part of a trial. An inspiring summation could work a miracle. A lame one could lose a case.

But Barry Slotnick had laryngitis. It had gotten so bad that he could barely talk. If he couldn't complete his summation, the judge would tell him to step aside and have Mark Baker finish it. But this was Slotnick's moment, and he felt almost a moral imperative to deliver the closing himself.

During the previous week, while the trial was on hiatus, Slotnick had spoken with Elizabeth Dixon, a Broadway vocal coach who'd worked with Katharine Hepburn, Margaret Thatcher, and Michael Douglas, about ways to make it through his closing without losing his voice entirely. She gave him exercises, which she called tonal drills, to do.

Slotnick had read phrases she gave him to say out loud.

"Wandering winds were wistfully playing o'er the meadow."

She told him to repeat "Oo-*a*, oo-*aw*, oo-*ah*, oo-*oh*" several times.

Dixon also advised him to avoid whispering, which would actually make his voice worse, so all week with his family, when Slotnick spoke at all it was in a low but regular voice. He drank mug after mug of hot water with honey.

Slotnick considered the upside of his ailment: his hoarseness might humanize him with the jury.

"I warn you now," Slotnick told the Goetz jury when he began speaking at 10:35 a.m. "It will be long. It will be tedious. Hopefully it will be not that educational because you will have seen it, but I must do it." He reminded the jurors that Waples had framed his case around the confession: "The most unreliable source in the world, the statement of Bernhard Goetz...Well, that is unreliable and that is untrustworthy and that is not what people are convicted of in this country." Slotnick reminded the jurors of the promises he'd made in his opening, including that he'd remind them of what Waples had said in his own opening.

"I apologize for hanging on to the mike," Slotnick said, milking his laryngitis. "It is either that or my voice goes."

"Mr. Waples indicated to you that there was another shot—that same evidence he said, at page 4762, 'We will show beyond the slightest shadow of a doubt that when the defendant fired the second of these shots at Cabey, Darrell Cabey was sitting down in the subway seat.'"

Page 4762. It was the first of many times in his closing that Slotnick would refer to a specific page in the ten-thousand-page trial transcript. If his opening had been intentionally vague, his summation would be hyperspecific. All the evidence was in. Later, when the jury deliberated, he didn't want any of their requests for "the testimony Slotnick referenced" to require a decision by the judge about exactly what it was they wanted to see.

Now Slotnick walked around the courtroom with his "curious rocking gait, his arms held slightly out from his sides as if his shirt was too starched," as a juror later described it. He spoke without notes, pausing frequently to take a sip of water. While Slotnick performed, Bernhard Goetz doodled and whispered to paralegal Gillian Coulter.

Slotnick was going to debunk Goetz's own confession and Christopher Boucher's corroboration of it. He pointed out that

Boucher's account was different from every other witness's. He suggested that Boucher, his denials notwithstanding, had been traumatized, which explained his "impossible" version of events. "Am I undermining my client? The answer is no, and I'll tell you why." Slotnick talked about Dr. Bernard Yudowitz and the phenomenon of automatic pilot. He talked about the nine days between the shooting and Goetz's surrender in New Hampshire. "[Goetz] knew about as much about Ramseur and his bullet wound as you all before you came in here." Waples "framed his case around post-traumatic statements."

Slotnick believed that a summation should have a clear point, and the point of this one was fear. He no longer spent much time talking about how awful the four kids were. The jury had seen that for themselves, and Slotnick kept the four photos of the youths on their easels throughout his summation. Instead, Slotnick wove in snippets of witness testimony to support the idea that Goetz had reasonably been afraid, pointing especially to Andrea Reid's testimony—not only because she said she'd been afraid but also because, as Slotnick painted it, she was so afraid of Darrell Cabey's mother that she'd essentially thrown her chances of becoming a police officer out the window by perjuring herself. She was "a very sad witness," Slotnick said. "She came here and lied, and we will forgive her for that and so will everybody because we understand why she did it."

"Thank God for Bernhard Goetz" that Slotnick's investigator had recorded Andrea Reid, Slotnick said, because otherwise he wouldn't be able to prove she'd lied. He reminded the jury of her comment to her husband that "they got what they deserved," hoping the jury would see in Andrea Reid the reaction they themselves might have had—a reasonable one, the one Goetz had had.

Slotnick liked to have a mantra in his closings. If he was careful not to overstate it, it could be an effective tactic in selling a theory. Now the phrase he repeated over and over was "rapid succession." He was drilling it into jurors' heads: *Boom. Boom. Boom. Boom. Boom.* Before the closing was done, Slotnick would repeat the phrase "rapid succession" forty-six times, or an average of once every six minutes. In a close second place, he would say the words *surrounded* and *surrounding* forty-one times, or an average of once every seven minutes.

Occasionally, Slotnick's summation felt like a race to see which would be exhausted first: his vocal cords or the jurors' patience. Slotnick considered the duration of some of his closings almost boastworthy. Frank King, in singing his boss's praises, would talk about the impassioned, thirteen-hour summation Slotnick gave in his own case.

But some observers at the Goetz trial found Slotnick's summation tedious, long-winded, and repetitive, as if he were trying to bore the jury into acquitting his client. Jurors fidgeted and yawned. Slotnick asked for a break.

"You will bring this tragedy to an end, because the true tragedy, and I ask you to look at it in its proper perspective, is Bernhard Goetz's tragedy," Slotnick said after his closing resumed. "Let us not be shanghaied by the rhetoric of an assistant district attorney who tells you not to be swayed by rowdy behavior that was an annoyance to more gentle sensibilities."

"Louder, Mr. Slotnick. The jurors can't hear you," Justice Crane said.

Slotnick tried to raise his voice but after another minute said, "Shall we take our lunch break now, Your Honor?"

At first, the judge said it was too early for lunch, allowing

Slotnick another five-minute break instead, but then he relented and said the trial would adjourn until 2:00 p.m. Over lunch, Slotnick rested his voice, drinking water and popping cough drops and jotting notes to his team.

At 2:00 p.m., the jurors came back in, and Slotnick resumed his closing. "I will be very quick," he lied.

After talking about Andrea Reid again, Slotnick asked for another break. It was his third and would be, he said, his last. This time, when his closing resumed, he was practically whispering, and the judge asked him to use the microphone. Slotnick pressed it to his lips and loomed over the jury, pointing at the easel photos.

"Now I can't come back; it is over," Slotnick said as he neared an end. "They came in here without a case. Please let him walk out without a conviction." He reminded the jury that he had no burden to prove Goetz's innocence; Waples had the burden of proving him guilty. Slotnick noted that once he finished his summation and Waples started his, Slotnick wouldn't have a chance to address the jury again. And then, although he believed it was important to be humble in one's closing, Slotnick croaked, "I ask you to do one thing when he raises a point, strikes a chord. Please say, 'What would Slotnick say about that?'"

Waples appeared to stifle a laugh.

Finally, at 4:35 p.m., having said everything he wanted to in a closing that had lasted six hours, Slotnick said, "Providence has sent me a message. My voice is about gone."

And he rested.

CHAPTER 82

Mr. Slotnick is many things," Gregory Waples told the jury, "including an ingenious and resourceful lawyer, but he isn't an alchemist. He can't spin gold from straw, nor can he transmute a totally sadistic, hateful attempt to murder into a perfectly legitimate and blameless act of self-defense."

It was the next day, and Waples had begun his closing argument at 8:30 a.m. To the end, he was staying in character, wearing a rumpled gray suit with a loosely tucked-in blue button-down shirt, his backpack on the prosecution table nearby. His father had flown in, as he had for Waples's opening, to see his son's closing argument.

Slotnick hated sitting through these. He hated that under New York State rules, the prosecutor's words would be the last ones the jury heard. His own role in the trial was nearly done, and whatever control he had previously been able to exercise—through cross-examination, and then through the defense case—was reduced to an occasional objection. Slotnick would at least take advantage of those. He had recovered enough of his voice to repeatedly interrupt Waples with objections, such as to his "obvious appeal to the jury's emotions."

But superficially, the argument Waples was making seemed more compelling than the defense case. The jury was visibly more alert than they had been during Slotnick's marathon.

Whereas the defense case had sharpened over the course of the trial into an almost monomaniacal focus on "rapid succession," the prosecution case remained essentially the same as it had been at the opening. Waples again relied heavily on Goetz's confessions, cherry-picking those pieces of other witnesses' testimony that corroborated them. He argued that Slotnick was asking the jury to hold Goetz above the law, to say that four hoodlums were less deserving of legal protection than Goetz was. Waples framed the verdict as a choice for the jury between judging with their hearts or their heads. He had heard the same conflicting testimony everyone else had and seen the same unimpressive testimony by Canty and Ramseur. He was clearly hanging his whole case on Cabey and the idea that he'd been shot sitting down. He said that even if the jury found no crime with regard to Canty, Ramseur, or Allen, it had to convict Goetz on Cabey.

Then Waples started talking about the kids as merely rambunctious, suggesting that anyone who couldn't deal with such "petty annoyances" should "pack his bags" and leave New York. Slotnick and Baker looked at each other. They were both thinking the same thing. Waples was from the land of corn and cows. Slotnick, from the Bronx, and Baker, from Long Island, knew New York, and they knew New Yorkers. The idea that what Goetz had experienced was merely a "petty annoyance," and that he should love it or leave it and docilely accept the city's flaws as unchangeable, offended them, and they knew it would offend the jurors, too. In fact, one of the jurors, Michael Axelrod, audibly said: "This guy is insulting my intelligence."

Before Waples sat down, he used some showmanship of his own. He brought out Darrell Cabey's jacket, announcing that he would prove that Cabey must have been sitting down when he was shot. He held the jacket up before the jury, pointing out two bullet holes. He said that one of the holes, with blood around it, was made by the bullet that paralyzed Cabey.

Waples suddenly took off his own jacket and put on Cabey's.

He explained that because of the position of the bloodless hole on the jacket relative to the position of the dent in the conductor's cab, the bloodless hole had to have been made by the fourth shot, while Cabey was standing. Meaning that the fifth shot—the one Waples was arguing had been premeditated and fired while Cabey was sitting down—was the one that paralyzed Cabey.

Four hours after Waples had begun, he sat down.

Slotnick then stood and asked the judge to let him present rebuttal witnesses of his own, or a resummation, on the question of Cabey's jacket, arguing that Waples had improperly introduced it for the first time during his summation. Justice Crane denied the request.

As Slotnick returned to his seat, he passed ADA Robert Pitler, who headed up the DA's appellate bureau and was sitting among the press.

"We beat your ass," Pitler said. "You were outfoxed."

"No, no," Slotnick replied. "Dirty pool."

Despite his outward confidence, Slotnick was far from certain about what the jury was thinking.

CHAPTER 83

Barry Slotnick's agony began on Friday, June 12, at 1:20 p.m. Before the jury would begin its deliberations, Justice Crane gave them two and a half hours of instructions. Slotnick had skirmished with Greg Waples, behind the scenes, over precisely what Crane would tell the jurors. Crane had agreed, among other things, to tell the jury that it could draw a negative inference from the failure of Barry Allen to appear as a witness. And he agreed with Slotnick's objection about the show-and-tell with Darrell Cabey's jacket during Waples's summation, instructing the jurors that they shouldn't speculate about how many shots hit the jacket if there had been no trial testimony about it. Waples, angry, stood and said, "That was the most one-sided, unwarranted instruction I've ever heard. I cannot fathom how Your Honor can give that instruction in good conscience."

The topic Crane spent more time on than any other, though, was the precise definition of self-defense and the elements of the law of justification. Crane had intended to say that if the jury found Bernhard Goetz guilty beyond a reasonable doubt, they "must convict"; after a sidebar in which Mark Baker vigorously pressed his case, Crane had agreed to say only that the jury "may convict." It was a subtle distinction, but one that hinted to the jury that it had the power to "nullify" the law—essentially ignore it if they felt that the law as it existed was unfair to Goetz. Finally, Crane turned over the case to the jurors so they could begin their deliberations and Slotnick's suspenseful anxiety could kick into overdrive.

The pressure of waiting for a verdict is hard for outsiders to understand. After two and a half years of work and six and a half weeks of sustained performance, Slotnick had to wait an unknown length of time to hear in an instant the only judgment of his work that mattered. What hinged on that moment wasn't simply a salve or blow to his ego or a thumbs-up or thumbs-down that could affect his reputation and his business. What happened would also determine whether a man who'd entrusted his liberty and, in many ways, his life to Slotnick would go free or go to prison—for years.

In this case, which had grown into something much larger than itself, Slotnick believed that if he lost, he would also be letting down "the good people of New York and all over the world."

During the trial, a reporter had asked him about "your client." Slotnick had snapped, "Don't talk to me about my client. I have no client. The people of the state of New York are my client."

As the jury began to deliberate, Slotnick found it hard to work on anything else, and he waited in the courtroom with his team and Goetz, ready in case the jury came back with a question or a decision. Goetz mostly sat at the defense table, his head bent over an electrical-engineering schematic that confounded Baker, while Slotnick kept moving around, animated by nervous energy. He alternately wandered the hallways, kibitzed with reporters, leaned back in his chair, and called in to his office. He took off his suit jacket. He put it back on. He chewed his paper clips. He smoked his cigarettes.

Every time the jury sent out a request, Slotnick tried to stifle the urge to speculate what it meant, but invariably he and Frank King and Mark Baker and Gillian Coulter would try to read the tea leaves. Around 3:30 p.m. on Saturday, the jury sent out two notes. One asked for the scale drawing of the subway car that had been submitted as evidence by Waples as well as the plastic overlays on which various witnesses had marked their versions of where they and others had been positioned in the car. The other requested that the law concerning the assault and attempted murder charges, including "all the justification tests," be read back to them.

Clearly, the jury was struggling with the justification question. Struggle meant uncertainty. Uncertainty meant lack of clarity, which meant the presence of doubt. Doubt was good for the defense. While an acquittal would be best, a hung jury would also be good for Goetz. Defense lawyers were always better off trying a case twice. With all the evidence on the table, a defendant went into the second trial in a much stronger position. But what if the struggle meant something else? Maybe all the jurors were leaning toward a conviction and they just needed to persuade one holdout.

Slotnick and Baker moved for the judge to change his description of the law of justification, arguing that his previous

inclusion of an example of the way Goetz might have dees-
calated the situation—by simply "drawing and displaying his
weapon"—was prejudicial and that the instructions should also
specifically mention defense witness Dr. Bernard Yudowitz's
theory of automatic pilot in traumatized shooting situations.
This was an unusual request, and Waples objected, but Slotnick
and Baker were more aggressive in making their case, and
Crane "capitulated," as he'd later say.

The jury filed back into the courtroom, where the court
reporter spent an hour rereading the requested law, this time
with a few changes. The new instructions mentioned Yudowitz
by name, and although they didn't include the words *automatic pilot,* they did refer to Yudowitz's testimony about "the
autonomic nervous system." And this time, the explanation of
the law's requirement that a person facing a lethal threat must
retreat, if it's possible to safely do so, excluded the "drawing
and displaying his weapon" example. The new instructions
were more favorable to the defense, enlarging the circumstances
under which Goetz should be considered to have been justified
in his actions. Slotnick felt that they would make it much easier
for the jury to acquit.

Fifteen minutes after the jury filed back out, Slotnick and
Baker interviewed alternate juror Augie Ayala, who had been
been excused by the judge a day earlier for personal reasons
(he couldn't tolerate the isolation of being sequestered). When
he stopped by the courthouse that Saturday afternoon, Slotnick
and Baker approached him.

"How are we doing?" Slotnick asked.

"We're doing great," Ayala said, possibly misunderstanding
the question.

The jury had Sunday off.

On Monday afternoon, just before lunch, the jury asked for Darrell Cabey's jacket, the screwdrivers found in it, and a re-reading of testimony about the jacket. During a long argument, Slotnick pressed the judge, over Waples's objections, to expand and reinforce his instructions about the jacket, reminding the jury that they could consider only evidence, not the surprise story about the bullet locations, which Waples had sprung on them in his summation. "Absent the jury being told that the district attorney's version was impossible to prove," Baker said, "I submit to the Court, most respectfully, if there is a conviction on this count it's absolutely reversible error."

The next day, Tuesday, the jury sent out another note. Now they wanted to have Christopher Boucher's testimony about Cabey's position reread. Slotnick didn't know what to make of this, but murmurs rippled through the courtroom, with people audibly speculating that the jury was going to find Goetz guilty of assault or attempted murder.

After the jury filed back out of the courtroom, Slotnick professed confidence, saying, "I feel good that the jurors understand what happened that day." He was bluffing. "The most painful experience that I've had as a lawyer was waiting for the Goetz verdict," Slotnick would say later. "The jury took so long."

Around 4:00 p.m. that day, Robert Hamkalo, the court clerk, informed the judge that, after thirty hours of deliberations, the jury was ready to render its verdict.

CHAPTER 84

G reg Waples walked over to Barry Slotnick and Mark Baker and shook their hands.

Bernie Goetz sat quietly at the defense table, wearing his usual uniform of jeans, a button-down white shirt with unbuttoned sleeves, a black belt, brown lace-up shoes, and glasses. He was reading a book called *Connections,* about links in history.

Then the jury came out. The room was hushed. More than a dozen court officers ringed the room.

At 4:10 p.m., the jury foreman, James Hurley, stood and began to speak.

On the first count, illegal possession of a weapon, Hurley read: "Guilty."

Goetz seemed, in that moment, to visibly deflate.

On the second count, Hurley read: "Not guilty."

Goetz sighed, and his shoulders rose and fell; he repeated this over the next few counts.

"Not guilty."

"Not guilty."

"Not guilty."

At 4:14 p.m., it was time for the final count, the attempted murder of Darrell Cabey. It was the most serious count, with the longest potential prison sentence, and concerned the most controversial of Goetz's actions.

"Not guilty."

Goetz had been acquitted of twelve out of thirteen counts.

A collective *Phew* could be heard in the room. Ten minutes after the jury foreman had begun speaking, he sat down. For the first time, Goetz looked relieved. Frank King gave him a big smile, and Goetz gave a small smile back. Waples stared blankly ahead.

Goetz bent his head toward Baker's. "Can I go home now?" he asked quietly.

Gillian Coulter and Baker both started crying. "On the one hand, I was so relieved," Coulter says, "and legally it was a massive victory. On the other, he did get a conviction that was going to result in him going to jail, so it was still upsetting, and I was a little scared for him. Bernie Goetz going to jail? Really? That may not go that well." She had become close to him and cared for him.

"This has been the most difficult case of our time," Justice Crane said. "Its emotions will last beyond this verdict."

As Crane adjourned the trial until sentencing, Goetz said of the jury, to no one in particular: "How does one ever thank these people?"

Waples came back over to Slotnick and Baker and shook their hands again. "It's been quite an experience," he said.

Reporters ran out of the room to file stories, and radio and

TV stations broke into their regular programming to announce the verdict. Jurors began to line up to get Goetz's autograph on their jury-service certificates, but Goetz had already left through a side door.

Downstairs, Slotnick was surrounded by two hundred reporters and camera operators, and he gave an impromptu news conference. "All he wants right now is to fade into the woodwork," he said of Goetz. "This has been a terrible chapter in his life—he would like to go back to being an anonymous stranger in the streets of New York."

Manhattan DA Robert Morgenthau, in his own news conference at his office, said, "I think it was a fair trial. It was fair to the people, and it was fair to Mr. Goetz... This was a case that had to be tried. The public was entitled."

Goetz and his legal team piled into Slotnick's chauffeured Cadillac (Slotnick called it the Goetzmobile), which raced away, flanked by Guardian Angels and court officers running alongside it as camera operators tried to keep up. Before Slotnick reached his office, calls had already begun to pour in by the dozen, from well-wishers including James Earl Jones; Benny "Uncle Benny" Ong, the Godfather of Chinatown; and John Carneglia.

That night, Slotnick took Donna to Jim McMullen's, a pub on the Upper East Side. When they walked in, the room applauded. With their friend the reporter John Miller, they shared a Champagne toast.

The next morning, the cover of the *New York Post* blared GOETZ OFF THE HOOK and A TRIUMPH FOR COMMON SENSE. Inside, on opposing pages, were a photo of a beaming Barry being kissed by Donna over the word WINNER and a photo of a taciturn Waples, in profile, over the word LOSER.

For the next several weeks, people in New York and across the country debated the verdict. "The whole city loses," Jimmy Breslin said. "If it wasn't race, what the hell was it?" William Kunstler, the prominent left-wing lawyer who was representing Darrell Cabey in his civil suit, called it "an absolute disgrace. It is open season on black males." The *New York Times* published an article headlined BLACKS SEE GOETZ VERDICT AS BLOW TO RACE RELATIONS. Newspapers reported that two of the jurors, James Mosely and Diana Serpe, had begun dating each other.

For a certain set of New Yorkers, Slotnick's victory in the Goetz case made Slotnick himself a hero. To people who were tired of feeling scared in the city, questions of Goetz's guilt or innocence took a back seat to the feelings his acquittal channeled. The Goetz case would enter the history books, changing the standard on self-defense in New York from a subjective idea of what was reasonable to a more objective one. It's a case that's still taught in law schools. "To a great extent," Slotnick says, "it made my career. Everything changed. This was the most widely known case ever."

Slotnick started making the monthly payment on Baker's leased 1987 Isuzu Trooper.

Three weeks later, Slotnick was attacked by the masked man with a baseball bat.

PART SEVEN

CHAPTER 85

After the attack on Barry Slotnick, police came to the house in Scarsdale and watched it for a couple of days, just in case the culprit decided to make a second pass. Slotnick hired some private security at the house, which suggested that even he suspected the assault might not have been random.

For several weeks, a giant guy named Joe sat sentry in the Slotnick living room, holding a weapon. "He was scary looking," Stuart remembers. "At night I'd come down; he'd be sitting on the couch with a huge gun that looked like a sawed-off shotgun. He was there 24-7."

Condolences poured in to Slotnick. US attorney Rudy Giuliani wrote to offer his help in any investigation and to say that "all of us here at the U.S. Attorney's office know that this will only make you even more tenacious." Slotnick, wearing a cast and beginning physical therapy, looked into whether any of his insurance policies might cover the loss of his Piaget Polo watch.

But his main concern was the mystery of who had done this to him and whether that person still intended him harm.

One day, Slotnick noticed that his car had stopped running. When he had it looked at, the mechanic found that several tubes under the hood had been disconnected. The mechanic asked whether Slotnick knew anyone who might want to sabotage him. Slotnick suspected it was a valet at the garage where he parked. When the same thing happened again, Slotnick found a new garage.

Whoever was to blame for the bat attack, it was understandably distressing to Slotnick's family. Soon afterward, Slotnick started carrying a gun: Donna got one, too, a purse-size Walther PPK, James Bond's weapon of choice. Stuart, then eighteen, also decided he wanted a gun. He got a .38 Smith & Wesson and started going to the shooting range with his parents and cleaning his gun alongside them.

Slotnick would claim that the bat attack had merely been an unfortunate mugging, but that belief, if it was sincere, put him in a distinct minority. At the hospital, New York City's chief of detectives, Robert Colangelo, had said of the attack: "It didn't have the classic indications of a robbery. At this point, we are at a loss for a motive."

Everyone who knew Slotnick had a theory about who was behind the attack and why. Donna thought it was a simple robbery and that Barry had been targeted because of all the Goetz coverage; at least one write-up had specifically mentioned what kind of watch Slotnick wore. Stuart at first thought it might be backlash from the Goetz verdict, given how racially polarizing the case had been, but later decided the attack had been too organized to have stemmed simply from someone's angry impulse.

Most people thought it had something to do with the Mafia. John Gleeson, who'd prosecuted John Gotti alongside Diane Giacalone, thought Slotnick's client John Carneglia was behind it. Bruce Cutler disagreed, because Carneglia's brother happened to love Slotnick. Mark Baker thought it was a message from the Gambino family, angry that Slotnick had moved on so quickly to the Goetz trial. A lot of people thought that it was a message from John Gotti, who'd never liked Slotnick. Bernhard Goetz himself would come to believe it was organized crime–related.

Twenty years later, when an FBI agent named Lindley DeVecchio went on trial for allegedly helping a Mafia informant commit four murders, there'd be testimony that one of his informants, Gregory "the Grim Reaper" Scarpa, had told him, a week after the attack on Slotnick, that it had been ordered by Colombo family boss Carmine "the Snake" Persico, who held some kind of grudge about work Slotnick had done for the family. (But Cutler, for one, is skeptical even of this confession, which he thinks was likely part of a scheme to smear Persico.)

For Donna, the attack was the straw that broke the camel's back. She put her foot down. "I said, you have to transition into clean work. I felt like the tides were changing. Juries wouldn't be as apt to give him a not guilty verdict. He moved into white-collar. And then when he got to Buchanan"—Buchanan Ingersoll & Rooney, the large corporate firm he'd join a few years later—"they discouraged that kind of work ... I just know I felt better when he wasn't trying those cases anymore."

Donna was speeding, with Barry in the passenger seat, when she heard a police siren behind her. She looked in the rearview mirror and saw the dreaded flash of dome lights. Donna pulled over.

The cop asked to see her license and registration. When he recognized the name on it, he looked past Donna to Barry and said, "Oh, Mrs. Slotnick; have a nice day."

Donna did a double take. "You aren't giving me a ticket because he's famous?"

"It's a courtesy," the cop said.

Barry Slotnick had become a celebrity. Part of his brand, paradoxically, was that he was someone who'd stick up for the little guy. Even police officers, who usually had little affection for defense lawyers, made an exception for Slotnick. He had turned the Goetz trial into a trial about a city overrun with thugs—a theme he continued as he went on to campaign for victims' rights—so cops loved him. Though he'd run lights and get pulled over all the time—"My dad didn't really obey traffic regulations," Stuart recalls, "especially after the Goetz case"—he'd never get a ticket.

Now Donna kept arguing with the cop. "That's not right."

"You married her," the cop said to Barry as he wrote up a ticket and gave it to Donna.

At airports, the Slotnicks started getting upgrades. People would cross the street to say, "Hey, Barry." Walking in New York City, trailing his parents, Stuart would hear passersby whispering, "That's Barry Slotnick." The family couldn't go to dinner without people approaching the table to ask for an autograph or just to speak with Barry. In college, Stuart encountered people who were either overly nice to him or strangely hostile because of the polarized reactions to the Goetz case. Donna would be talking to people—a taxi driver, a manicurist, a 411 operator—who, when they heard the name Slotnick, would ask if she was related to *Barry* Slotnick.

A *New Yorker* cartoonist drew a cartoon captioned: "This is the greatest news we've had since we hired that brilliant Barry Slotnick!"

The game Trivial Pursuit came out with a card that included the question: "What infamous subway rider was defended by Barry Slotnick in 1987?"

Rapper Sean Price's song "Rising to the Top," which would later be featured in the video game Grand Theft Auto III, name-checked Slotnick.

Slotnick seriously considered running for Congress.

He relished his success.

CHAPTER 86

Barry Slotnick may no longer have been defending organized crime cases, but in the court of public opinion, his clients didn't necessarily belong to a higher class of people. But they were wealthy and well connected.

In the wake of the Goetz trial, Slotnick briefly represented Radovan Karadzic, the so-called Butcher of Bosnia. He also represented Dewi Sukarno, widow of Indonesia's autocratic first president, after she was arrested for slashing the face of a fellow socialite with a broken Champagne glass at a party in Aspen.

His most notorious client may have been Panamanian strongman Manuel Noriega, who was looking for a lawyer to help get his US assets unfrozen.

A man and his wife were sitting in the front row when Slotnick boarded the plane on his way to visit Noriega, and one of Slotnick's Panamanian escorts told the couple to vacate the seats.

The man protested, saying he had paid for these specific

seats, but Slotnick's escort repeated his demand: "These are guests of the general, and they're sitting in these seats."

The escort began animatedly speaking in Spanish to the man, who then started looking scared and stood up. At that point, an increasingly uncomfortable Slotnick said he didn't want to sit in these seats and that he didn't mind sitting elsewhere on the plane. But the man, who had terror in his eyes, gestured insistently for Slotnick to take his seat. Slotnick refused. Finally, Slotnick's escort told him that the man was terrified and no longer wanted to sit there—he'd be scared for the rest of his life if Slotnick didn't accept the seat. So Slotnick sat down, and the plane departed for Panama.

In Panama the next day, Slotnick was picked up at his hotel at 5:00 a.m. and delivered to the general's headquarters. Noriega came into the conference room where Slotnick was waiting, and they spoke about Noriega's legal issue. Then Noriega said he had to confer with his people, and he left the room.

After an hour, Noriega hadn't returned, and Slotnick began to get nervous. He wondered if he'd made a terrible mistake. If Noriega didn't like him, or didn't want him as his lawyer, maybe he would just have him killed. Slotnick tried to walk out of the room, and a guard told him he couldn't leave. Slotnick said he just wanted a cigarette. Downstairs, he scanned the perimeter. He was inside a compound. This couldn't be good.

Finally, Noriega returned and said, "You will be my lawyer."

Slotnick's reputation as a legal miracle worker had preceded him.

That reputation also came into play when he represented Joseph Porto, a Long Island teenager who had confessed to fatally strangling his seventeen-year-old girlfriend, Kathleen Holland.

Holland was the pretty daughter of a Nassau County police sergeant. She was starting her freshman year of college at C. W. Post, a school near her childhood home, on Long Island. On the afternoon of Saturday, September 27, 1986, she told her roommates that she was going out for ice cream with Porto, whom she'd been dating for nine months. The couple, both seventeen, had met at Locust Valley High School. Just three months earlier, when they attended the prom together, Porto had worn white tails, and his mother had sewn Kathleen's white dress. As she left her dorm now, Holland told her roommates to wait for her before going out. She didn't plan to be gone for more than an hour.

But many hours later, close to midnight, Porto showed up at the dorm room. He said he was looking for Holland. He said he'd dropped her off earlier in the evening only to later receive a call from her, saying, "Get me out of here," and now he was here to find out what was going on. Her roommates said they hadn't seen her. Porto called Holland's house to tell her family she was missing. He helped them search for her, without success. Detective Holland, Kathleen's father, said later, "I realized that really something drastically was wrong." Police questioned Porto, and at 10:45 on Monday evening, he was arrested.

At 1:30 a.m. on Wednesday, September 30, Porto led police to Holland's body in the woods in North Hills, Long Island. There were deep ligature marks on her neck. There were bruises on her head and chest, and her buttocks and feet had abrasions from being dragged along the ground both facedown and faceup.

An hour and a half later, at 3:00, Porto was at the Nassau County DA's office eating a cheeseburger detectives had bought for him. Then, seated with hands folded, as a video camera recorded him, he emotionlessly confessed to killing Kathleen Holland. He said they'd been on their way back to her college campus in his Chevy Suburban after their date when she told him she wanted to see other men. In Brookville, he'd pulled over, they'd argued, and, in a jealous rage, he'd choked her with his hands. He then restated this confession in writing, adding that when his hands grew tired he finished the job using the tassel from his high school graduation cap. Police charged him with second-degree murder.

Slotnick took the case because he was still a "door lawyer"; he'd take almost any paying client. But with the trial two weeks from starting, in the spring of 1988, Slotnick didn't know how he was going to convince a jury that there was reasonable doubt. There was a confession, but it didn't necessarily match the injuries, and Slotnick's theory was that the police had drugged Porto and made him confess. The plan was to argue that Kathleen's death had actually been an accident.

CHAPTER 87

Prosecutor Kenneth Littman, in his opening statement, presented a straightforward case that closely tracked with Porto's confession: he had strangled Kathleen Holland in a fit of jealous rage because she "had outgrown this seventeen-year-old boy."

When it was Slotnick's turn to speak, he began on a deadpan, almost literary note. "It was a beautiful spring evening when Joseph Porto strangled Kathleen Holland and then disposed of her body," Slotnick said, as he eased into his opening statement to the jury. "The next morning Denis Holland Sr.—the chief investigator for the Nassau police department—woke up to find that his daughter was not home."

Slotnick went on to ask the jurors to "withhold all of your judgment until all the evidence is in…Joseph Porto did not commit the act of murder." He asked the jury to "keep your word" about remaining impartial (obtained during jury selection) and said they'd have "no choice" but to acquit his client on all charges. He conceded only that Kathleen had died of asphyxiation, that she and Porto had been lovers, and that her father was a detective. But Slotnick didn't elaborate on his theory of what had really happened on the night she died.

As the prosecution presented its case, Detective John Sharkey testified about Porto's confession. When Sharkey had first questioned him, Porto changed his story midstream to say that Holland *hadn't* called him after he dropped her off. "I told him that I was disturbed because the phone call had been the very reason he went back to C. W. Post that night," Sharkey told the courtroom. "I told him, 'I don't think you're telling the truth'... Joseph lowered his head and started to cry. He blurted out, 'I killed her. I gave her one good shot'... He said he had to get this off his chest." Sharkey said Porto had described back-handing Kathleen in the head as they sat in his van because she told him she wanted to see other men. He then crawled on top of her and strangled her with his hands until "she went limp." Later he dragged her outside the van, he told Sharkey, and tried to revive her.

As Slotnick began to cross-examine Sharkey, he got him to acknowledge that Porto, in his initial confession, hadn't mentioned the tassel. Porto had only acknowledged it and added it to a second written statement after Sharkey confronted him with evidence of ligature marks on Kathleen's neck. "He apologized to me," Sharkey recalled. "He told me that he had forgot."

On April 13, 1988, Slotnick cross-examined Nassau County medical examiner Dr. Leslie Lukash, trying to get Lukash to admit that the tassel was "inconsistent with the mark left on

Kathleen Holland's body." He got Detective Thomas Kubic, of the police department's Scientific Investigation Bureau, to admit that the tassel had no trace of skin fibers or blood on it and that the fibers on Holland's neck didn't match the fibers of the tassel. Slotnick hammered Sharkey about discrepancies between Porto's videotaped and written confessions, such as the location of the store where he bought the sapphire ring that he gave Kathleen the night she died. These were small dings in the prosecution's case—puzzling, even troubling questions about the evidence—but would they be enough to establish reasonable doubt?

It was hard to see how Slotnick could get around the prosecution's evidentiary centerpiece: the video confession. As all twenty-four minutes of it were played in the courtroom, Porto kept his head down. On the tape, Porto, speaking to Barry Grennan, head of the Nassau County DA's Major Offense Bureau, said: "She said she fooled around behind my back and I just lost it there...I lost control...After she started screaming, I got so nervous...She was gasping for air and she couldn't...At one point, I let her go because my hands got tired and I got on top of her" and strangled her more. After she was limp, "I took her out of the van...I knew she was dead." In a second two-minute statement the jury heard, Porto described how he then used the tassel: "I took it and just applied it to her throat. I pushed it up under her like that."

It sounded incontrovertibly damning, but as the prosecution rested, Slotnick seemed to have something up his sleeve. "Are you aware," he asked Grennan as he cross-examined him, "that 85 percent of what Joseph Porto said to you on the videotape is a lie?"

* * *

And then Slotnick revealed what he was up to. A week before trial, Frank King had confronted Porto about the ligature not being able to have killed Holland. There was some sisal found on her neck. But there was no rayon—the material the tassel was made out of—in her wounds. Slotnick, with King, had told Porto he was lying to them. Porto had then broken down and cried, confessing to a markedly different version of Kathleen's death: he had strangled her accidentally during an attempted voluntary sexual asphyxiation. He didn't want to embarrass her, so he'd made up a story about killing her out of jealousy.

On the stand, on Monday, April 18, Slotnick started to walk Porto through his testimony. Porto, weeping, contradicted his prior confessions, testifying that he accidentally strangled Holland. He claimed Kathleen had told him she'd heard about sexual asphyxia from a friend and wanted to try it. "She got on top of me and she said, 'Put it around my neck.' She said, 'Let's try it,' and I did. I just placed it around her neck...All of a sudden, I was just pulling. I guess I pulled too tight." He only realized that she was dead, he testified, after she fell backward. He claimed he drove to Community Hospital at Glen Cove, but didn't go in. "When I first met with Mr. King"—Frank King—"he said I was lying and that there was no way she could have died from a tassel. He said there was a rope involved."

Slotnick also entered into evidence cards Holland had sent Porto a few days before her death. "I am so happy that we are still together," she had written. "I hope we will be together for a long time...you are so sweet and so special and I am very lucky to have you all to myself. If I don't see you for a day, I feel like I am going to die."

Prosecutor Ken Littman could hardly believe what was happening. As Littman cross-examined Porto, he reminded him of a conversation in the DA's office only five weeks earlier, when Porto had repeated his earlier confession to a psychiatrist retained by the prosecutor. Porto at first denied making that confession, but after a break for lunch, he acknowledged he had done so, claiming it had been to maintain his cover-up.

"So for the past year and a half, you were lying to your own lawyer—lying to the Holland family—but now you're telling these twelve people the truth," Littman said, his voice dripping with disbelief.

"Yes," Porto said. "I am."

It was a distasteful but effective strategy. Slotnick was using a defense similar to that used in another recent notorious case—the "rough sex" that Robert Chambers, the so-called Preppy Killer, had claimed was the accidental cause of Jennifer Levin's death in Central Park. In fact, Levin's father and stepmother appeared at the Nassau County courthouse during the Porto trial to support Kathleen's parents. Levin called Detective Holland at home, and "we discussed the similarity of tactics—the sleaziness, the outrageous testimony...The cases are similar as to the sex involved, except that Chambers always claimed it was accidental during sex and Porto said it was murder and then changed course."

Outside the courthouse one day, after Porto's about-face, Detective Holland told reporters: "It's incredible that anybody would think they could feed such lies to the twelve intelligent people sitting here to save their own skin. It's a strategy that others have used, in which Mr. Slotnick is putting the victim on trial." Friends of Kathleen who attended the trial were outraged: "Anybody who knows Kathy knows that she would never do anything like this."

In his seven-hour summation, Slotnick took pains to distinguish his Porto defense from the rough-sex defense used by Chambers's lawyer. "I vilify no one," Slotnick said. "I tried not to harm anyone. I'm trying to save the life of Joseph Porto...I know this is painful. I know this is difficult." This was a case, he said, of "two kids in love and a tragic accident happened."

When it was time for Littman, the prosecutor, to make his closing argument, he took only two hours. He clearly thought the jury would give as little credence as he did to Porto's sexual asphyxia defense, which he dismissed as "this nonsense of an accidental homicide," and "the oops defense." Kathleen's death was "cold-blooded murder," and Littman told the jury to "use your common sense...Did any of you ever accidentally strangle your dates?...That's what he's selling. But I don't think you're buying."

Littman called Slotnick's Porto defense a copycat of the Chambers defense.

The jury deliberated for three days, eventually acquitting Porto of murder, finding him guilty only of the much less serious charge of criminally negligent homicide, which carried a maximum prison sentence of just one and a third to four years. With the crowd riled up, the defense team had to be escorted outside to their cars.

During the trial, Porto had been free on one million dollars' bail. Now he was going to jail. But the verdict was widely seen as a miscarriage of justice. "He absolutely got away with murder," prosecutor Littman said. This was, according to *Newsday,* "the first time in the county that a jury has acquitted a defendant of murder after he has confessed to the crime in both writing and on videotape." Detective Holland said, "If this is justice, then society is in trouble," and in the parking lot, Kathleen's brother yelled at the jury foreman: "You're scum!" When Porto was sentenced, six weeks later, even the judge said that the jail time "does not fit the crime."

Porto began serving his sentence at the Collins Correctional Facility, near Buffalo, New York. When he came up for parole after a year, he was denied it on grounds of "callous indifference." But under sentencing rules, he could be held no longer than two-thirds of his sentence, and at 7:00 a.m., on December 21, 1990, after just thirty months in prison, he was released from the Mid-Orange Correctional Facility, in Warwick, New York. He stepped into a limousine that contained his parents and a crew from the tabloid TV show *A Current Affair.* He was giving his first interview to correspondent Steve Dunleavy, Slotnick's friend.

On the day of the verdict, Slotnick made his usual triumphant phone call to Donna—"Not guilty"—but he was muted in his public statements. "I guess people will be saying that this is a great victory for the defense. But in cases like this, there are no winners or losers," he said.

Public sentiment wasn't with Slotnick this time around. Despite some similarities to the Goetz case—a videotaped confession, a defense that asked jurors to disregard their eyes—Slotnick received a different kind of attention in the wake of the Porto verdict. Goetz, for better or worse, had become a public hero, and Slotnick had been the hero's champion. But now Slotnick had worked his magic for a very different sort of defendant with a very different kind of victim. Goetz was a stand-in for every New Yorker who'd ever been mugged or feared being mugged; Porto wasn't anything of the sort.

Even the Guardian Angels' Lisa Sliwa, a victims' rights advocate who'd been an ally to Slotnick in the Goetz case, told a reporter: "I think Slotnick has hit a new low with this."

Slotnick was bothered by the criticism, but he felt that he'd done his job well. It was yet another rabbit out of a hat for Slotnick, and it wasn't the last one.

CHAPTER 88

A round 1:40 p.m. on May 15, 1988, police converged on a church in Manhattan. The True Church of God in East Harlem served a mostly poor, mostly Black congregation, but it was led by a tall, thin, fifty-nine-year-old white man, Pastor Thomas Streitferdt, who had founded it as a storefront church in 1964. Streitferdt had just ended church services when he was arrested and charged with rape and sodomy for allegedly having sexually abused two children in his congregation: a fourteen-year-old girl and a sixteen-year-old girl. Police said he had threatened to expel them from the church if they told anyone what he'd done.

In the days after Streitferdt's arrest, he became a tabloid sensation as reporters revealed him to be a not-so-simple man of the cloth. The New York *Daily News* splashed him across its cover: MYSTERY CLOAKS SEX-RAP PASTOR: HARLEM MINISTER A PARADOX OF PIETY, LUXURY. He lived in Old Field, an exclusive enclave on Long Island, in a 1.4-million-dollar waterfront house with a pool and electric security gates displaying the word SERENITY in gold lettering. He drove a blue Mercedes sedan. At the same time, he demanded that every congregant give 10 percent of their annual income to the church—and 30 percent of it every three years. In addition, on Streitferdt's birthday, each member of the church had to give him a dollar for every year of his age (when Streitferdt turned forty-nine, for example, each parishioner gave him forty-nine dollars).

He was authoritarian in other ways. One time, he told all male congregants to shave off their beards. Congregants who got married had to honeymoon at a church-owned condo in Acapulco, Mexico, and congregants' savings had to be placed with a church-owned bank. Congregants were forbidden from celebrating Christmas, which Streitferdt deemed a "pagan rite." And always there lurked the threat of disfellowship—being cast out from the community if you did something the pastor didn't like. These weren't the kinds of details that would endear him to a jury.

Slotnick believed that he could establish reasonable doubt by impeaching Streitferdt's accusers, who, his investigator Frank King learned, had credibility issues. During the trial, one of the victims said of Streitferdt that "nobody believed him." The law was clear: if a prosecution witness says something like that about a defendant, defense counsel may call another witness to rebut the testimony. But in this case, the judge wouldn't allow it. On May 26, after a three-week jury trial, Streitferdt was convicted of raping a twenty-one-year-old woman and sexually abusing the fourteen-year-old girl and a forty-four-year-old woman. A month and a half after that, Streitferdt was sentenced to seven to twenty-one years in prison.

* * *

Slotnick was certain the verdict would be reversed on appeal. His associate Michael Shapiro was so confident that the appellate court would shoot down the trial court's decision that for the first and last time in his career, he guaranteed that that was what would happen. Their certainty was well founded, and on July 2, 1991, a five-judge panel of the state supreme court's appellate division reversed Streitferdt's conviction and sentencing and ordered a new trial, finding that the lower court had improperly excluded testimony about the veracity of the complainants. "We're very pleased the case has been reversed," Slotnick said. "The alleged victims were people who were dissatisfied with the church, had been thrown out of the church, and had real good reasons for testifying against him."

At the retrial, which began in March of 1992, Slotnick locked one of the witnesses into testifying that she had been called to Streitferdt's office on a particular day and at a particular time and been sexually abused by the pastor, after which she had spent the rest of the day distraught and weeping. Slotnick then showed the jury a magnified photograph taken of the witness on the date of the alleged attack. Her watch showed that it was 4:30 p.m., mere hours after the alleged attack, and she was smiling brightly.

Streitferdt was acquitted.

CHAPTER 89

One morning in 2004, at the offices of Slotnick's law firm, at 100 Park Avenue, the usual hum of phones ringing and copy machines collating and staplers stapling and employees chitchatting had a more excited pitch than usual.

Did you see who's in the office?

Have you walked past the conference room lately?

Do yourself a favor and take the long way to the restroom.

One by one, everyone in the office managed to walk past the conference room as casually as they were able to, hoping to catch a quick glimpse inside when the door briefly opened to let someone enter or leave.

Barry Slotnick was meeting with a statuesque woman with brown hair and eastern European features who was, recalls a lawyer who caught one of those glimpses, "stunningly gorgeous."

Melania Knauss was getting married, and the man she was engaged to was insisting that she sign a prenuptial agreement.

Donald Trump knew that his fiancée needed to be represented

by a well-regarded lawyer so that she wouldn't be able to challenge the contract, should it ever come to that, on the basis of ineffective counsel. So he'd sent her to Slotnick.

Liberty's last champion still handled some big criminal cases—notably representing Vyacheslav "Yaponchik" Ivankov, the Russian John Gotti—but he'd largely moved away from the kinds of cases in which he'd made his name. More often now he had a tonier class of clients.

He represented Anthony Quinn in his divorce and June Gumbel in hers.

He represented Kim Porter in her child-support suit against Sean "P. Diddy" Combs.

He was the lawyer for Fred Tepperman in his wrongful-termination suit against billionaire Ron Perelman and for B. Gerald Cantor's widow, Iris Cantor, in her decade-long litigation against Cantor Fitzgerald, the firm her husband had founded.

When casino owner Steve Wynn sued Lloyd's of London after the blind billionaire put his elbow through a Picasso he had just agreed to sell for more than one hundred million dollars, Slotnick was his lawyer.

Later, Melania Trump would explain, in her pronounced Slovenian accent, why she'd chosen Slotnick to handle her prenup: "Donald said he was a killer."

"He really was a killer," Donald Trump would add.

"Donald was very generous," Slotnick would say diplomatically.

Several of Slotnick's clients continued to need his expertise in later years. One such case involved his old client Vincent "Chin" Gigante, who, the government maintained, had been the boss of the Genovese crime family for decades. In recent years, Gigante had become a tabloid character, shuffling around Greenwich Village in his bathrobe talking to parking meters, earning him the *New York Post* sobriquet the Oddfather. His detractors said his strange behavior was a ploy designed to avoid prison time (Jimmy Breslin even wrote a satiric novel based on Gigante, titled *I Don't Want to Go to Jail*); Slotnick spent seven years fighting to establish that Gigante was in fact incompetent to stand trial. (Gigante eventually admitted that it had been an act, but not until 2003—and with a different lawyer.)

But the most unexpected client to reappear—in a most unexpected case—was Bernhard Goetz.

Creme Puff was loose.

This would have been less of a problem if the animal hadn't chosen to make its escape in the buttoned-down midtown law offices of Buchanan Ingersoll & Rooney, the staid corporate law firm Barry Slotnick joined in 2005.

And, of course, if the animal in question weren't a squirrel. In the years since his historic trial, Bernie Goetz had largely disappeared from public view. After serving a six-month sentence on his weapons charge, he'd briefly surfaced in 2001, when he launched a quixotic campaign to become mayor of New York City, but otherwise his focus was on small animals such as chinchillas and squirrels. He spent much of his time strolling around Central Park searching for rodents in distress. When he found one, he'd take it home to his apartment, on 14th Street, and nurse it back to health.

Goetz's concern for furry critters was what had brought him to see his old lawyer all these years later. Having a squirrel in the apartment was a violation of Goetz's lease, and when his landlord found out, he'd moved to evict his famous tenant.

In the austere modern conference room at Buchanan's offices, Goetz had thought it would be harmless to give Creme Puff some room to run around, but now the bushy-tailed creature was making a mad dash for freedom. They were able to close the door in time to block the exit, but Creme Puff did a 180 and began racing furiously around the conference table.

Barry Slotnick, more salt than pepper in his hair now, but still dapper in a three-piece Fioravanti suit, anticipated the squirrel's route and headed it off before it could hide behind a filing cabinet.

At that point, Goetz managed to coax Creme Puff into his hand and return it to his pocket after giving it some soothing strokes. Eventually, Barry and Stuart were able to come to terms with the landlord: Goetz could stay in the apartment, and he would no longer bring squirrels there.

CHAPTER 90

One day, Slotnick grabbed a document out of his son's hand and scrawled a note on it. It was a witness deposition from a lawsuit against a major pharmaceuticals company that Stuart's client was suing, and Slotnick wrote: "I met with a client today, who basically said, 'It's two weeks and you still can't talk?'"

A few months earlier, Slotnick had noticed that his voice, normally a silky tenor, was becoming increasingly low and hoarse. Finally, he had it checked out by a doctor, who found a polyp growing on his vocal cords. A surgeon operated and removed the polyp, but there was a real question about whether he'd be able to speak again. For the first two weeks after the operation, he wasn't allowed to try, and during this period, he was writing notes instead.

Slotnick had gone through a similar health scare a few years before, when at fifty-eight he was diagnosed with colon cancer. Fearful that clients would drop him if they thought he was distracted by a fight for survival, he didn't want anyone to know. Slotnick then underwent a colon resection and chemo-therapy. To explain his absence from the office each Friday, he told colleagues he had diverticulitis.

Now Stuart, an accomplished lawyer himself, was on the verge of joining his father's firm after years as a prosecutor and then a defense attorney, but Slotnick had put the brakes on the process. He was the firm's rainmaker, and without him the practice would collapse. He didn't want to bring his son on until he was sure the firm would survive.

In his scrawled notes to Stuart, his anxiety was unmistakable: clients were getting antsy. They weren't going to stick with a lawyer who couldn't speak.

Slotnick's voice did come back in the end, and from then on, he and Stuart worked side by side on a number of cases, first at Slotnick's firm and then at Buchanan, which they both joined.

When Barry and Stuart Slotnick and their client showed up at the federal courthouse in Manhattan on a Friday morning, Judge Robert Sweet growled: "Slotnick strikes again."

A few nights earlier, Stuart had received a call from a friend he met back in his days in the DA's office saying he needed Stuart's help. His sister's fiancé, Jay Ferriola, had been a soldier in Iraq, served his commitment of six years, gotten out as a member of the IRR (Individual Ready Reserve), and then, having secured another job, put in a request to resign. The request had been approved one or two levels up, but it hadn't yet gotten approved all the way up, and now the army was trying to pull him back in. He was being redeployed the following Tuesday.

"Okay," Stuart said, "so why are you calling me?"

"We need to sue the army."

The friend had already contacted several other lawyers, and everyone had said there was nothing to be done.

Stuart discussed the case with Barry, and they agreed to take it. The Slotnicks wrangled a bunch of other lawyers from the firm, and the group pulled a series of all-nighters. Filing a complaint late the night before, in the southern district of New York, they'd sued the army; the secretary of defense, Donald Rumsfeld; and everyone else in Ferriola's line of command. It was a classic Slotnick case—a chance to do something legally innovative and make headlines—but now he was doing it alongside his son, ready to pass the torch to the next generation.

Slotnick had appeared before Judge Sweet dozens of times, but the jurist's remark on this Friday morning—"Slotnick strikes again"—was clearly about the gathering media mob outside, which had grown to two hundred people.

Time was of the essence, and although Sunday was normally a day when the federal courts were closed, Judge Sweet scheduled a hearing for that day. There the Slotnicks argued that Ferriola's resignation had been approved, so he should be allowed to resign. The army's position was that Ferriola served at the pleasure of the president, but the Slotnicks interpreted that to also mean that if Ferriola *wanted* to serve, the president could block him from doing so. Ultimately, the Slotnicks worked out a deal with the US attorney whereby the government's order was stayed: Ferriola would report to the fort to be redeployed for the second time in Operation Iraqi Freedom, but he'd be honorably discharged.

After the success with Ferriola, the Slotnicks took on a similar case. Then they took on a third, fourth, and fifth. In each case, using the same argument, they won a discharge for the client. Eventually, the army changed its policy to state that if a soldier was in the IRR and was called up for duty, he'd be given an opportunity to resign.

In later years, as Barry edged into retirement, he acceded to Donna's request that they buy a home in South Florida to "try it out." Barry wasn't great at seeing himself as old, and he viewed Florida as a place for old people. But after a few seasons of flying back and forth from New York, Barry began to think Florida wasn't so bad after all. And in truth, for better or worse, New York wasn't the same city he'd grown up in. He'd always be a boy from the Bronx and a New Yorker through and through, but he found himself enjoying the Florida weather and unencumbered time with his wife. He'd sit on the veranda of the condo he and Donna bought, taking calls from friends. It was good to talk about his old cases. He'd been a defender of the people of the city he loved and of the place itself. Law had been his first love.

But when he'd hang up, he'd look over at his true love. He and Donna had been married for more than fifty years. They had four children and nine grandchildren. It was then that he found himself thinking about the present, and he said to Donna: "We won."

ACKNOWLEDGMENTS

This book would have been impossible to write without the help of Barry Slotnick, Donna Slotnick, and especially Stuart Slotnick. Thanks also to Cindy Adams, Mark Baker, Jay Breakstone, Steven Brounstein, Shoshana Slotnick Buchanan, Gillian Coulter, Stephen Crane, Bruce Cutler, Jim Druker, Melissa Fertig, George Gabriel, Lawrence Herrmann, Jeff Hoffman, Joanne Eboli Julien, Susan Kellman, Ed McDonald, John McNally, John Miller, Gianni Russo, Bettina Schein, Joel J. Seidemann, Michael Shapiro, and Chani Slotnick Tegnalia.

ABOUT THE AUTHORS

James Patterson is the world's bestselling author and most trusted storyteller. He has created many enduring fictional characters and series, including Alex Cross, the Women's Murder Club, Michael Bennett, Maximum Ride, Middle School, and I Funny. Among his notable literary collaborations are *The President Is Missing*, with President Bill Clinton, and the Max Einstein series, produced in partnership with the Albert Einstein estate. Patterson's writing career is characterized by a single mission: to prove that there is no such thing as a person who "doesn't like to read," only people who haven't found the right book. He's given over three million books to schoolkids and the military, donated more than seventy million dollars to support education, and endowed over five thousand college scholarships for teachers. For his prodigious imagination and championship of literacy in America, Patterson was awarded the 2019 National Humanities Medal. The National Book Foundation presented him with the Literarian Award for Outstanding Service to the

American Literary Community, and he is also the recipient of an Edgar Award and nine Emmy Awards. He lives in Florida with his family.

Benjamin Wallace is a features writer at *New York* magazine, a contributing editor at *Vanity Fair,* and the author of *The Billionaire's Vinegar,* a *New York Times* nonfiction bestseller.

For a complete list of books by

JAMES PATTERSON

VISIT
JamesPatterson.com

 Follow James Patterson on Facebook
@JamesPatterson

 Follow James Patterson on Twitter
@JP_Books

 Follow James Patterson on Instagram
@jamespattersonbooks